A STRAIGHTFORWARD GUIDE
TO
JOB AND CAREER OPPORTUNITIES

Jeanette Benisti

www.straightforwardco.co.uk

Contents

Introduction

Introduction

Choosing the right career constitutes one of the most important decsions that a person can make, whether you are young, i.e. a school leaver or a graduate or whether you are older and looking for a career change.

This book deals with the main areas of employment and offers a breakdown of a number of key jobs within that field plus also the main contacts for you if you choose to further your line of enquiry. A main contact number and website is also included so that you can discuss the wide range of careers on offer that are not listed in this book. To list every career on offer, and do the main jobs justice, which has been done in the various sections, is beyond the scope of this book.

We have listed 21 main areas of work in the book, that encompass most careers, including: accountancy;a advertising; the armed forces; banking and finance; catering; civil service and local government; construction; engineering; farming and land jobs; health service; information technology; journalism and printing; the legal profession; marketing; music radio and tv; the police force; retail; social work; sport and liesure; teaching; travel and tourism and vetinary.

Out of these areas you are sure to find a career that might suit you and your particular skills and abilities, plus what you want to devote your working life to.

Some people look for money, regardless of the job and others look for a more socially orientated job, one that provides a degree of material reward but also provides greater personal satisfaction.

The National Careers Service website https://nationalcareersservice.direct. gov.uk provides very useful information on career choices and also outlines a wide variety of jobs.

Good luck with your career search.

Jeanette Benisti
October 2012

1. ACCOUNTANCY

This section covers:

* The Accounting profession
* The Actuarial Profession

Mention accountancy to people, particularly non-accountants, and they groan. Accountancy is perceived as a very conservative and rather boring profession. However, it is anything but. Accountancy is at the heart of all business and is a great way to learn the machinations of any industry whatever it may be. It is also a profession that pays well.

Accountancy is central to all business, whether large or small. The complexities, however, change with the nature and size of businesses and their environments.

An accountant is involved in the financial transactions of particular businesses and also the preparation of accounts and also auditing. Accountants deal with a wide variety of areas, such as taxation, business forecasting, business modelling, financial performance, investments and acquisitions and mergers. Because the work is so diverse accountancy is split into specialist areas, in the main three specialist areas.

MANAGEMENT ACCOUNTING

The nature of the work
Management accountants work mainly in commerce and industry. There work is integral to a company's operation, dealing with planning budgets, monitoring ongoing expenditure and preparing reports for external bodies. Management accountants may be qualified Chartered Accountants, Chartered Certified Accountants or Management Accountants.

ACCOUNTANTS IN PRIVATE PRACTICE

As the name suggests, accountants working for private practice will offer their services to all types of business, small organisations, fee paying clients and so on. Basically, they are freelance. They are either qualified as Associate Members of the Institute of Chartered Accountants in England and Wales (CAEW), the Institute of Chartered Accountants in Scotland (CAS), The Institute of Chartered Accountants in Ireland (CAI) or the Association of Chartered Certified Accountants (ACCA).

PUBLIC SECTOR ACCOUNTANTS

This is a different area of accountancy, employing the same essential skills but operating in a very different environment which encompasses local and national government finance. Public Sector accountants control and assess the expenditure within local authorities, health trusts, universities and central government. As you can imagine, this is a complex and varied area of accountancy.

Entry requirements

Most trainee accountants are graduates. maths is obviously an important element of accountancy and if you have a degree which involves maths, for example business studies, this will stand you in good stead. Most employers will set numeracy tests as part of the overall selection process. There are other entry requirements, for example, some professional bodies mentioned above, before accepting a person onto their trainee programme will require 5 GCSE's grades A or B and two A levels as a minimum.

Accountants who are qualified with any of the professional bodies can practice in the public sector. However, the most relevant organisation is the Chartered Institute of Public Finance and Accountancy (CIPFA). If, however, you don't have another accountancy qualification you must, as a minimum have three GCSE's Grade A to C and two A levels. Maths and English will be a requirement.

The best advice is to identify which area of accountancy most attracts you, identify the relevant professional body and then make enquiries about entry qualifications. The most important thing is to gain a job in the appropriate area and then, through the employer, gain day release onto the required course.

What can you earn?

Salaries within the accountancy profession will vary with industry and location, also size of the firm. As a trainee you can expect £24,00-£28,000 in London and the South east, with starting salaries varying elsewhere. After qualifying salaries will increase significantly. A good accountancy qualification will always hold you in good stead.

Other areas of accountancy

A less qualified area of accountancy is that of accountancy technician. Accountancy technicians work in a variety of roles, usually assisting qualified Chartered Accountants. There are no set entry level qualifications but people wanting to work within this area must be confident in maths. Good IT skills are also valuable as Information technology is integral to accountancy. Salaries are lower than qualified accountants but can still be attractive.

More information

The following are the important bodies within accounting and they can offer all the advice that you will need.

Chartered Institute of Management Accountants (CIMA)
0208 8849 2251
www.cimaglobal.com

Chartered Institute of Public Finance Accountants (CIPFA)
020 7543 5600
www.cipfa.org.uk

Association of Certified Accountants
020 7059 500
www.accaglobal.com

Association of Accounting technicians (AAT)
0845 863 0800
www.aat.org.uk

ACTUARY

The nature of the work
This is a distinct area of finance, dealing with the assessment of financial risks and probabilities. Typically, you might find actuaries working in areas such as pension forecasting, life assurance and other areas of insurance. They will also be involved in other areas of business where risks are involved. Actuaries will use their skills in mathematics and statistics to create models to analyse past events and predict future outcomes. Actuaries can be found either in private practice, typically consultancies and also government and the health service.

Entry requirements
To qualify as an actuary you must become a student member of one of the professional bodies, which are either the Faculty or the Institute of Actuaries. Minimum qualifications for entry are usually three GCSE's Grades A-C including English and two A levels one of which must be maths at grade B. If you have a second class honours degree in any subject then a grade C in maths is usually acceptable. If you have a degree in maths or actuarial science you do not need maths A level.

Once you have completed your professional training you become a fellow of either the Institute or Faculty. To become a Fellow you must pass 15 professional examinations. Depending on your prior qualifications you may be exempt from some of the exams at the Core technical stage and some at the other stage.

What can you earn?
Actuaries earn high salaries, with a trainee beginning at around £30,000. This will rise significantly as training and qualifications progress.

More information
The Association of Consulting Actuaries

020 73824954
www.aca.org.uk

Faculty of Actuaries
0131 240 1300
www.actuarites.org.uk

Financial Services Skills Council
020 7216 7366
www.fssc.org.uk

Government Actuaries Department (GAD)
020 7211 2601
www.gad.gov.uk

The Actuarial Education Company
01235 550005
www.acted.co.uk

2. ADVERTISING

Advertising is a very attractive profession. It is also a complicated profession and if you get it right it can provide enormous benefits both to an employee but also clients. It can be a very worthwhile career. In this section, we cover the following:

- Advertising account executive
- Copywriters

Their are numerous other positions within advertising, for more information contact:

Institute of Practitioners in Advertising (IPA)
44 Belgrave Square
London
SW1X 8QS
Tel: 020 7235 7020
www.ipa.co.uk

ADVERTISING ACCOUNT EXECUTIVE

The nature of the work
As an account executive, you would find out about the client's advertising goals then work with your agency's creative and planning staff to ensure that effective advertising campaigns are produced.

Your tasks would include:

- meeting clients to discuss their advertising needs
- working with account planners to come up with a campaign that meets the client's brief (instructions) and budget
- presenting campaign ideas and costs to clients
- briefing the creative team that produces the words and artwork

- negotiating with clients, solving problems and making sure that deadlines are met
- checking and reporting on the campaign's progress
- keeping in contact with the client at all stages of the campaign
- managing the account's budget and invoicing the client
- trying to win new business for the agency.

You would normally handle about three or four accounts at the same time.

What can you earn?

Starting salaries are around £18,000 to £24,000 a year. With experience, this normally rises to between £30,000 and £45,000 a year. Top salaries can reach £90,000 a year.

Entry requirements

Employers will usually be more interested in your personal qualities, such as creativity, quick thinking and business sense, than your formal qualifications. However, competition for jobs in advertising is very strong so it may help you if you have a BTEC HND or degree in one of the following subjects:

- advertising
- marketing
- statistics or operational research
- communication and media studies
- business or management
- psychology.

Any previous work experience that you have in communications, marketing, sales or the media would also be useful.

In smaller advertising agencies you may be able to start in a more junior position such as administrator, and work your way up as your experience in the industry grows. It is a good idea to try to find work experience in an advertising agency before looking for your first job. You could contact agencies directly to ask about placements, and make industry contacts through relevant groups on social networking sites. See the Work Experience section of the Institute of Practitioners in Advertising (IPA) website for more information and a list of member agencies. To become an advertising account executive, you will need to have good spoken and written communication skills

More information

Institute of Practitioners in Advertising (IPA)
44 Belgrave Square
London
SW1X 8QS
Tel: 020 7235 7020
www.ipa.co.uk

Account Planning Group (APG)
16 Creighton Avenue
London
N10 1NU
Tel: 020 8444 3692
www.apg.org.uk

Communication Advertising Marketing Foundation group
Tel: 01628 427120
www.camfoundation.com

Creative Skillset
Focus Point
21 Caledonian Road
London
N1 9GB
www.creativeskillset.org

Creative Skillset Careers
Tel: 08080 300 900 (England and Northern Ireland)
Tel: 0845 850 2502(Scotland)
Tel: 08000 121 815 (Wales)
www.creativeskillset.org/careers

COPYWRITERS

The nature of the work

As a copywriter, you would work as a team with an art director, who would provide the visual images to go with your words. Your job would begin with a briefing about the client, their product, the target audience and the advertising message to be put across. Your work could then involve:

- creating original ideas that fit the brief (working closely with the art director)
- presenting ideas to the agency's creative director and account team
- helping to present ideas to the client
- making any changes that the client asks for
- writing clear and persuasive copy
- making sure that ads meet the codes of advertising practice
- proofreading copy to check spelling, grammar and facts
- casting actors for TV and radio advertisements
- liaising with photographers, designers, production companies and printers.

You would often work on several projects at once, usually under the supervision of a creative director.

What can you earn?

Starting salaries can be around £18,000 to £25,000 a year. With experience this rises to between £25,000 and £50,000 a year. Senior creatives in leading agencies can earn up to £100,000 or more.

Entry requirements

Employers will usually be more interested in your creativity, writing skills and business sense than your formal qualifications.

However, advertising is a very competitive industry to join, so you may have an advantage with a qualification that includes some copywriting, such as:

- a foundation degree, BTEC HND or degree in advertising

- Communication, Advertising and Marketing Education Foundation (CAM) Diploma in Marketing Communications.
- Other useful courses include BTEC HNDs or degrees in journalism, English, media studies and marketing.

Most people get their first copywriting job as a result of work experience. This can give you the chance to make industry contacts and impress potential employers.

You could contact agencies directly to ask about placements, and make industry contacts through relevant groups on social networking sites. See the Work Experience section of the Institute of Practitioners in Advertising (IPA) website for more information and a list of member agencies. The

IPA also runs a Graduate Recruitment Agency, and D&AD runs a Graduate Placement Scheme.

When looking for jobs, you will need to show a portfolio of your work (known as a 'book') to potential employers, as you will be employed on the strength of your creative ideas, versatility and writing ability.

It's a good idea to team up with a would-be art director and work together on campaign ideas for your portfolio, as this can help prove your ability to fulfil a client's 'brief'. See D&AD's website for details of their advertising workshops, aimed at helping people build a portfolio and make contacts in the advertising industry. If you join the IPA, you can also showcase the best of your portfolio online on their All Our Best Work website. Visit the Diagonal Thinking website to find out if you have what it takes for a career in advertising.

More information

Institute of Practitioners in Advertising
44 Belgrave Square
London
SW1X 8QS
Tel: 020 7235 7020
www.ipa.co.uk

3. ARMED FORCES

Careers in the armed forces are many and varied. These will include civilian as well as non-civilian roles. In this section we look at:

- Army Officer
- Army Soldier
- Territorial Soldier
- RAF Officer
- RAF Airman or Woman
- Royal Marine
- Royal Marine Officer
- Royal Navy Officer
- Royal Navy Rating

For further information concerning the variety of jobs available in the armed forces go to:

British Army
Tel: 08457 300111
www.army.mod.uk

ARMY OFFICER

The nature of the work

The army's work can range from fighting in combat zones to providing peacekeeping duties. They can also provide disaster relief and help civil communities during difficult times, such as floods. The army officer plays an important role in the safety of the nation.

To be an army officer, you will need to have a willingness to go into combat. You need to be able to lead and motivate others. You will also need excellent teamworking skills.

To become an officer you must be aged between 17 years and 9 months and 28 years. You must pass a full army medical. You must also have at least five GCSEs and two A levels.

What can you earn?

Your pay as an army officer depends on your rank and how long you have served. Non-Graduate Officer Cadets earn around £15,300 a year while training. Graduate Officer Cadets earn £24,100 during training. Lieutenants earn between around £29,000 and £32,000 a year.

Salaries of higher ranks (from Captain to Brigadier) range from £37,200 up to £98,900 a year.

Entry requirements

To become an officer you must

- be aged between 17 years and 9 months and 28 years (upper limit could be higher depending on the role
- meet the army nationality requirement
- pass a full army medical
- have at least five GCSEs (A-C) including English, maths and a science or foreign language, plus two A levels or equivalent qualifications (180 UCAS points).

Once you show an interest in becoming an Army Officer you would be interviewed by an experienced Careers Adviser. If you show the required potential the next stage is to attend the Army Officer Selection Board (AOSB) Briefing. This is a one-and-a-half day filter selection. Successful applicants would then be invited to attend the AOSB Main Board, which is a rigorous three-day selection process that tests your physical and mental abilities and your suitability to potentially become an officer. If you pass this phase you would then be offered a place on the 44-week Commissioning Course at the Royal Military Academy Sandhurst (RMAS).

There is a separate entry process and shortened commissioning course of only four weeks for professionally qualified applicants (i.e. nurse, doctor, medical/dental officer, lawyer, veterinary surgeon or chaplain). Additional financial incentives are offered to encourage professionally qualified individuals to consider the Army as a career. For those still in education the Army offers financial incentives to progress through A levels (or attend the

Defence Sixth Form College at Welbeck), Army Scholarship Scheme, Undergraduate Cadetship or Undergraduate Bursary.

For those at university you can gain Army experience, and get paid, by joining the University Officer Training Corps. This gives a real feel for Army life but without any commitment on joining at the end of your time.

An Army Officer career is open to all applicants, but currently females cannot apply for commissions in the Household Cavalry, Royal Armoured Corps or Infantry.

More information

Wellbeck Defence Sixth Form College
Forest Road
Woodhouse
Loughborough
Leicestershire
LE12 8WD
www.dsfc.ac.uk

British Army
Tel: 08457 300111
www.army.mod.uk

ARMY SOLDIER

The nature of the work
The British army's work can range from fighting in combat zones to providing peacekeeping and humanitarian duties. If you are looking for a challenging and active job, this could be ideal for you.

To become an army soldier, you will need to have self-discipline and confidence. The Army needs people with good teamwork skills. You'll need to be able to think and react quickly in changing situations.

To join the army, you must be aged between 16 and 33. You need to meet the Army's strict nationality requirements. You must pass a full army medical examination.

What can you earn?

Your pay as a soldier in the army depends on your rank, how long you have served and the pay band for your particular job.

New recruits in training start on around £13,400 a year. On completion of 26 weeks training, this rises to over £17,000 a year.

Private soldiers can earn between £17,000 and £28,000 per year, Corporals can earn up to £35,000 a year, and those with higher ranks can earn up to around £46,000 a year.

There are additional allowances, for example whilst serving overseas, and subsidised food and accommodation. Housing for married soldiers is also subsidised to enable families to accompany their partner throughout their careers unless serving on Operations.

Entry requirements

To join the army, you must:

- be aged between 16 and 33 on the day you enlist (if you are under 18, you will need consent from a parent or guardian)
- meet the army nationality and residency requirements (see the Citizenship page of the British Army website for details)
- pass a full army medical examination.

You may need some qualifications for certain technical roles, such as in engineering or communications, but for many army jobs you will not need any. You can check the entry criteria for each job role on the British Army website, or discuss your options in detail with your local Armed Forces Careers Office. You could also take army practice tests, which aim to match you with the jobs best suited to your skills. See the British Army website for more information.

The next stage involves spending two days at your nearest Army Development and Selection Centre, which includes an interview, taking a series of physical and aptitude tests, and having a full medical examination. If you are successful, you can sign up and start the Phase One training programme. See the Training and Development section below for details.

If you are aged between 16 and 17 years and one month, you could apply for the 42-week school leavers' course at the Army Foundation College at Harrogate. See the College website for more information.

When you join the army, your contract will be for about four years. You can leave any time after this point, as long as you give 12 months' notice.

Territorial Army

You may prefer to become a part-time soldier with your local Territorial Army (TA) unit as a volunteer. You can apply to join the TA between ages 17 and 43. TA soldiers are committed to serving a minimum of 27 training days per year plus a two-week annual camp, but you can serve every weekend if you wish. Many TA soldiers choose to go on operations serving alongside regular soldiers for 6-month tours of duty. See the British Army website for details.

More information

British Army
Tel: 08457 300111
www.army.mod.uk

RAF OFFICER

The nature of the work
RAF officers are responsible for the welfare, discipline and career development of their team of non-commissioned RAF personnel (airmen and airwomen).

As an RAF officer you could choose to work in one of 20 specialist areas, each with different responsibilities, for example:

- Air Operations – pilots and weapons systems officers – flying sorties, carrying out reconnaissance, and taking part in search and rescue duties
- Operations Support – air traffic and aerospace battle managers, and flight operations officers – providing target information, coordination refuelling, digitally mapping terrain and planning missions

- Engineering and Logistics – aircraft and communications engineers – commissioning new aircraft, servicing fleets and managing resources and supplies
- Support Services – catering, security and training officers – providing day-to-day services for staff at RAF bases and in the field during operations
- Professions – medical, dental and nursing officers – managing specialist teams working in support of the service.

The areas of responsibility are split into squadrons and you would manage a squadron with other officers who have also earned their rank or 'commission'.

What can you earn?

New pilot officers earn £24,130 a year. Flying officers earn between £29,000 and £32,000.
Flight lieutenants can earn up to £44,200. Squadron leaders can earn around £56,000.
Salaries are independently reviewed each year, so check the latest rates with your local AFCO.

If your job involves flying, you are entitled to flying pay as well as your basic salary. If you live in RAF accommodation, a charge for rent is automatically taken from your salary.

Entry requirements

To join the RAF as an officer you must:

- be aged at least 17 years and six months
- be a UK, Republic of Ireland or Commonwealth citizen, or have dual nationality with Britain and another country
- have at least five GCSEs (A-C), including English language and - for some roles - grade B in maths, plus two A levels or similar qualifications.

For some jobs, you would need a degree or professional qualification.

Selection tests

Before you can join the RAF, you would have to pass a series of tests held at the Officers and Aircrew Selection Centre at RAF College, Cranwell in Lincolnshire. This is a three-day process that includes tests for aptitude, practical initiative and fitness, and is followed by interviews and a medical.

Scholarships and bursaries

If you are still at school or preparing to go to university, you may be eligible for an RAF sixth-form scholarship, or medical, dental or engineering sponsorship.

Check the RAF Careers website for more details about entry requirements, funding opportunities and details of your nearest Armed Forces Careers Office (AFCO).

More information

RAF Careers
Tel: 0845 605 5555
www.raf.mod.uk/careers

RAF AIRMEN AND WOMEN

The nature of the work

Royal Air Force (RAF) airmen and airwomen make up the largest number of RAF personnel. They use specialist skills in a wide range of mostly ground support roles.

As an RAF airman or airwoman, you would provide specialist support in one of the following categories:

- aircrew – which includes non-commissioned aircrew and weapon systems operators
- engineering and technical – including roles like aircraft technician
- catering and hospitality – which includes roles such as catering officer
- security and defence – with jobs in firefighting and the RAF police
- medical and medical support – dental, nursing, medical and laboratory roles
- personnel support – including administration, bands, and training

- air operations support – for example air traffic controllers
- communications and intelligence – such as photographers and intelligence analysts
- logistics and equipment – which includes drivers and supply officers.

While your exact role would vary according to your specialist skill or trade, you would also carry out military tasks like guard duties, and take part in military exercises and training.

You can contact your local Armed Forces Careers Office (AFCO) through the RAF Careers website for a full list of the trades available.

What can you earn?

Pay during training is around £13,400 a year, rising to £16,700 after training. Senior airmen/airwomen earn up to £28,400 a year. Corporals and sergeants can earn between around £25,000 and £36,200 a year.

Salaries are independently reviewed each year – check the latest rates with your local AFCO. If you are living in RAF accommodation, a charge for rent is automatically taken from your salary.

Entry requirements

Before you apply or make contact with the RAF, you should check the RAF Careers website which includes advice on exploring your options in the force.

If you decide to join the RAF as an airman or airwoman, you must be:

- at least aged 16 (upper age limits vary according to the job – check with your local AFCO and the RAF Careers website)
- a citizen of the UK, Republic of Ireland or the Commonwealth, or have dual nationality with Britain and another country.

You will also need to pass a series of tests, covering:

- aptitude
- practical initiative
- health and fitness.

You would then be interviewed and have a medical assessment.

Tests usually take place at an AFCO. For some of the trades you will need GCSEs and BTEC or City & Guilds qualifications.

Most trades are open to men and women. However, women are not able to join the RAF Regiment, which involves combat. For more details on all requirements, check the RAF Careers website.

More information

RAF Careers
Tel: 0845 605 5555
www.raf.mod.uk/careers

ROYAL MARINES COMMANDO

The nature of the work

Royal Marines are part of the Royal Navy. They take part in front-line combat (on land and at sea) and are sent at short notice to deal with emergency situations, which may include military operations or natural disasters. If you are physically fit, resourceful and have self-discipline, this could be for you.

In this job you will need to be resilient and determined. You will need to follow orders. You will also need to think and react quickly under pressure.

To become a Royal Marines commando you must be male and a British citizen. You do not need any formal qualifications, however, you must pass the Royal Navy selection process.

What can you earn?

On entry, Royal Marines earn around £13,337 a year. This can rise to between £16,681 and £28,372 a year. Non-Commissioned Officers (corporals and sergeants) can earn around £32,000 to £36,200. Senior Non-Commissioned Officers (colour sergeants and warrant officers) can earn up to £45,800.

Extra allowances may be paid for family separation and special service. All medical and dental care is free. Where housing is provided, deductions may be made from the monthly income.

Entry requirements

As a first step to joining the Royal Marines you should visit your local armed forces careers office (AFCO), where you will be able to pick up free leaflets and have an informal chat about your career options. You can search for your local AFCO on the Army Jobs website.

To become a Royal Marines commando you must be male and a British citizen. You do not need any formal qualifications, however, you must pass the Royal Navy selection process. This involves:

- aptitude tests for reasoning, English language, numeracy and mechanical comprehension
  an interview and medical check
- a pre-joining fitness test, including two 2.4km runs on a treadmill, to be completed within 12 minutes 30 seconds and 10 minutes 30 seconds respectively
- the Potential Royal Marine Course (PRMC), which lasts three days and includes physical tests, classroom-based work and an interview.

As a commando you will serve an open engagement which lasts for 18 years (this can be extended up to the age of 55). You will usually be able to hand in 12 months' notice if you wish to leave after serving a minimum of three years.

See the Royal Navy website for more information and a list of specialist areas of work.

More information

Ryal navy
Careers Enquiries: 0845 607 5555
www.royalnavy.mod.uk

Armed Forces Careers Office (NI)
Royal Navy and Royal Marines
Palace Barracks
Holywood
Co Down
BT18 9RA
Tel: 028 9042 7040

ROYAL MARINES OFFICER

The nature of the work

Royal Marines (RM) officers lead teams of commando-trained soldiers in combat situations, at sea or on shore. Increasingly, RM officers are involved in leading peace-keeping and humanitarian missions.

As an RM officer, you would be responsible for the day-to-day welfare and discipline of the marines under your command. You would usually start out as a troop officer in charge of 28 men. Your duties would involve leading the troop and making decisions about their training and deployment.

What can you earn?

Trainees can earn between £15,300 and £24,150 a year. Captains earn between £36,160 and £43,000. Colonels can earn up to £85,300.

Extra allowances may be paid, for example when overseas or on flying duties. Deductions may be made where accommodation is provided.

Entry requirements

To apply for Royal Marine officer training, you will need:

- a minimum height of 1.51 metres and weight in proportion to your height
- to pass a medical assessment
- to meet the Royal Marines nationality and residence requirement
- to be at least age 17 (upper age limits vary depending on your specialism)
- a minimum of five GCSEs (A-C) including English and maths, plus two A levels (alternative qualifications may also be accepted).

If you have a UK degree you can apply for marine officer training through direct graduate entry. Financial support through scholarships, sponsorships and bursaries is sometimes available to help with sixth-form and degree-level study. Check with your Armed Forces Careers Office for full details of all criteria.

You must also pass a three-day Potential Officers Course, which will test your physical ability, endurance, mental aptitude and leadership skills. This is followed by an interview.

You will join the service as an officer on a 12-year Initial Commission. You would usually need to serve a minimum of between three and five years.

More information

Royal Navy
Careers Enquiries: 0845 607 5555
www.royal-navy.mod.uk

Armed Forces Careers Office (NI)
Royal Navy and Royal Marines
Palace Barracks
Holywood
Co Down
BT18 9RA
Tel: 028 9042 7040

ROYAL NAVY OFFICER

The nature of the work

Royal Navy officers are senior managers in the Royal Navy, working onboard ships and submarines.

As an officer, you would be responsible for the welfare and management of those serving in your squadron or unit. You would also have a specialist role such as:

- warfare officer – controlling weapons and defence systems, and assisting with navigation
- air engineering officer – making the ship's aircraft ready to fly when needed, and working with industry to improve aircraft design
- weapons engineering officer – overseeing the maintenance of weapons delivery systems, detection sensors, and communications equipment
- logistics officer – managing the delivery of supplies and equipment, and giving advice on the legal and financial implications
- medical or nursing officer – providing medical care on ships, submarines and ashore.

For details on the full range of officer specialisms, see the Royal Navy website.

What can you earn?

Lieutenants earn from £37,915 to £45,090 a year. Lieutenant commanders earn from £47,760 to £57,199. Commanders earn between £67,031 and £77,617. Captains can earn up to £89,408.

Deductions may be made if accommodation is provided. Extra allowances are paid for family separation, special service and flying duties.

Entry requirements

To get on to Royal Navy officer training, you will need:

- to be at least age 17 (the upper age limit varies according to the specialism)
- a minimum height of 151.5cm
- to meet strict eyesight standards
- to pass a medical
- to meet the Royal Navy nationality and residence requirements.

You will also need qualifications equivalent to:

- five GCSEs (A-C), including English and Maths two A levels.
- If you have a degree you could apply through Direct Graduate Entry.

Check with your local Armed Forces Careers Office (listed on the Royal Navy Careers website) for a full explanation of all criteria.

Financial support through scholarships and bursaries is sometimes available to help with sixth-form and degree-level study; see the Royal Navy Careers website for details.

For all officer roles you need to pass the Admiralty Interview Board at HMS Sultan in Hampshire. This is a two-day assessment which includes interviews and tests in communication, maths, mental agility, spatial orientation and physical fitness.

You can get full information and advice on Royal Navy officer careers by ringing the Royal Navy Career Enquiries helpline.

More information

Royal Navy
Careers Enquiries: 0845 607 5555
www.royal-navy.mod.uk

Armed Forces Careers Office (NI)
Royal Navy and Royal Marines
Palace Barracks
Holywood
Co Down
BT18 9RA
Tel: 028 9042 7040

ROYAL NAVY RATING

The nature of the work
Royal Navy ratings work in a variety of job roles onboard ships or submarines at sea, or in a Royal Navy shore base.

As a royal navy rating, your work will vary depending on which branch of the service you support and your specific trade. Branches and related duties include:

- warfare – operating and maintaining the ship's weapons, electronic systems and sensors; co-ordinating the ship's communications systems
- engineering – operating, maintaining and refitting the Royal Navy's ships, submarines and aircraft
- logistics – operating and co-ordinating a range of office, accounting, stores and catering systems
- naval air branch – ensuring that Navy aircraft are prepared for action and giving navigation information based on weather and ocean conditions
- submarine service – operating and maintaining a submarine's weapons, electronic systems and sensors.

What can you earn?

Starting salaries are from £13,895 a year. Able ratings can earn between £17,265 and £28,939 a year. Warrant officers can earn up to £46,753 a year.

Submariners, divers and anyone required to fly, may receive additional pay. Extra allowances are also paid for family separations. Where accommodation is provided, deductions may be made from monthly pay.

Entry requirements

To join the Royal Navy you will need to pass a selection test, interview and medical examination. For many jobs or trades within the Navy, there are no formal academic entry requirements and you will receive training on the job. However, you will have a wider choice of careers if you have some GCSEs (A-C). Your local Royal Navy Careers Office can advise you further on your options, and the exact requirements.

- Entry to the Royal Navy is possible from the age of 16 for most trades. The exceptions are:
- medical assistants, dental surgery assistants and dental hygienists (17)
- divers (18)
- student naval nurses (17 years, 6 months)
- direct entry registered general nurses (21).

For all trades, the upper age limit at entry is 36. The upper age limit may be waived for exceptional candidates. You will need to apply at least six months in advance of the age limit.

The minimum height for all entrants is 151.5 centimetres and your weight must be in proportion to your height. There are strict eyesight standards and, for some jobs, normal colour vision is essential. You must also meet nationality and residence requirements.

More information

Royal Navy
Careers Enquiries: 0845 607 5555
www.royal-navy.mod.uk

Armed Forces Careers Office (NI)
Royal Navy and Royal Marines
Palace Barracks
Holywood Co Down BT18 9RA
Tel: 028 9042 7040

****

4. BANKING AND FINANCE

Like accountancy, banking is a very diverse industry. Bankers have come to the forefront since the onset of the credit crunch and not in a favourable way. However, you should ignore the negative publicity as banking is a very worthwhile and rewarding career.

There are several different types of bank. Firstly, there are the traditional retail banks which are high street banks with branches across the country, these are the banks that most people deal with on a day to day basis. Then there are the investment banks dealing with large companies and other investment organisations.

There are many different types of role in the banking world, ranging from cashiers through to more senior roles such as bank managers and brokers.

In this section, we look at:

- Cashiers and Customer Services Advisors
- Bank Management
- Building Society Jobs
- Commodity Brokers
- Financial Advisors

CASHIERS OR CUSTOMER SERVICE ADVISORS

The nature of the work
The above deal with all general queries, made in person or by phone or in writing or via the web. They will, typically, work in either branches or call centres. They will be responsible for a wide variety of functions, such as processing cash and cheques and dealing with foreign currency. Senior cashiers will work in a supervisory role. All in all, those who enter the world of banking via a cashier role will gain valuable experience of work at the ground floor, experience that will stand them in good stead for more senior roles later on.

Entry requirements

Banks will set their own entry requirements but most will set entry tests which will assess the level of maths, English and IT skills. These are the most important attributes which will help a candidate gain entry to the world of banking. Most banks will require GCSE grades A-C. Once having gained entry training is on the job. Training to a higher level is provided to enable candidates to progress to manager level.

BANK MANAGER

The role of the bank manager is rather more complex. The manager will be involved in strategic planning and they will usually be placed in a branch, being responsible for the running of a branch. The manager will be involved also in putting together sales strategies and offering advice to clients.

Entry to management level

There are two main routes into management-as mentioned above through promotion from cashier/customer services advisor or buy joining a training scheme run by the bank. Most banks will expect a good honours degree in a business or finance related subject, but some will accept good A levels.

Managers will normally work towards a professional qualification, including The Professional Diploma in Financial Services Management, The Applied Diploma in Corporate Banking and the Applied Diploma in Retailing Financial Services. Banks will also run their own management courses in house as the job progresses.

What can you earn?

Cashiers will start on a salary of between 14,000-16,500 which will rise with experience. Managers will usually start on 21,000-25,000 which again rises with experience. Many roles will incorporate bonuses although these have now been moderated following the general and ongoing furore over bankers pay.

More information

British Bankers Association (BBA)
020 7216 8000
www.bba.org.uk

Financial Services Skills Council
0845 257 3772
www.fssc.org.uk

BUILDING SOCIETY JOBS

Although building societies are structured differently to banks, in terms of their legal structure, the jobs available largely mirror those within banks. For more information concerning jobs in building societies contact:

Building Societies Association
020 7520 5900
www.bsa.org.uk

Outside of the banks, there are other important and rewarding roles, such as:

COMMODITY BROKERS

The nature of the work
Commodity brokers buy and sell a variety of commodities , which will include grain, coffee, oil, gas and metals. In addition to trading actual products they will also deal in what are known as futures, which are commodities that will be produced in the future. Prices are fixed way into the future and gains or losses can be made. There is an element of risk involved here. Commodity brokers will work in conjunction with a variety of organisations such as transport, shipping and insurance.

Entry requirements
Most successful applicants in this field will be highly numerate and have a good degree in a relevant subject such as economics or maths. Applicants can earn high salaries, with new entrants earning between 35,000 to 50,000. Experienced brokers can earn many times this amount.

More information
Financial Services Skills Council
0845 257 3772

www.fssc.org.uk
Intercontinental Exchange
020 7481 0643
www.theice.com

The London Metal Exchange
020 7264 5555
www.lme.co.uk

FINANCIAL ADVISORS

Financial advisers help their clients choose financial products and services. These might be investments, savings or pensions. They can also be mortgages and insurance. If you are interested in finance and you want to help people make decisions, this could be an ideal job for you.

A financial adviser needs to be able to explain complex information clearly and simply. They need to have good maths and computer skills. They also need to be trustworthy.

The nature of the work
As a financial adviser, your work would normally involve:
- having meetings with clients
- talking to clients about their current finances and future plans
- researching financial products
- explaining details of products so that clients can make informed choices
- preparing clear recommendations
- meeting performance and sales targets
- negotiating with providers of financial products
- keeping detailed records
- dealing with client enquiries
- producing financial reports
- keeping clients regularly updated about their investments
- keeping up to date with new products and changes in the law.

You could work as a 'tied', 'multi-tied' or independent financial adviser:

- tied – usually working for banks, building societies or insurance companies, and only offering your own company's financial products
- multi-tied – dealing with a number of companies and only selling products from those companies
- independent financial adviser (IFA) – offering products and giving advice on all financial products on the market.

You would need to follow strict financial industry rules and guidelines. These make sure that you act fairly and that you are properly qualified to give appropriate financial advice.

What can you earn?

Financial advisers working for a company are usually paid a basic salary plus commission. Independent financial advisers can be paid either a fee or commission. Basic salaries without commission for trainee and newly qualified advisers can be around £22,000 to £30,000 a year. As an experienced financial adviser, you may earn up to £40,000 a year. Successful advisers, especially those working in wealth management or private client advice, may earn between £50,000 and £70,000 or more a year, with commission.

Entry requirements

You could become a financial adviser with various qualifications and experience. Many employers consider 'people skills' and a strong background in customer service, sales or financial services to be more important than formal qualifications.

A common way to start this career is as a tied adviser in a bank, building society or insurance company. You would do this job after being promoted from a customer service role and achieving an industry-regulated qualification. These qualifications are known as 'appropriate qualifications'. See the Financial Skills Partnership (FSP) website for details.

You could also start as a paraplanner – a person who provides administrative support and research for independent financial advisers. If you are not already working in financial services, you could take an approved qualification for trainee financial advisers before you join the industry. See the Training and Development section below for details.

Some banks, building societies and large firms of independent financial advisers (IFAs) offer graduate training schemes for new advisers who have degrees or similar qualifications.

You may be able to start this career through a Level 4 Higher Apprenticeship in providing financial advice. You will need to check if there are schemes available in your area. For more information, visit the Apprenticeships or FSP websites.

More information
Financial Skills Partnership
51 Gresham Street
London
EC2V 7HQ
Tel: 0845 257 3772
www.financialskillspartnership.org.uk

Chartered Insurance Institute
42-48 High Road
South Woodford
London
E18 2JP
Tel: 020 8989 8464
www.discoverrisk.co.uk
www.cii.co.uk

Personal Finance Society
42-48 High Road
South Woodford
London
E18 2JP
Tel: 020 8530 0852
www.thepfs.org

5. CATERING

Catering is a diverse profession, with many opportunities on offer. In this section we look at the roles of:

- Catering Manager
- Chef
- Food Scientist
- Consumer Scientist
- Baker

For details of other jobs within the industry go to:

People first
2nd Floor
Armstrong House
38 Market Square
Uxbridge
Middlesex
UB8 1LH
Tel: 01895 817 000
www.people1st.co.uk

CATERING MANAGER

The nature of the work

As a catering manager, you could work in hotels, small independent restaurants, eateries that are part of a large chain, and fast food outlets. Your role would be to make sure that the restaurant runs smoothly, overseeing the business side as well as ensuring high standards for customers.

As a catering manager you would work in larger catering operations, such as business or factory canteens, hospitals or schools. You would have less contact with customers than a restaurant manager, and spend more time behind the scenes.

Your duties as a restaurant or catering manager would include:

- planning menus
- advertising vacancies and recruiting staff
- making sure that all staff are fully trained
- keeping staff motivated to provide the highest standard of service
- organising shifts and rotas
- managing stock control and budgets
- running the business in line with strict hygiene, health and safety guidelines.

What can you earn?

Entry requirements

To apply for a trainee manager job, you will usually need a good standard of general education plus relevant experience.

You could work your way up to a management position, for example by starting as a waiter/waitress. With experience and qualifications you could take on more responsibilities and supervise less experienced colleagues. You could then apply for a head of waiting staff or assistant manager post. Qualifications include:

- Level 2 NVQ Diploma in Food and Beverage Service
- Level 3 Advanced Apprenticeship in Hospitality & Catering (Supervision & Leadership).

Many large restaurants, fast food chains and catering companies run management trainee schemes that can lead to management roles. You would usually need a qualification such as a foundation degree, BTEC HNC/HND or degree, or relevant experience, in order to be accepted on a scheme.

More information

Springboard UK
Http://springboarduk.net

People first
2nd Floor
Armstrong House
38 Market Square
Uxbridge
Middlesex
UB8 1LH
Tel: 01895 817 000
www.people1st.co.uk

UKSP
www.uksp.co.uk

CHEF

The nature of the work

Chefs prepare food using a variety of cooking methods. In large kitchens they normally work as part of a team, and look after one food area, like bread and pastries, or vegetables. The head chef (also known as executive chef, kitchen manager or chef de cuisine) runs the entire kitchen.

Your main tasks as a chef would include:

- preparing, cooking and presenting food in line with required standards
- keeping preparation at the right level
- making sure that food is served promptly
- monitoring food production to ensure consistent quality and portion size
- stock control

- following relevant hygiene, health and safety guidelines.

You would usually start as a kitchen assistant or trainee chef (also known as commis chef). At this level you would spend time in each area of the kitchen, learning a range of skills and how to look after kitchen equipment.

With experience, you could progress to section chef (also known as station chef and chef de partie), where you would be in charge of an area of the kitchen. The next step would be sous chef, where you would be running the entire kitchen for the head chef when needed. At head chef level, you would be responsible for creating and updating the menus, and for producing and meeting financial budgets.

What can you earn?

A trainee (commis) chef may start on a salary of around £12,200 a year. Section chefs (chefs de partie) can earn up to £16,000 a year, and a second chef (sous chef) may earn around £22,000 a year.

Head chefs (chefs de cuisine) can earn up to £30,000 a year. An executive head chef in a top hotel can earn between £40,000 and £50,000.

Entry requirements

You may not need any academic qualifications to start work as a trainee (commis) chef. However, some employers will prefer you to have a good general standard of education, possibly including a hospitality or catering qualification.

Another way to prepare for this work would be to take one of the following qualifications. Some of these also combine classroom study with practical experience and work placements:

- Level 1 Diploma in Introduction to Professional Cookery/Level 2 Diploma in Professional Cookery
- Level 1 NVQ Certificate in Food Production and Cooking/Level 2 NVQ Diploma in Food Production and Cooking
- Level 2 NVQ Diploma in Professional Cookery

- Level 2 Certificate in Hospitality and Catering Principles (Professional Cookery) or (Food Production and Cooking).

Check with colleges for details of course entry requirements.

Another option is to progress as a chef through a Level 2 Apprenticeship in Hospitality and Catering (Food Production & Cooking) or (Professional Cookery). You will need to check which schemes are available in your area. To find out more about Apprenticeships in hospitality, visit the Apprenticeships and UKSP websites.

More information

Springboard UK
http://springboarduk.net

People first
2nd Floor
Armstrong House
38 Market Square
Uxbridge
Middlesex
UB8 1LH
Tel: 01895 817 000
www.people1st.co.uk

FOOD SCIENTIST/TECHNOLOGIST

The nature of the work
As a food scientist, you would use scientific techniques to:

- provide accurate nutritional information for food labelling
- investigate ways to keep food fresh, safe and attractive
- find ways of producing food more quickly and cheaply
- test the safety and quality of food.

As a food technologist, you would plan the manufacture of food and drink products and your duties may include:

- working on newly discovered ingredients to invent new recipes and ideas
- modifying foods, for example creating fat-free products
- conducting experiments and producing sample products
- designing the processes and machinery for making products in large quantities.

Some jobs (for example carrying out research for a supermarket chain) may involve quality control as well as product development.

As a food scientist or food technologist you would also gain knowledge and experience of areas like chemical engineering, production planning, market and consumer research, and financial management.

What can you earn?
Starting salaries for food scientists and technologists can be between £20,000 and £25,000 a year. With experience and increased responsibilities, this can rise to between £30,000 and £45,000.

Entry requirements
You will need a strong background in science, usually through a BTEC HNC/HND or degree in a subject such as food science, food studies, or food technology.

To get on to a degree you will usually need:

- five GCSEs (A-C), and
- two or three A levels, preferably in chemistry or biology.

For a BTEC HNC/HND, entry requirements are usually one or two A levels or equivalent.
You can search for courses on the Universities and Colleges Admissions Service (UCAS) website, and you should check directly with course providers for exact requirements.

If you have a degree in an unrelated subject, you could improve your chances of employment by taking a postgraduate course in a subject such as food safety or food quality management.

Visit the Institute of Food Science and Technology careers website for more information including details of relevant courses.

Alternatively, you could begin as a lab technician and work towards further qualifications whilst in employment. For this level you would need at least four GCSEs (A-C) including English, maths, and a science subject. See the laboratory technician job profile for more information.

Another option could be to enter through an apprenticeship scheme. The range of Apprenticeships available in your area will depend on the local jobs market and the types of skills employers need from their workers. The most suitable Apprenticeship in Food and Drink (Food Industry Skills). To find out more, visit the Apprenticeships website.

More information

Improve Ltd
Providence House
2 Innovation Close
York
YO10 5ZF
Tel: 0845 644 0448
www.improveltd.co.uk

Institute of Food Science and Technology (IFST)
5 Cambridge Court
210 Shepherd's Bush Road
London
W6 7NJ
Tel: 020 7603 6316
www.ifst.org

IFST Careers
www.foodtechcareers.org

Chartered Institute of Environmental Health
Chadwick Court
15 Hatfields
London
SE1 8DJ
Tel: 020 7928 6006
www.cieh.org

CIEH Careers Website
www.ehcareers.org

The Food and Drink Federation
6 Catherine Street
London
WC2B 5JJ
Tel: 020 7836 2460
www.fdf.org.uk

CONSUMER SCIENTIST

The nature of the work

As a consumer scientist, you would provide a key link between consumers and manufacturers. Your work would involve:

- researching the tastes, needs, aspirations and preferences of consumers
- giving advice (for example to retailers) on how to improve the quality, design, production, delivery and popularity of an item or service.

You could use your knowledge of consumer behaviour in a variety of industries. For example in food product development, you would work with a supermarket chain or manufacturer, researching and designing new dishes to attract consumers.

Other areas you could be involved with include:

- marketing – using market research to help marketing professionals develop, package, advertise and distribute a product or campaign
- quality assurance – developing tests to make sure products meet quality standards and legal requirements
- consumer advice – representing consumers' rights, using knowledge of relevant legislation
- catering – advising hotels, restaurants, schools, residential care homes or hospitals on the type of food to provide
- product and service development – advising on products ranging from household goods to public amenities
- publishing and public relations – producing information on cookery, family health and new products, or liaising with the media
- education – advising on healthy living, in schools or further and higher education
- government departments – working for bodies such as the Food Standards Agency or Trading Standards to enforce food safety and consumer protection laws.

Your main duties are likely to involve researching and writing reports, carrying out experiments (for example, developing recipes), recruiting and training panels or focus groups, and conducting interviews with consumers.

What can you earn?

- Starting salaries can be between £17,000 and £22,500 a year.
- With experience, earnings can rise to around £30,000.
- Managers may earn around £40,000 to £50,000.

Entry requirements

Many employers will want you to have a degree or BTEC HND in a subject such as:

- consumer studies
- consumer product management
- food and consumer management
- food science or technology
- psychology

- marketing
- statistics.

To get on to a degree you will usually need five GCSEs (A-C) and two A levels. However, you should check with course providers because alternative qualifications may also be accepted. Some employers may prefer you to have a postgraduate qualification, for instance in behavioural psychology or consumer behaviour. Experience in food manufacturing or market research could be an advantage or an alternative way of getting into consumer science.

More information

Improve Ltd
Providence House
2 Innovation Close
York
YO10 5ZF
Tel: 0845 644 0448
http://www.improve-skills.co.uk/
www.improveltd.co.uk

Food Standards Agency
Aviation House
125 Kingsway
London
WC2B 6NH
Tel: 020 7276 8000
www.foodstandards.gov.uk

BAKER

The nature of the work

At a plant bakery, you would use machinery and production lines to manufacture large amounts of baked goods for shops, supermarkets and other large customers.

As an in-store baker, for example with a supermarket, you would use some automated machinery to make fresh bread products to be sold in the store.

At a craft bakery, you would create a smaller amount of products to be sold in a shop, delicatessen or chain of specialist shops. This work would be more varied, and although some machinery is used, you would do much of the work by hand.

What can you earn?

Bakers can earn between £11,600 and £16,000 a year. With experience, specialist skills or supervisory responsibilities, this could rise to around £20,000 to £25,000 a year. Additional payments may be made for working overtime or shifts.

Entry requirements

You can apply for work as a trainee in a bakery without any specific qualifications. However, having GCSEs in English, maths, science or food technology could help you.

You could learn bakery skills and develop your knowledge through part-time and full-time courses at further education colleges. Qualifications you could gain include:

- Level 2 Certificate/Diploma in Professional Bakery
- Level 3 Diploma in Professional Bakery
- Level 3 Diploma in Professional Bakery, Science and Technology.

You may be able to do this job through an Apprenticeship scheme. The most suitable Apprenticeship is the Improve Proficiency Apprenticeship in Food and Drink (Bakery Industry Skills). You will need to check which schemes are available in your area. To find out more, see the Apprenticeships website.

More information

Improve Ltd
Providence House

2 Innovation Close
York
YO10 5ZF
Tel: 0845 644 0448
www.improveltd.co.uk

Federation of Bakers
6 Catherine Street
London
WC2B 5JW
Tel: 020 7420 7190
www.bakersfederation.org.uk

****

6. CIVIL SERVICE AND LOCAL GOVERNMENT

The civil service is vast and forms the backbone of government. There are numerous opportunities within the civil service, many of them concentrated in London but also many in various departments in the UK as a whole from local government to administration of passports and driving licences. In this section we look at:

- Civil Service Administrative Officer
- Civil Service Executive Officer
- Diplomatic Services Officer
- Local Government Administrative assistant
- Town Planning Support Staff
- Registrar of Births, Deaths and marriages and Civil Partnerships

For further information about the variety of jobs in the civil service you should go to www.civilservice.gov.uk

CIVIL SERVICE ADMINISTRATION OFFICER

The nature of the work
Your main tasks at administrative officer (AO) or administrative assistant (AA) grade would be to deal with customers, update records and carry out routine clerical duties. Your day-to-day work would depend on which department or agency you worked for, but might include:

- handling enquiries from the public in person, by telephone or by letter
- updating computerised and paper-based records
- processing benefit payments
- researching information
- filing, photocopying and other administrative tasks.

With experience, you could deal with more complex enquiries or complaints, or take on more specialist work related to your department.

What can you earn?

Administrative assistants start on around £12,000 a year. Administrative officers start on around £14,500 a year. With experience and good performance this can rise to between £16,000 and £20,000 a year.

Entry requirements

Each department and agency organises its own recruitment and sets its own entry requirements.

You do not need formal qualifications for many jobs. Instead, you would take an aptitude test to prove your ability in areas like teamwork, communication and number skills. However, some departments may ask for five GCSEs (A-C) or similar qualifications for certain jobs.

You must also meet the nationality requirement. All jobs are open to British nationals and around 75% are also open to Commonwealth citizens or European Union nationals. See the Civil Service website for more information.

More information

There aren't any central telephone number for information - see the Civil Service Website for contacts for individual departments.

CIVIL SERVICE EXECUTIVE OFFICER

The nature of the work

Executive officers are the first level of management in the civil service. As an executive officer, you could work in any of the 170 civil service departments and agencies that deal with developing policies and delivering services to the public. All departments and agencies employ people at executive officer (EO) grade, although job titles can vary widely.

Your exact duties would depend on the department you worked for, but could include:

- managing a team of administrative officers being responsible for motivating, training and appraising team members
- training in a specific area of work such as tax or immigration control
- handling a caseloads

- applying complex laws and procedures to deal with problems and enquiries
- using computer systems and databases
- preparing and presenting reports.

What can you earn?

Salaries at EO grade are between around £21,000 and £24,000 a year. Salaries are higher in London. There may be extra allowances for working unsocial hours.

Entry requirements

You could join a civil service department in an administrative grade and work your way up, or you could be recruited directly as an executive officer.

Each department organises its own recruitment and sets its own entry requirements. You may need two A levels or equivalent qualifications for some jobs at EO grade, but in many cases you will not be asked for any formal qualifications. Instead, when you apply you would go through various stages, which might include:

- filling in an application form based on your skills and life experience
- taking a written test to check your level of English and maths
- passing more selection tests and an interview.

If you have a first or second class honours degree, you can apply to the Fast Stream Development Programme. This is a four-year training scheme that leads to senior management posts. Your degree can be in any subject, although some departments may prefer degrees in subjects that are relevant to their work.

Competition for places on the Fast Stream is very strong, and you must pass a series of selection tests and interviews. Fast Stream is usually only open to UK nationals. See the Civil Service website for more information on the Fast Stream.

For all jobs you must also meet the nationality requirement – all jobs are open to British nationals and around 75% are also open to Commonwealth citizens or European Union nationals. You can find more information on the Civil Service website.

More information

No central telephone number for information, see <u>Civil Service Jobs Online</u> for contacts for individual departments.

DIPLOMATIC SERVICE OFFICER

The nature of the work
The work of the FCO is very varied and covers every area where British interests and citizens are involved internationally, for example:

- political – monitoring political and economic developments in the host country, and representing Britain to that country's government and media
- commercial – helping British companies to trade in the host country, and promoting investment into Britain
- consular – helping British citizens in the host country, and processing visa applications from local people who wish to come to Britain.

Your day-to-day duties would depend on your grade. For example:

- Policy Officers (grade C4) – researching issues and helping to develop policy and strategy
- Executive Assistants (A2) – drafting letters, handling accounts and invoices, and providing clerical support
- Administrative Assistants (A1) – providing clerical support.

As a UK-based Policy or Operational Officer, you might be responsible for one country or geographical area, or for a specific foreign policy issue that affects many countries.

What can you earn?
Administrative Assistants start on £16,635 a year (plus London allowance where appropriate). Executive assistants start on £18,885 a year. Operational Officers start on £21,432. Policy (Fast Stream) Officers start on £26,102 a

year. All London-based staff are also awarded an extra allowance of £3,000 a year for when working in London. Staff working overseas may be paid additional allowances.

Entry requirements

The qualifications and experience that you need to join the Foreign and Commonwealth Office will vary depending on the grade of job you are applying for.

To join as a C4 Policy Entrant through the civil service's Fast Stream programme, you must have at least a second class degree in any subject. You must then pass a series of skills-based online and practical tests. See the Faststream website for more information on the Fast Stream recruitment process.

For Executive Assistant (A2) posts you will need at least five GCSEs (A-C) including English and maths, or equivalent qualifications. For Administrative Assistant (A1) posts you will need two GCSEs (A-C) including English, or equivalent.

To join the FCO at any grade, you must meet the nationality and residency requirements, and pass a strict security vetting process. See the Careers section of the FCO website for full details of these.

Each job's selection process involves several stages, and can take several months to complete especially at the higher grades.

For the policy grade, previous work experience in management, business or public administration would be useful, though not essential.

You will find it useful to have experience of office work for the administrative grades, and your typing skills will be tested during the selection process.

More information

Foreign and Commonwaelth Office
www.fco.gov.uk

Civil Service Jobs Online
No central telephone number for information, see website for contacts for

individual departments
www.civilservice.gov.uk

Careers in operational delivery- helps you to explore the different career pathways you would need to follow to get to specific job roles within Operational Delivery

www.civilservice.gov.uk/my-civil-service/networks/professional/operational-delivery/leading-opdel-profession.aspx

---

LOCAL GOVERNMENT ADMINISTRATIVE ASSISTANT

The nature of the work
You could work in any local authority department, for example housing, social services, education or planning.

Your duties would vary according to the department you worked in, but they might include:

- dealing with enquiries by phone, in writing or in person
- looking up information on a computer system
- filing and photocopying
- producing and sending letters
- sorting, recording and distributing mail
- dealing with cash and payments
- updating computerised and clerical records
- acting as a secretary or personal assistant (PA) to a manager or department
- liaising with staff in other departments.
- You may also be known by a number of different job titles such as administrative officer, clerical officer, customer service assistant, or support officer.

What can you earn?
Salaries are usually between £13,000 and £19,000 a year, depending on experience and responsibilities.

Entry requirements

For most jobs, you will need a good standard of general education, and good computer or keyboard skills. You will usually find it useful to have experience of customer service or office work.

Although you may have an advantage with some GCSEs including maths and English, many councils do not ask for formal qualifications. Instead, they will test you in the skills you need for the job, for example communication, IT and ability with numbers.

You should check with individual councils about the exact qualifications and experience needed for each job.

You may be able to get into this job through an Apprenticeship scheme. The range of Apprenticeships available in your area will depend on the local jobs market and the types of skills employers need from their workers. To find out more, visit the Apprenticeships website.

More information

LG careers
www.lgcareers.com

Skills CFA
6 Graphite Square
Vauxhall Walk
London
SE11 5EE
Tel: 020 7091 9620
www.cfa.uk.com

LOCAL GOVERNMENT OFFICER

The nature of the work

You could work in a variety of departments and roles, such as planning council services in a policy section, or delivering services in a department like education or housing. Job titles at this level could include best value officer, external funding officer, policy officer and democratic services officer.

Your day-to-day tasks would vary according to the department and your level of responsibility. They may include:

- managing and evaluating projects
- writing reports and briefing papers
- dealing with enquiries and giving advice
- presenting information at meetings
- supervising administrative work and managing clerical staff
- keeping records
- preparing and managing contracts
- liaising with other agencies
- managing budgets and funding.

What can you earn?

Starting salaries can be between £16,000 and £20,000 a year, depending on the job. With experience this can rise to between £22,000 and £38,000.

Entry requirements

The skills and experience that are needed will vary depending on the duties and level of responsibility, so you should check the entry requirements carefully for each job. For some jobs, employers will ask for qualifications to degree standard, or equivalent work experience. Most councils value life experience and may accept you without the exact qualifications that they have asked for, as long as you have enough relevant experience and the skills needed for the job.

If you have a good degree in any subject, you may be able to join many local authorities in England and Wales through the National Graduate Development Programme. Some other local authorities run their own graduate or management training schemes for new entrants. See the National Graduate Development Programme website for more information.

More information

LG Careers
www.lgcareers.com

Institute of Chattered Secretaries and Administrators (ICSA)
16 Park Crescent

London
W1B 1AH
Tel: 020 7580 4741
www.icsa.org.uk

Institute of Administrative Management
Caroline House
55-57 High Holborn
London
WC1V 6DX
Tel: 020 7841 1100
www.instam.org

TOWN PLANNING SUPPORT STAFF

The nature of the work
Town planning support staff help to process planning applications submitted by individuals and businesses. This is a broad role that includes everything from giving advice to the public, to technical planning and office duties.

- As a support staff member, your responsibilities would include:
- preparing reports for internal and external publications
- recording minutes at meetings
- building and managing technical libraries, filing systems and databases
- drawing up designs, using computer-aided design (CAD) software
- carrying out data surveys, for example traffic impact assessments
- supplying information and data to planners for applications
- recording the progress and outcomes of planning applications
- organising public meetings
- answering enquiries about application procedures.

You might also work in planning enforcement, which would involve:

- working with individuals and businesses to make sure that they comply with the conditions set out in their application decisions
- gathering information to use as evidence in disputes

- presenting reports on breaches to planning committees or, where necessary, to magistrates and judges.

You would usually work for a local authority, independent planning consultancy, government department or a private company, for example a property developer.

What can you earn?

Starting salaries are between £14,000 and £18,000 a year. Experienced staff can earn between £18,500 and £23,000. Qualified technical staff with supervisory duties can earn up to £28,000.

Entry requirements

Most employers will expect you to have GCSEs or A levels, in relevant subjects such as maths, English, geography, IT or economics, or equivalent qualifications.

Specific qualifications and/or experience in surveying, CAD design, construction, information management, administration or law may also be useful skills for getting into this career.

See the Royal Town Planning Institute (RTPI) website for more details about careers in this field, and the Local Government careers website for information about local government planning.

More information

Royal Town Planning Institute
41 Botolph Lane
London
EC3R 8DL
Tel: 020 7929 9494
www.rtpi.org.uk

LG Jobs
www.lgcareers.com

REGISTRAR OF BIRTHS MARRIAGES AND CIVIL PARTNERSHIPS

The nature of the work

In this job your main duties would include:

- interviewing parents and relatives after a birth or a death
- completing computerised and paper records
- issuing birth or death certificates
- informing the coroner (or procurator fiscal in Scotland) if there are any suspicious circumstances surrounding a death
- collecting statistics to send to the General Register Office
- taking payment for copies of certificates
- keeping accurate records
- performing civil ceremonies.

You could also be employed as a celebrant, conducting civil ceremonies such as marriages, civil partnerships and civil funerals without the responsibility of registering births and deaths. You could be employed by a local council, or you could work independently (see the Association of Independent Celebrants for information). If you share humanist beliefs, you could also become an officiant or celebrant of the British Humanist Association.

What can you earn?

Assistant registrars usually start on around £17,000 a year. Registrars can expect to earn around £25,000 a year. Superintendent registrars may earn up to £40,000 a year. Part-time celebrants usually earn a set fee for each ceremony they conduct.

Entry requirements

To become a registrar, you will need experience of dealing with a wide range of people, and you should be computer literate. You may find it useful to have some experience of public speaking. A driving licence is also useful.

Employers look for a good standard of general education and will usually prefer you to be qualified to at least GCSE standard or equivalent, including English and maths. In Scotland applicants need three S-Grades (1-3) including English. Doctors, midwives, ministers of religion, funeral directors and anyone working in the life assurance industry are not allowed to become registrars.

More information

LG careers
www.lgcareers.com

****

7. CONSTRUCTION

Although the construction industry is contracting at this point in time, there are always many opportunities within this area for a variety of different skills. One truism about this industry is that it expands and contracts regularly and the government is always using construction to try to get the economy going.

The following jobs are outlined below:

- Architect
- Bricklayer
- Building surveyor
- Building control officer
- Carpenters/joiners
- Civil engineer
- Clerk of works
- Electrician
- Gas service engineer
- Painter/decorator
- Plasterer
- Plumber
- Quantity surveyor
- Town planner

For more information on all jobs in the construction industry go to:

Construction Skills
Bircham Newton
King's Lynn
Norfolk
PE31 6RH
Tel: 0344 994 4400
www.cskills.org

ARCHITECT

The nature of the work

Architects draw plans for new buildings, and for restoring and conserving old ones. Their work also involves planning the layout of groups of buildings and the spaces around them.

To be an architect you will have to finish a five-year university course and complete at least two years' professional experience.

You would be responsible for a building project from the earliest stage through to completion. On larger jobs, you could work in a team alongside other architects and architectural technicians or technologists.

What can you earn?

As an architect's assistant during the trainee stages, you could earn between £17,000 and £30,000 a year.

Newly registered architects may earn between £30,000 and £35,000. With three to five years' post-registration experience, you may earn between around £34,000 and £42,000.

Entry requirements

The most common way to qualify as an architect involves:

- five years' study on a university course recognised for registration with the Architects Registration Board (ARB) **and** at least two years' professional experience.

See the RIBA and ARB websites for full details of qualifications and alternative routes to becoming an architect.

More information

Royal Institution of British Architects (RIBA)
66 Portland Place
London
W1B 1AD
Tel: 020 7580 5533
www.architecture.com

Architects Registration Board
Tel: 020 7580 5861
www.arb.org.uk

BRICKLAYER

The nature of the work

Bricklayers build and repair walls, chimney stacks, tunnel linings and decorative stonework like archways. They might also refurbish brickwork and masonry on restoration projects. As a bricklayer the projects you might work on can range from a house extension to a large commercial development. If you enjoy doing practical things and you are interested in construction, this could be the perfect job for you.

What can you earn?

A bricklaying labourer can earn up to £15,000 a year. Qualified bricklayers can earn between £16,000 and £23,000 a year. Experienced bricklayers, including instructors, can earn up to £30,000 a year. Overtime and various allowances can add to your income. Self-employed bricklayers set their own pay rates.

Entry requirements

You do not need formal qualifications to become a bricklayer, but employers usually want people who have some on-site experience. If you have not worked in construction before, you could find a job as a labourer to get site experience. Once you are working, your employer may be willing to offer you training in bricklaying.

You may be able to get into this job through an Apprenticeship scheme with a building company. Some building companies may want you to have GCSEs in subjects like maths, English, and design and technology, or vocational qualifications such as the BTEC Introductory Certificate or Diploma in Construction. You will need to check which schemes are available in your area and what the requirements are. To find out more, visit the Apprenticeships website.

Another option is to take a college course in bricklaying. This would teach you some of the skills needed for the job, but employers may still want you to have some site experience.

Courses include:

- BTEC Level 2 Certificate/Diploma in Construction (bricklaying options)
- City & Guilds Certificate in Basic Construction Skills: Bricklaying
- CSkills Intermediate/Advanced Construction Award (Trowel Occupations – Bricklaying).

For more information about bricklaying qualifications, see the ConstructionSkills website and contact your local college. ConstructionSkills also has general information on careers and qualifications in building. www.cskills.org

Traditional Building Skills Bursary Scheme

The aim of the Traditional Building Skills Bursary scheme is to reduce the shortage of skills in the traditional crafts and built heritage sector. It is doing this by offering bursaries and organising work-based training placements for suitable applicants.

To find out more about the scheme, suitability and available placements, visit the Traditional Building Skills Bursary Scheme website.

BUILDING SURVEYOR

The nature of the work

As a surveyor, you would usually focus on three main areas – surveying, legal work, and planning and inspection. Your work could include:

- surveying properties, identifying structural faults and making recommendations for repairs
- assessing damage for insurance purposes, for example following a fire or flooding
- establishing who is responsible for building repair costs

69

- advising clients on issues such as property boundary disputes
- acting as a client's supporter or standing as an expert witness during legal proceedings
- checking properties to make sure that they meet building regulations, and fire safety and accessibility standards
- dealing with planning applications and with improvement or conservation grants.

Depending on the size of the company, you may cover all of these tasks or you might specialise in just one.

Other duties would include supervising a surveying team made up of assistants and technicians.

What can you earn?

Newly-qualified graduates earn between £18,000 and £22,000 a year.

Experienced surveyors earn between £23,000 and £38,000 a year, and senior staff with chartered status can earn over £50,000 a year.

Entry requirements

To qualify as a building surveyor, you will need to complete a degree course accredited by the Royal Institution of Chartered Surveyors (RICS), followed by professional development. surveying

To search for accredited qualifications, see the RICS Courses website.

You could also start work in a trainee position with a surveying firm, and study for qualifications while you are working.

If you have a non-accredited degree, you will need to take a postgraduate course in surveying. You can do this through a company graduate traineeship, or by studying full-time at a RICS-accredited university. If you are working in engineering or construction, you could take a distance learning postgraduate conversion course with the College of Estate Management (CEM). For more details, see the CEM website.

With an HNC/HND or a foundation degree in surveying or construction, you may be able to start working as a surveying technician and take further qualifications to become a building surveyor.

For more information about surveying careers, accredited degree programmes and membership routes, contact the RICS and the Chartered Institute of Building's (CIOB) Faculty for Architecture and Surveying.

More information

Royal Institution of Chartered Surveyors (RICS)
Parliament Square
London
SW1P 3AD
Tel: 020 7334 3875
www.rics.org

College of Estate Management
Whiteknights
Reading
Berkshire
RG6 6AW
Tel: 0800 019 9697
www.cem.ac.uk

BUILDING CONTROL OFFICER

The nature of the work

As a building control officer, you would work on the planning and construction phases of building projects. These could range from a small housing extension to a large city centre redevelopment.

You would also be responsible for surveying buildings that have been damaged by fire or bad weather. If necessary, you could approve their demolition. Other responsibilities may include authorising entertainment licences, and checking safety at sports grounds, open-air events, cinemas and theatres.

On all projects you would have to take into account the implications of your decisions on contractors' time and costs. If you decided that a building project no longer meets regulations, you could start legal proceedings to change or stop the work.

What can you earn?

Starting salaries can range from £21,000 to £26,000 a year.

Experienced inspectors can earn between £27,000 and £38,000, and senior inspectors can earn up to £50,000 a year.

Rates tend to be higher in the South East, particularly in the private sector.

Entry requirements

You would normally need at least two A levels, a BTEC National Diploma, HNC/HND or a degree to work as a building control officer. Relevant subjects include:

- building studies
- civil engineering
- building control
- building surveying.

Employers' entry requirements can vary so you would need to check with them for exact details.

More information

www.lgcareers.com
Parliament Square
London
SW1P 3AD
Tel: 020 7334 3875
www.rics.org

Association of Building Engineers
Lutyens House
Billing Brook Road
Weston Favell
Northampton
NN3 8NW
Tel: 0845 126 1058
www.abe.org.uk

Chartered Institute of Building
Englemere
Kings Ride
Ascot
Berkshire
SL5 7TB
Tel: 01344 630700
www.ciob.org.uk

CARPENTER OR JOINER

The nature of the work

As a carpenter or joiner, you may work in one or more of the following areas:

- cutting and shaping timber for floorboards, skirting boards and window frames
- making and assembling doors, window frames, staircases and fitted furniture
- fitting wooden structures, like floor and roof joists, roof timbers, staircases, partition walls, and door and window frames (first fixings)
- installing skirting boards, door surrounds, doors, cupboards and shelving, as well as door handles and locks (second fixings)
- building temporary wooden supports for concrete that is setting, for example on motorway bridge supports or building foundations (formwork)
- making and fitting interiors for shops, hotels, banks, offices and public buildings.

You could be skilled in all of these or you may specialise in just one or two.

What can you earn?

Starting salaries are between £13,000 and £16,000 a year.

Qualified joiners earn between £17,000 and £23,000 a year, and experienced joiners can earn up to £28,000 a year.

Overtime and shift allowances will increase your income. Self-employed carpenters and joiners set their own rates.

Entry requirements

You do not need any formal qualifications to become a carpenter or joiner, but employers usually want people with some on-site experience. If you have not worked in construction before, you could work as a joiner's mate or labourer to get site experience. Once working, your employer may offer you training in carpentry and joinery.

You may be able to become a carpenter or joiner through an Apprenticeship scheme. To be eligible, you may need GCSEs in subjects such as maths, English and design and technology, or vocational qualifications such as a BTEC Certificate or Diploma in Construction (carpentry options). To find out more about Apprenticeships, visit the Apprenticeships website.

Another route in is to take a college course in carpentry and joinery. This would give you some of the skills needed for the job, but employers may still want to see some site experience.

Courses include:

- City & Guilds Award in Basic Construction Skills (carpentry options)
- CSkills Level 2 Diploma in Site Carpentry.

For more details about courses, contact ConstructionSkills and your local college. ConstructionSkills also has general information on building careers and qualifications.

Traditional Building Skills Bursary Scheme

The Traditional Building Skills Bursary scheme aims to increase the number of skilled people in the traditional crafts and built heritage sector. It is doing this by offering grants (bursaries) and organising work-based training placements for suitable applicants. To find out more, visit the Traditional Building Skills Bursary Scheme website.

More information

National Heritage Training Group
www.nhtg.org.uk

Institute of Carpenters (IOC)
32 High Street
Wendover
Buckinghamshire
HP22 6EA
www.instituteofcarpenters.com

Construction Skills Certification Scheme (CSCS)
Tel: 0844 576 8777
www.cscs.uk.com

Construction Skills
Bircham Newton
King's Lynn
Norfolk
PE31 6RH
Tel: 0344 994 4400
www.cskills.org

CIVIL ENGINEER

The nature of the work
You could work in any one of the following specialist areas of engineering:

- structural – dams, buildings, offshore platforms and pipelines
- transportation – roads, railways, canals and airports
- environmental – water supply networks, drainage and flood barriers
- maritime – ports, harbours and sea defences
- geotechnical – mining, earthworks and construction foundations.

What can you earn?

Graduate salaries are between £17,000 and £25,000 a year. Experienced engineers earn between £25,000 and £40,000 a year, and senior Chartered Engineers can earn between £60,000 and £100,000 a year.

Entry requirements

You would normally need to gain a three-year Bachelor of Engineering (BEng) degree or four-year Masters (MEng) degree in civil engineering for this career. These qualifications are important if you want to work towards incorporated or chartered engineer status. See the Training and Development section below for details. You could study other engineering-related subjects, but it may take you longer to fully qualify.

To do a degree course, you will need at least five GCSEs (A-C) and two or three A levels, including maths and a science subject (normally physics), or equivalent qualifications. Check exact entry requirements with individual colleges and universities, as they may accept a relevant Access to Higher Education award.

If you already work in the industry as a technician, you could qualify as a civil engineer by studying part-time for a BTEC HNC/HND, foundation degree or degree in civil engineering.

More information about engineering careers and courses is on the Institution of Civil Engineers (ICE) website.

More information

Institution of Structural Engineers (ISE)
11 Upper Belgrave Street
London
SW1X 8BH
Tel: 020 7235 4535
www.istructe.org.uk

The UKRC
Listerhills Park of Science and Commerce
40-42 Campus Road
Bradford
BD7 1HR
Tel: 01274 436485
www.theukrc.org

Institution of Civil Engineers
Great George Street
London
SW1P 3AA
Tel: 020 7222 7722
www.ice.org.uk

Construction Skills
Bircham Newton
King's Lynn
Norfolk
PE31 6RH
Tel: 0344 994 4400
www.cskills.org

Tomorrows Engineers
EngineeringUK
Weston House
246 High Holborn
London
WC1V 7EX
Email: careers@engineeringuk.com
Tel: 020 3206 0400
www.tomorrowsengineers.org.uk

Engineering Training Council (NI)
Interpoint
20-24 York Street
Belfast
BT15 1AQ
Tel: 028 9032 9878
www.etcni.org.uk

CLERK OF WORKS

The nature of the work
As a clerk of works, or site inspector, you would oversee the quality and safety of work on a construction site, making sure that building plans and specifications are being followed correctly.

Your duties would include:

- performing regular inspections of the work on site and comparing completed work with drawings and specifications
- measuring and sampling building materials to check their quality

- recording results either on paper or a hand-held Personal Digital Assistant (PDA)
- identifying defects and suggesting ways to correct them
- liaising with other construction staff, such as contractors, engineers and surveyors
- monitoring and reporting progress to construction managers, architects and clients

You may also be responsible for supervising the workforce on the building site during a project.

What can you earn?

A clerk of works can earn between £21,000 and £40,000 year. With substantial experience, this can rise to around £50,000 or higher, depending on the contract.

Entry requirements

You would usually become a clerk of works after gaining experience in the construction or engineering industries, at craft or technician level.

You could look for work as a trainee after taking a BTEC HNC/HND, foundation degree or degree in construction or engineering, and work your way up. To search for colleges and universities offering these courses, visit the UCAS website.

Employers may insist that you hold membership of the Institute of Clerks of Works and Construction Inspectorate (ICWCI), which is the recognised industry body for this area of work. See the further training section below for more details.

To find out more about this career, visit the CITB-ConstructionSkills websites.

More information

Institute of Clerks of Works and Construction Inspectors
28 Commerce Rd
Lynch Wood
Peterborough
PE2 6LR

Tel: 01733 405160
www.icwgb.org

Construction Skills CITB
Bircham Newton
King's Lynn
Norfolk
PE31 6RH
Tel: 0344 994 4400
www.cskills.org

Construction Skills Certification Sceme
Tel: 0844 576 8777
www.cscs.uk.com

ELECTRICIAN

The nature of the work
If you are interested in electrics and like the idea of diverse and exciting work, this could be a great career for you.

Electricians work on a very wide range of projects, from bringing power to homes to taking part in major engineering projects. Their tasks can range from transporting data along fibre optic cables to programming computer-controlled 'intelligent' buildings and factories. They can also work with renewable technology, such as wind turbines or photovoltaic systems that turn the sun's energy into electricity.

As an electrician, you would install, inspect and test equipment, ensure that electrotechnical systems work, and spot and fix faults.

Electrotechnical careers are divided into different areas:

Installation electrician - Installing power systems, lighting, fire protection, security and data-network systems in all different types of buildings.

- Maintenance electrician - Checking systems regularly to ensure that they keep on working efficiently and safely.
- Electrotechnical panel builders - Having responsibility for the building and installing control panels that operate the electrical systems inside buildings.

- Machine repair and rewind electrician - Repairing and maintaining electrical motors and other machinery such as transformers to make sure that they work correctly.
- Highway systems electrician - Installing and maintaining street lighting and traffic management systems that tell the public what they need to know when they're on the roads and motorways.

You could be working in all types of buildings, such as homes, offices, shops or sports stadiums. You may also supervise other people in a team.

Depending on your exact role, you may work on a construction site, which can be noisy, dusty and cold. You might have to work in cramped and uncomfortable spaces to reach the electrical cabling and equipment, and you may sometimes work at heights using a variety of equipment such as scaffolding.

What can you earn?

First year apprentices may start on around £8,000 a year.

Newly-qualified electricians may earn over £17,000 a year, and experienced electricians may earn over £30,000 a year.

Some employers pay more, and you might get bonuses and overtime pay. Your salary will vary depending on your employer and where you live in the UK.

There are national set rates to cover travelling time, travel expenses and accommodation costs.

Entry requirements

To work as a qualified electrician, you will need to gain an NVQ Diploma or Scottish Vocational Qualification (SVQ) at Level 3. You may also need additional training if you want to do specialist work such as installing environmental technology systems.

You could start as an apprentice straight from school or college. You would combine training on the job with going to a college or training centre. It normally takes between three and a half and four years to complete training and an apprenticeship.

If you're not able to do an apprenticeship straight away, there are programmes around the UK that can help you to progress to an apprenticeship, further learning or a job. Speak to your local careers adviser to find out more.

Some apprenticeship schemes are open to people over 25, although the number of places might be limited. If you are over 25 and employed, or you could be assessed on site, you could work towards the NVQ Diploma/SVQ without doing an apprenticeship.

The range of Apprenticeships available in your area will depend on the local jobs market and the types of skills employers need from their workers. To find out more, visit the Apprenticeships website.

Electricians qualified before 1996

If you qualified as an electrician before 1996, you should contact the Joint Industry Board for the Electrical Contracting Industry (JIB). They will assess your experience and qualifications to decide whether you meet their requirements. They will be able to tell you if you need to take further qualifications.

Overseas qualified electricians

If you have qualified as an electrician outside the UK, you could register with the JIB Electrotechnical Card Scheme (ECS). You will need to do three things to register:

- contact UK NARIC to find out what your qualifications match in the UK
- complete the City & Guilds 17th Edition IEE Wiring Regulations (2382)
- pass the ECS Health and Safety Assessment.

You may also need to contact the certification schemes listed below for details of how to meet Part P requirements of the Building Regulations (see Training and Development section below for more about Part P).

You may need a driving licence.

Portable Appliance Testing (PAT)

If your job involves carrying out portable appliance testing (also known as PAT testing), you will need to have relevant training. The City & Guilds In-service Inspection and Testing of Electrical Equipment (2377) course is a common choice. Any course that meets the IEE Codes of Practice would be suitable.

You do not always have to be a qualified electrician to carry out PAT testing, however, you would need to show your capability. This is normally shown by qualifications and/or relevant experience. For more details, visit the PAT Testing Information website.

Electrical Safety and Part P

Part P of the Building Regulations states that certain types of household electrical work must be approved by a certified contractor or building inspector. You can certify your own work by completing a short Part P training scheme. See the Part P contacts in More Information below for details about certification training, entry requirements and information about the electrical work that requires approval.

Entry requirements for a training scheme will depend on your qualifications and experience. Some providers offer extra training if you need it, for instance, 17th Edition Wiring Regulations. Some do not, so please check with the providers.

Traditional Building Skills Bursary Scheme

The aim of the Traditional Building Skills Bursary scheme is to reduce the shortage of skills in the traditional crafts and built heritage sector. It is doing this by offering bursaries and organising work-based training placements for suitable applicants.

To find out more about the scheme, suitability and available placements, visit the Traditional Building Skills Bursary Scheme website.

Environmental Technologies

The government has set targets for greater energy efficiency. With further training, you may be able to install and maintain renewable energy technologies like solar electric systems. Some employers may also pay half the cost of training for qualifications in environmental technologies like fitting solar heating systems.

To find out more about this growing area of work, see the following websites:

You could continue your professional development by gaining higher qualifications such as NVQ Diploma/SVQ Level 4, a foundation degree, HNC, HND or degree in Building Services Engineering. If you want to do a degree course, many universities or similar institutions will accept a relevant qualification, or take your work experience into account, instead of traditional academic qualifications.

You can search for full-time courses on the Universities and Colleges Admissions Service (UCAS) website, or contact individual universities or colleges for information about part-time courses.

The Institution of Engineering and Technology (IET) offers a membership scheme at various grades. Membership would give you access to a variety of professional development workshops and training courses. See the IET website for more information.

More information

Summit Skills
Tel: 08000 688336
www.summitskills.org.uk

Electrical Contractors Association
www.eca.co.uk

Part P Self-Certification Schemes:

NICEIC Domestic Installer Scheme
Tel: 0870 013 0382
www.niceic.org.uk

ELECSA
Tel: 0870 749 0080
www.elecsa.org.uk

British Standards Institution
Tel: 01442 278607
www.bsi-global.com

National Association for Professional Testers and Inspectors
Tel: 0870 444 1392
www.napit.org.uk

GAS SERVICE TECHNICIAN

The nature of the work

As a gas service technician, you would mainly work at customers' homes, or at businesses like cafes and hotel kitchens. Your job could include:

- installing appliances and systems
- carrying out planned maintenance checks on systems and equipment
- testing controls and safety devices to make sure that they are working properly
- finding and repairing gas leaks using computerised fault-finding equipment
- replacing or repairing faulty or old parts
- ordering new parts when necessary
- keeping records of work you have carried out
- giving customers advice about gas safety and energy efficiency.

You would also give customers quotes for jobs and tell them how long they would take, sell additional company services and occasionally deal with complaints. Gas service technicians are also sometimes known as gas installation engineers or gas maintenance engineers.

What can you earn?

British Gas apprenticeship salaries are around £15,000 a year. Qualified technicians can earn between £19,000 and £30,000 a year.

Bonuses, shift allowances and overtime will increase basic salaries.

Entry requirements

To qualify as a gas service technician you will need:

- NVQ Level 3 in Domestic Natural Gas Installation (you normally need to be employed by a company to complete this); or
- appropriate work experience and training leading to safety certification through the Accredited Certification Scheme (ACS).

You will also need to have Gas Safe Registration (this used to be called CORGI registration).

See the Training and Development section below for more details.

You may be able to start this career through an Apprenticeship scheme. You will need to check which schemes are available in your area. To find out more, visit the Apprenticeships website.

Some utility companies offer national apprenticeship schemes in a variety of technical and engineering roles. For more information, see the Energy and Utility Skills website.

Industry organisations strongly recommend that you gain a work placement or job with a gas servicing firm as soon as possible after starting the Technical Certificate (the theory part of the NVQ). This would allow you to work towards the full NVQ. Your college may help you to find a placement, but you could also contact companies directly.

You may need a driving licence, as this job normally involves travelling to customer's premises.

Accredited Certification Scheme (ACS)

If you have experience in the gas industry or related fields, you may be able to follow the ACS scheme. This would enable you to demonstrate your ability to work safely with gas systems and equipment, and be eligible to join the Gas Safe Register. You will need to complete safety assessments covering your specific areas of work and the types of appliances you work on every five years.

If you have qualifications from any other fields, you will have to be trained and satisfy safety assessments at an approved ACS centre.

You will be classed as being in one of three categories when you apply for ACS assessment:

Oil-fired equipment

If you work with oil-fired equipment, such as heating systems and oil storage tanks, you could gain accreditation with the Oil Firing Technical Association for the Petroleum Industry (OFTEC). Contact OFTEC for more information.

Energy efficiency

You could also gain the City & Guilds Certificate in Energy Efficiency for Domestic Heating, which will give you the knowledge and competence you need to meet Part L of the Building Regulations concerning energy efficiency.

More information

Gas safe Register
Tel: 0800 408 5500
www.gassaferegister.co.uk

Oil Firing Technical Association for the Petroleum Industry
Foxwood House
Dobbs Lane
Kesgrave
Ipswich
IP5 2QQ
Tel: 0845 658 5080
www.oftec.co.uk

British Gas Jobs
The Harrow Way
Basingstoke
Hampshire
RG22 4AR
www.britishgasjobs.co.uk

Energy and Utility Skills
Friars Gate

1011 Stratford Road
Shirley
Solihull
B90 4BN
Tel: 0845 077 9922
www.euskills.co.uk

Tomorrows Engineers
EngineeringUK
Weston House
246 High Holborn
London
WC1V 7EX
Email: careers@engineeringuk.com
Tel: 020 3206 0400
www.tomorrowsengineers.org.uk

PAINTER AND DECORATOR

The nature of the work

As a painter and decorator, you would work on a variety of domestic and industrial projects ranging from re-decorating homes to applying heavy-duty finishes to large structures like bridges.

On a domestic job, you would use paint, varnishes and wallpaper to decorate rooms. You would follow the householder's instructions about choice of colour, finishing texture and wallpaper patterns. Your main tasks would include:

measuring surface areas to work out how much paint or wall covering you need

- stripping off old wallpaper or paint
- filling holes and cracks and making sure surfaces are level
- preparing surfaces with primer and undercoat
- mixing paint to the right shade, either by hand or using computerised colour-matching equipment
- applying layers of paint and hanging wallpaper
- tidying up after finishing a job.

On some jobs you might apply specialist finishes such as rag rolling, graining and marbling. You would often work from ladders or raised platforms to reach ceilings.

For industrial projects, such as bridges or ships, you would remove old paintwork with abrasive blasting methods before applying new coatings using industrial paint spraying equipment. You would use a cradle or safety harness when working.

Paints and solvents give off fumes, so you may have to wear a protective mask or use fume extraction equipment on some jobs, if in enclosed spaces.

What can you earn?

Starting salaries can be between £13,500 and £16,500 a year.

Average salaries for qualified painters and decorators are between £17,000 and £21,500 a year. Decorators with supervisor duties or specialist skills can earn over £23,000 a year.

Overtime and shift allowances can increase income. Self-employed painters and decorators set their own pay rates.

Entry requirements

Employers often prefer people with some relevant experience, so you could start by looking for work as a painter and decorator's labourer or 'mate'. Once you are working, your employer may give you the opportunity for further training in painting and decorating. See the Training and Development section below for more details.

Another option is to take a college course, which would give you some of the skills needed for the job. Relevant courses include:

- City & Guilds Level 1 Certificate in Basic Construction Skills (Painting and Decorating)
- CSkills Level 1 Diploma in Painting and Decorating
- CSkills Intermediate and Advanced Construction Award (Decorative Occupations – Painting and Decorating).

For more details about courses and entry requirements, contact your local colleges.

A common way into this career is through an Apprenticeship scheme. You will need to check which schemes are available in your area. To do an Apprenticeship, you may need GCSEs in subjects such as maths, English and design and technology, or equivalent qualifications such as the BTEC Introductory Certificate and Diploma in Construction. This course includes options in painting and decorating.

To find out more about Apprenticeships, see the Apprenticeships website.

For more information about careers and qualifications in painting and decorating, see the bConstructive website.

The Know Your Place campaign promotes the construction trades as a career choice for women. See the Know Your Place website for details.

Traditional Building Skills Bursary Scheme

The aim of the Traditional Building Skills Bursary scheme is to reduce the shortage of skills in the traditional crafts and built heritage sector. It is doing this by offering bursaries and organising work-based training placements for suitable applicants.

To find out more about the scheme, suitability and available placements, see the Traditional Building Skills Bursary Scheme website.

More information

Industrial Rope Trade association
Kingsley House
Ganders Business Park
Kingsley
Bordon
Hampshire
GU35 9LU
Tel: 01420 471619
www.irata.org

National Heritage Training Group
www.nhtg.org.uk

Construction Skills Certification Scheme (CSCS)
Tel: 0844 576 8777
www.cscs.uk.com

ConstructionSkills
Bircham Newton
King's Lynn
Norfolk
PE31 6RH
Tel: 0344 994 4400
www.cskills.org

PLASTERER

The nature of the work

You would normally be part of a small team, and work in one of the following:

- solid plastering – applying wet finishes to surfaces and putting protective coverings like pebble-dashing on external walls
- fibrous plastering – creating ornamental plasterwork, such as ceiling roses, cornices, and architraves, using a mixture of plaster and short fibres shaped with moulds and casts
- dry lining – fixing internal plasterboard or wallboard partitions by fastening them together on a timber or metal frame ready for decorating.

You could work on small-scale domestic jobs, repairs and restoration or on big commercial developments such as schools or hospitals.

What can you earn?

Starting salaries can be between £14,000 and £17,000 a year. Qualified plasterers can earn from £17,500 to over £25,000 or more. Experienced plasterers can earn around £28,000 a year.

Overtime and shift allowances will increase earnings. Self-employed plasterers negotiate their own rates.

Entry requirements

You do not usually need qualifications to become a plasterer, but employers usually look for people with some on-site experience. If you have not worked in construction before, you may be able to get this experience by working as a plasterer's 'mate' or labourer.

A common way into plastering is through an Apprenticeship scheme with a plastering, drylining or building firm. The range of Apprenticeships available in your area will depend on the local jobs market and the types of skills employers need from their workers. For more information, visit the Apprenticeships website.

For an Apprenticeship, you may need some GCSEs in subjects such as maths, English and design and technology, or equivalent qualifications.

Alternatively, you could learn some of the skills needed for the job by taking a college course in plastering, but employers may still want to see some site experience. Relevant courses include:

- City & Guilds (6217) Certificate in Basic Construction Skills (Plastering)
- CSkills Awards Diploma in Plastering
- ABC Certificate in Preparation for Employment in Plastering
- Ascentis Preparation for Employment in the Construction Industries (Plastering).

Visit the ConstructionSkills website for information on construction careers and qualifications.

The Know Your Place campaign aims to promote the construction industry as a career choice for women.

More information

National Heritage Training Group
www.nhtg.org.uk

Construction Skills Certification Scheme (CSCS)
Tel: 0844 576 8777
www.cscs.uk.com

Construction Skills CITB
Bircham Newton
King's Lynn
Norfolk
PE31 6RH
Tel: 0344 994 4400
www.cskills.org

PLUMBER

The nature of the work

Depending on whether you work in homes, industrial or commercial locations, your job could include:

- installing and repairing water supplies, heating systems and drainage
- servicing gas and oil-fired central heating systems, boilers and radiators
- installing and fixing domestic appliances like showers and washing machines
- servicing air-conditioning and ventilation units
- fitting weather-proof materials, joints and flashings to roofs, chimneys and walls.

On all jobs you would use hand and power tools, which could include welding equipment.

As an experienced plumber, you might specialise in sheet metal work for industrial, commercial or historical buildings.

What can you earn?

Starting salaries for newly qualified plumbers can be between £16,500 and £21,000 a year. Experienced plumbers can earn between £21,000 and £35,000 a year.

Rates vary in different regions. The highest average salaries are in London and the South East.

Self-employed plumbers set their own rates.

Entry requirements

To become a qualified plumber you will need to achieve Level 2 and 3 NVQ Diplomas from City & Guilds or EAL. These are:

- City & Guilds (6189) NVQ Diploma in Plumbing and Domestic Heating, at levels 2 and 3
- EAL NVQ Diploma in Domestic Heating and Plumbing at levels 2 and 3.

If you are not working in plumbing at the moment, you would start at level 2. At this level you would first need to gain passes in a series of knowledge units. You would then move on to practical units, which you would mainly complete in the workplace.

Note: These qualifications replace the City & Guilds (6129) Technical Certificate and the NVQ levels 2 and 3 in Mechanical Engineering Services – Plumbing (City & Guilds 6089). If you are already part way through these qualifications, you will be able to finish them and they will still be valid for you to work as plumber.

There is strong competition for places on plumbing courses, and college entry requirements will often include an aptitude test. Due to health and safety regulations, you may not be able to do a training course if you are colour blind. Check with your chosen college and ask if they can offer you a colour vision assessment test.

Industry organisations strongly recommend that you get a work placement or employment with a plumbing firm soon after starting your training. This would allow you to complete the practical units of the NVQ Diplomas. Your college may help you find a placement but you could also contact plumbing firms directly.

The Chartered Institute of Plumbing and Heating Engineering (CIPHE) has useful information for anyone wanting to train as a plumber. Visit the CIPHE website for more details.

See the SummitSkills website for further information on entry routes into plumbing, training providers and new qualifications.

Entry into plumbing in Northern Ireland is similar to training in England and Wales. For more details contact ConstructionSkills (NI) and SNIPEF.

Apprenticeships

You may be able to become a qualified plumber through an Apprenticeship scheme. To get on to a scheme you will normally need four GCSEs (grades A-C). You will need to check if there are schemes running in your areas. To find out more, visit the Apprenticeships website.

Short courses

A number of organisations offer short intensive training courses, some with home study options. You should check whether the course you choose is recognised and accredited by the industry. Your regional City & Guilds office will be able to check this for you. You should also ask the course provider what would happen if you fell behind or dropped out of an intensive course.

Overseas qualifications

If you qualified outside the UK, contact the Joint Industry Board for Plumbing for information about how to register as a qualified plumber. You will need to tell them which qualifications you have from your home country.

More information

SummitSkills
Tel: 08000 688336
www.summitskills.org.uk

CITB ConstructionSkills (NI)
17 Dundrod Road
Nutts Corner
Crumlin
Co Antrim
BT29 4SR
Tel: 0800 587 2288
http://www.citbni.org.uk

Scottish and Northern Ireland Plumbing Employers Federation (SNIPEF)
2 Walker Street
Edinburgh

EH3 7LB
Tel: 0131 225 2255 www.snipef.org

Joint Industry Board for Plumbing Mechanical Engineering Services
Tel: 01480 476925
www.jib-pmes.org.uk

British Plumbing Employers Council Services Ltd (BPEC Services Ltd)
2 Walker Street
Edinburgh
EH3 7LB
www.bpec.org.uk/services

Institute of Plumbing and Heating Engineers
(including Women in Plumbing Group)
64 Station Lane
Hornchurch
Essex
RM12 6NB
Tel: 01708 472791
www.iphe.org.uk

Gas Safe Register
Tel: 0800 408 5500
www.gassaferegister.co.uk

QUANTITY SURVEYOR

The nature of the work
As a quantity surveyor, you might work on:

- housing and industrial sites
- retail and commercial developments
- roads, rail and waterways.

On most projects, your main responsibilities would be:

- carrying out feasibility studies to estimate materials, time and labour costs
- negotiating and drawing up bids for tenders and contracts

- monitoring each stage of construction to make sure that costs are in line with forecasts
- providing financial progress reports to clients
- advising clients on legal and contractual matters
- acting on clients' behalf to resolve disputes
- assessing the financial costs of new environmental guidelines, such as using sustainable timber.

You would use computer software to carry out some of these tasks, and to keep records, prepare work schedules and write reports. You might also deal with the maintenance and renovation costs once buildings are in use.

What can you earn?

Starting salaries can be between £20,000 and £25,000 a year. With experience this can rise to between £25,000 and £45,000. Senior chartered quantity surveyors can earn between £50,000 and £80,000 a year.

Entry requirements

You need a degree or professional qualification accredited by the Royal Institution for Chartered Surveyors (RICS) to qualify as a chartered quantity surveyor. Relevant subjects include:

- surveying
- construction
- civil engineering
- structural engineering.

If you are already working in engineering or construction, you could take a part-time distance learning postgraduate degree while working – many of RICS's accredited postgraduate degrees are available part-time or distance learning.

If you have a BTEC HNC, HND or foundation degree in surveying, you may be able to start work as a surveying technician then complete further study to qualify as a quantity surveyor.

You can find out more about careers and courses in surveying, by visiting the Royal Institution of Chartered Surveyors (RICS) and Chartered Institute of Building (CIOB) websites.

More information

Royal Institution of Chartered Surveyors (RICS)
Parliament Square
London
SW1P 3AD
Tel: 0207 334 3875
www.rics.org

College of Estate Management
Whiteknights
Reading
Berkshire
RG6 6AW
Tel: 0800 019 9697
www.cem.ac.uk

Chartered Institute of Building
Englemere
Kings Ride
Ascot
Berkshire
SL5 7TB
Tel: 01344 630700
www.ciob.org.uk

Construction Industry Council (CIC)
26 Store Street
London
WC1E 7BT
Tel: 0207 399 7400
www.cicskills.org.uk

ROOFER

The nature of the work
If you have a head for heights and are able to understand building plans, this job could suit you. As a roofer, your work could range from re-slating the roof on a house, to restoring the lead sheets on an old building.

In this job you will need good number skills to work out quantities of goods and prices. You will also need to work flexibly as part of a team.

It is common to start out as a roofing labourer and then get training on the job. Alternatively, you could do a course in roof slating and tiling first, which would teach you some of the skills you would need. You may be able to get into this job through an Apprenticeship.

What can you earn?

A roofing labourer or trainee can earn from £13,000 to £15,000 a year. Once qualified this can rise to between £16,000 and £24,000. Experienced roofers can earn up to £31,000 a year. Overtime and shift allowances will increase wages, while self-employed roofers set their own rates.

Entry requirements

Finding work as an entry-level roofing labourer is a common way into this career, as it will give you the on-site experience employers often ask for. Once you are working, your employer may be willing to give you further training in roofing techniques.

You may be able to get into this career by completing an Apprenticeship with a building or roofing company. The range of Apprenticeships available in your area will depend on the local jobs market and the types of skills employers need from their workers. To find out more, visit the Apprenticeships website.

To get on to an Apprenticeship, you may need GCSEs (grades A-C) in subjects like maths, English and design and technology. Equivalent qualifications like the BTEC Certificate or Diploma in Construction may also be accepted.

Alternatively, you could take a college course, such as the ConstructionSkills Awards Level 2 Diploma in Roof Slating and Tiling, which would teach you some of the skills needed. However, employers may still ask for some site experience. Check with local colleges for course availability and entry requirements.

See the ConstructionSkills website for more information on construction careers and qualifications.

The Know Your Place campaign aims to promote the construction trades as a career choice for women. Visit the website for more details.

Traditional Building Skills Bursary Scheme

The Traditional Building Skills Bursary Scheme aims to address skills shortages within the traditional crafts and built heritage sector by offering bursaries and organising work-based training placements for eligible applicants.

To find out more about the scheme, eligibility and which placements are available, visit the Traditional Building Skills Bursary Scheme website.

More information

National Heritage Training Group
www.nhtg.org.uk

Institute of Roofing
Tel: 020 7448 3858
www.instituteofroofing.org

Construction Skills Certification Scheme (CSCS)
Tel: 0844 576 8777
www.cscs.uk.com

Construction Skills CITB
Bircham Newton
King's Lynn
Norfolk
PE31 6RH
Tel: 0344 994 4400
www.cskills.org

TOWN PLANNER

The nature of the work
As a town planner (or spatial planner) you would help to shape the way towns and cities develop. This involves balancing the competing demands placed on land by housing, business, transport and leisure, and making sure plans meet

the economic and social needs of the community. If you are interested in urban environments, and you can see different viewpoints and make fair decisions, this job might suit you well.

To be good at this job you would also need to be a good communicator and negotiator. You would need knowledge of local planning policies and procedures. You would need report writing skills.

To work as a town planner you need a qualification accredited by the Royal Town Planning Institute (RTPI). You can qualify by studying for an RTPI-accredited degree in Town Planning. Alternatively, you can qualify by doing an RTPI-accredited postgraduate course, if you have a degree in a relevant subject such as surveying, architecture, statistics, geography or environmental science.

You would also assess the potential impact that developments, such as new road building, might have on an area. To do this, you would use surveying techniques, geographical information systems (GIS) and computer-aided design (CAD) to draw up plans and make recommendations to local and regional councils.

What can you earn?

For graduate or assistant planners this can be between £16,000 and £28,000 a year. Senior planners can earn up to £34,000. Planners with management responsibilities can earn up to £41,000. Chief planning officers can earn between £55,000 and £80,000.

Entry requirements

To work as a town planner you need a qualification accredited by the Royal Town Planning Institute (RTPI).

You can qualify by completing one of the following:

- a full-time RTPI-accredited degree course – these last for four years, which includes a three-year BA degree and a one-year postgraduate diploma (longer part-time courses are also available)
- an RTPI-accredited postgraduate course – If you already have a degree in a subject such as surveying, architecture, statistics, geography or environmental science

- a distance learning course at degree or postgraduate level – available jointly through the Open University and a consortium of the University of the West of England, Leeds Metropolitan University, London South Bank University and Dundee University.

Visit the RTPI website for a list of all accredited courses and information on town planning careers.

More information

Royal Town Planning Institute
41 Botolph Lane
London
EC3R 8DL
Tel: 020 7929 9494
www.rtpi.org.uk

LGcareers
www.lgcareers.com

Asset Skills
2 The Courtyard
48 New North Road
Exeter
Devon
EX4 4EP
Tel: 01392 423399
Careers Advice: careers@assetskills.org
www.assetskills.org

Local Government jobs
www.lgjobs.com

****

8. ENGINEERING

For those who want to join the long and illustrious line of great British engineers, this is the profession for you. However, there are many jobs within engineering and this chapter outlines the following:

- Civil engineer
- Mechanical engineer
- Design engineer
- Marine engineering technician

For more information on the many and diverse jobs in engineering, go to: www.tomorrowsengineers.org.uk

CIVIL ENGINEER

The nature of the work
You could work in any one of the following specialist areas of engineering:
- structural – dams, buildings, offshore platforms and pipelines
- transportation – roads, railways, canals and airports
- environmental – water supply networks, drainage and flood barriers
- maritime – ports, harbours and sea defences
- geotechnical – mining, earthworks and construction foundations.

You would normally work on projects alongside other professionals, such as architects, surveyors and building contractors. For more information about a career as a civil engineer see the Institution of Civil Engineers website.

What can you earn?

Graduate salaries are between £17,000 and £25,000 a year. Experienced engineers earn between £25,000 and £40,000 a year, and senior Chartered Engineers can earn between £60,000 and £100,000 a year.

Entry requirements

You would normally need to gain a three-year Bachelor of Engineering (BEng) degree or four-year Masters (MEng) degree in civil engineering for this career. These qualifications are important if you want to work towards incorporated or chartered engineer status. See the Training and Development section below for details. You could study other engineering-related subjects, but it may take you longer to fully qualify.

To do a degree course, you will need at least five GCSEs (A-C) and two or three A levels, including maths and a science subject (normally physics), or equivalent qualifications. Check exact entry requirements with individual colleges and universities, as they may accept a relevant Access to Higher Education award.

If you already work in the industry as a technician, you could qualify as a civil engineer by studying part-time for a BTEC HNC/HND, foundation degree or degree in civil engineering.

More information about engineering careers and courses is on the Institution of Civil Engineers (ICE) website.

For information on courses and careers in Northern Ireland, see the Engineering Training Council NI website.

More information

Institution of Structural Engineers
11 Upper Belgrave Street
London
SW1X 8BH
Tel: 020 7235 4535
www.istructe.org.uk

The UKRC
Listerhills Park of Science and Commerce
40-42 Campus Road
Bradford

BD7 1HR
Tel: 01274 436485
www.theukrc.org

Institution of Civil Engineers
Great George Street
London
SW1P 3AA
Tel: 020 7222 7722
www.ice.org.uk

Construction Skills
Bircham Newton
King's Lynn
Norfolk
PE31 6RH
Tel: 0344 994 4400
www.cskills.org

Tomorrow's Engineers
EngineeringUK
Weston House
246 High Holborn
London
WC1V 7EX
Email: careers@engineeringuk.com
Tel: 020 3206 0400
www.tomorrowsengineers.org.uk

Engineering Training Council (NI)
Interpoint
20-24 York Street
Belfast
BT15 1AQ
Tel: 028 9032 9878
www.etcni.org.uk

Construction Industry Council (CIC)
26 Store Street
London
WC1E 7BT
Tel: 020 7399 7400
www.cicskills.org.uk

MECHANICAL ENGINEER

The nature of the work
Your work would be divided into three key areas:

- research and development – assessing new products and innovations, and building prototypes
- design – turning research into technical plans using computer aided design/modelling (CAD/CAM) programs
- production – improving processes, and overseeing the installation of machinery and parts.

You could be working on large scale projects, for instance developing new ways to harness wave and tidal power; or at the small scale or micromechanical level, for example making prosthetic implants to help people become more mobile.

What can you earn?
Starting salaries can be between £19,500 and £22,000 a year. Experienced mechanical engineers can earn between £26,000 and £39,000. Engineers with chartered status can earn over £40,000 a year.

Entry requirements

To work as a mechanical engineer you will need a foundation degree, BTEC HNC/HND or degree in mechanical engineering, or a related engineering subject.

To search for foundation degrees, HNDs and degrees, see the Universities and Colleges Admissions Service (UCAS) website.

For a degree course you will usually need at least five GCSEs (grades A-C) and two or three A levels, possibly including maths and physics. Other science subjects such as biology would be useful for medical engineering. Check with colleges or universities for exact entry requirements, as alternative qualifications may be accepted.

Some courses, such as sandwich degrees, include a year in industry which may be useful when you start applying for work. Alternatively you could organise your own work placement with a relevant company.

You may also be able to get into this career starting off as an mechanical engineering technician apprentice with a manufacturer or engineering company and then after your Apprenticeship going on to higher education qualifications.

The range of Apprenticeships available in your area will depend on the local jobs market and the skills employers need from their workers. For more information, visit the Apprenticeships website.

To get on to an Apprenticeship, you are likely to need four or five GCSEs (A-C), including maths, English and a science subject.

For more information about careers in engineering, see the Institution of Mechanical Engineers and SEMTA websites.

More information

SEMTA (Sector Skills Council for Science, Engineering and Manufacturing Technologies in the UK)
14 Upton Road
Watford
Hertfordshire
WD18 0JT
Tel: 0845 643 9001
www.semta.org.uk

Women in Science Engineering and Construction
UK Resource Centre
Athlone Wing
Old Building
Great Horton Road
Bradford
BD7 1AY
Tel: 01274 436485
www.theukrc.org/wise

Institution of Mechanical Engineers
1 Birdcage Walk
Westminster
London
SW1H 9JJ
Tel: 020 7222 7899
www.imeche.org

Engineering Training Council (Northern Ireland)
Interpoint
20-24 York Street
Belfast
BT15 1AQ
Tel: 028 9032 9878
www.etcni.org.uk

Institution of Engineering and Technology (IET)
Michael Faraday House
Stevenage
Hertfordshire
SG1 2AY
Tel: 01438 313 311
www.theiet.org

Tomorrow's Engineers
EngineeringUK

Weston House

246 High Holborn

London

WC1V 7EX

Email: careers@engineeringuk.com

Tel: 020 3206 0400

www.tomorrowsengineers.org.uk

DESIGN ENGINEER

The nature of the work

As a design engineer you could work in a variety of industries, ranging from electronics to synthetic textiles, on projects as diverse as the redesign of a mobile phone to the construction of motorcycle parts from carbon fibre materials.

Your exact duties would depend on the project but could include:

- research – using mathematical modelling to work out whether new developments and innovations would work and be cost effective
- design – turning research ideas into technical plans for prototypes using computer-aided design (CAD) and computer-assisted engineering (CAE) software
- testing – collecting and analysing data from tests on prototypes
- modifying designs and re-testing – this process can go through several stages before a product is ready for manufacture or installation
- reporting – writing or presenting regular progress reports for project managers and clients.

What can you earn?

Starting salaries are between £20,000 and £25,000 a year. Experienced engineers can earn between £26,000 and £40,000. Senior design engineers can earn over £50,000 a year.

Entry requirements

You would normally need a foundation degree, BTEC HNC/HND or degree to become a design engineer.

Mechanical, electrical and civil engineering may also be acceptable to employers.

Contact the Institution of Engineering Designers (IED) and the Institution of Engineering and Technology (IET) for more details of accredited courses, as well as links to engineering careers information.

You may also be able to get into this career starting off as an engineering technician apprentice with a manufacturer or engineering company and then continuing after your Apprenticeship on to higher education qualifications.

To get on to an Apprenticeship, you are likely to need four or five GCSEs (A-C), including maths, English and a science subject.

For more general information about engineering as a career, see the Tomorrow's Engineers website.

More information

SEMTA (Sector Skills Council for Science, Engineering and Manufacturing Technologies in the UK)
14 Upton Road
Watford
Hertfordshire
WD18 0JT
Tel: 0845 643 9001
www.semta.org.uk

Women into Science, Engineering and Construction
Athlone Wing
Old Building
Great Horton Road
Bradford

BD7 1AY
Tel: 01274 436485
www.theukrc.org/wise

Tomorrow's Engineers
EngineeringUK
Weston House
246 High Holborn
London
WC1V 7EX
Email: careers@engineeringuk.com
Tel: 020 3206 0400
www.tomorrowsengineers.org.uk

Institution of Engineering Designers
Courtleigh
Westbury Leigh
Westbury
Wiltshire
BA13 3TA
www.ied.org.uk

Engineering Training Council (Northern Ireland)
Interpoint
20-24 York Street
Belfast
BT15 1AQ
Tel: 028 9032 9878
www.etcni.org.uk

Institution of Engineering and Technology
Michael Faraday House
Stevenage
Hertfordshire
SG1 2AY

Tel: 01438 313 311

www.theiet.org

MARINE ENGINEERING TECHNICIAN

The nature of the work

Marine engineering technicians (or shipbuilding technicians) design, build, service and repair boats and ships. They might also perform maintenance on offshore platforms, drilling machinery and equipment.

As a technician, you would use a broad range of engineering skills, such as welding, mechanical and electrical maintenance, and electronic equipment installation. Depending on where you work, your duties could include:

- fault-finding and repairing electronic, hydraulic and mechanical equipment on boats and ships
- assisting in the design and development of new marine equipment
- providing engineering support on board a dive support vessel
- refurbishing older craft with new navigation and communications systems
- using underwater craft (remotely operated vehicles – ROVs) to inspect undersea pipelines
- supervising a team of craftspeople in a ship or boatyard
- maintaining weapons systems, radar and sonar on board Royal Navy warships.
- You would usually work as part of a technical team under the direction of a marine engineer.

What can you earn? Starting salaries can be between £12,000 and £15,000 a year. With experience and qualifications this can rise to between £18,000 and £25,000. Senior technicians can earn over £30,000 a year.

Entry requirements

You could take various routes to becoming a marine technician. You may be able to get into this career as a marine industry apprentice. The range of

Apprenticeships available in your area will depend on the local jobs market and the types of skills employers need from their workers. To get on to an Apprenticeship scheme you may need GCSEs, or equivalent qualifications. To find out more about Apprenticeships, visit the Apprenticeships website.

To get on to an Apprenticeship, you are likely to need four or five GCSEs (A-C), including maths, English and a science subject.

Alternatively, you could take an engineering college course, which would teach you some of the skills needed, such as the BTEC Certificate and Diploma in Mechanical, Electrical or Electronic Engineering. You could also work towards a higher-level qualification, such as a BTEC HNC and HND in Marine Engineering.

You could train as an engineering technician with the Merchant Navy or Royal Navy. After completing your service with them, you could move into the commercial marine engineering industry. Visit the Merchant Navy and Royal Navy websites for more details.

For information about marine engineering as a career, see the Institute of Marine Engineering, Science and Technology (IMarEST) and British Marine Federation websites. For more information about engineering careers, visit the SEMTA website.

More information

SEMTA (Sector Skills Council for Science, Engineering and Manufacturing Technologies in the UK)
14 Upton Road
Watford
Hertfordshire
WD18 0JT
Tel: 0845 643 9001
www.semta.org.uk

Women into Science, Engineering and Construction
UK Resource Centre
Athlone Wing
Old Building
Great Horton Road
Bradford
BD7 1AY
Tel: 01274 436485
www.theukrc.org/wise

Tomorrow's Engineers
EngineeringUK
Weston House
246 High Holborn
London
WC1V 7EX
Email: careers@engineeringuk.com
Tel: 020 3206 0400
www.tomorrowsengineers.org.uk

Institute of Marine Engineering, Science and Technology (IMarEST)
80 Coleman Street
London
EC2R 5BJ
www.imarest.org.uk

Mercahnt Navy Training Board
Carthusian Court
12 Carthusian St
London
EC1M 6EZ
www.mntb.org.uk

British Marine Federation
Marine House

Thorpe Lea Road
Egham
Surrey
TW20 8BF
www.britishmarine.co.uk

Engineering Training Council (Northern Ireland)
Interpoint
20-24 York Street
Belfast
BT15 1AQ
Tel: 028 9032 9878
www.etcni.org.uk

****

9. FARMING AND LAND

Farming is an industry which finds it difficult to find talented recruits at this point in time. The hours are long and the work hard. The industry has gone through significant changes over the years and seeks talented and dedicated people to work within it. the rewards can be significant.

In addition to general farming jobs we look at a range of jobs associated with land management such as countryside rangers and gamekeeprs. the following jobs are outlined:

- Farm Manager
- Farm worker
- Aboriculturalist
- Countryside ranger
- Forest Officer
- Gamekeeper
- Groundperson/Groundskeeper
- Horse Groom
- Horticultural manager

For further information about farming and land jobs go to:

Lantra
Lantra House
Stoneleigh Park
Nr Coventry
Warwickshire
CV8 2LG
Tel: 0845 707 8007
www.lantra.co.uk

FARM MANAGER

The nature of the work

Farm managers run their own businesses or are employed by owners or tenants to run a farm efficiently and profitably. They may run a whole farm or just part of it, such as an arable (crops) unit.

As a farm manager, you could work on one of three main types of farm - livestock (animals), arable (crops) or mixed (animals and crops). Your work would depend partly on the type of farm, but could include:

- planning the running of the farm
- setting budget and production targets
- buying and selling animals or produce
- keeping financial records and records of livestock and/or crops
- recruiting, training and supervising staff.

On smaller farms, you may do practical farm work, such as looking after livestock, driving tractors and other machinery, and harvesting crops. You could also have responsibility for other activities, for example the farm may have a farm shop, horse riding facilities or provide accommodation for tourists. Farm managers work closely with the farm owner and often farm management consultants.

What can you earn?

These figures are only a guide, as actual rates of pay may vary, depending on the employer and where people live.

Minimum wage scales for agricultural work are set each year by the Agricultural Wages Boards for England and Wales. Individual employers may pay more according to the manager's skill and experience.

- Starting salaries for farm managers are at least £20,000 a year
- With experience, farm managers may earn between £26,000 and £30,000.

- The manager of a large farm with over ten years' experience may earn over £50,000 a year. Farm managers may be provided with rent-free accommodation and a vehicle. There may also be other benefits such as farm produce and a pension scheme.

Entry requirements

You will need comprehensive practical farming experience, and will probably start as a supervisor, assistant manager or the manager of a unit, such as dairy or arable.

Most farm managers have a qualification in agriculture. You can do courses at universities and agricultural colleges throughout the UK.

You may be able to get started through an Apprenticeship scheme. The range of Apprenticeships available in your area will depend on the local jobs market and the types of skills employers need from their workers.

Relevant qualifications include:

- City & Guilds Level 4 Diploma in Agricultural Business Management
- Foundation Degree in Agriculture, also available in Agricultural Business Management, Animal Studies, Crop Production.
- BSc (Hons) Degree in Agriculture, also available in areas such as in Agricultural Business Management, Animal Studies, Crop Production.

Entry to a degree course requires at least two A-level grades, normally including chemistry and maths, or another science subject. Alternative equivalent qualifications may be accepted. To search for foundation degrees, HNDs and degrees see the UCAS website. You should check with colleges and universities for entry requirements.

More information

Lantra
Lantra House

Stoneleigh Park
Nr Coventry
Warwickshire
CV8 2LG
Tel: 0845 707 8007
www.lantra.co.uk

City & Guilds
1 Giltspur Street
London
EC1A 9DD
Tel: 0844 543 0000
www.cityandguilds.com

ARBORICULTURALIST

The nature of the work

As an arboriculturalist, your duties will primarily include street or park tree pruning and removals. In some situations, work duties can also include tree planting, hazard tree assessment, diagnosis, and pest control. Work may also include other landscape and non-arboricultural duties.

An arboriculturist's work really begins once they have climbed into the tree. In addition to tree pruning, branch removal and felling, arboriculturists may also undertake work such as cable bracing to maintain the health of trees and inspections to assess the health of trees. Work is usually done from a rope and harness but may involve the use of elevated work platforms ('cherry-pickers').

An arboriculturist's duties may also include landscape and other non-arboricultural responsibilities such as tree and shrub planting and maintenance and snow removal.

What can you earn?

Arboriculturalists can earn between £18,000 and over £25,000 a year.

Entry requirements

If you are interested in becoming an arboricultural climber it is important that you:
- enjoy working outside
- have a good head for heights
- enjoy practical/physical work.

Individuals becoming climbers are likely have worked in the industry, usually as a groundworker or general arboricultural worker. Some may enter the industry having undertaken a full-time training programme and so already have some experience of climbing.

More information

Lantra
Lantra House
Stoneleigh Park
Nr Coventry
Warwickshire
CV8 2LG
Tel: 0845 707 8007
www.lantra.co.uk

Royal Forestry Society (RFS)
www.rfs.org.uk

International Society of Arboriculture (ISA)
www.isa-arbor.com

Institute of Chartered Foresters (ICF)
59 George Street
Edinburgh
EH2 2JG
Tel: 0131 240 1425
www.charteredforesters.org

The Arboricultural Association
Ullenwood Court
Ullenwood
Cheltenham
Gloucestershire
GL53 9QS
Tel 01242 522152
www.trees.org.uk

FARM WORKER

The nature of the work

Your work will vary depending on the type of farm and the time of year, but can include:

- looking after animals - such as feeding, cleaning (mucking out), caring for sick animals and using a milking ...ine to milk cows
- ploughing fields, sowing, looking after and harvesting crops, spreading fertiliser and spraying crops
- driving and looking after tractors, combine harvesters and other vehicles
- maintenance of farm buildings
- laying and trimming hedges
- digging and maintaining ditches
- putting up and mending fences.

You would be supervised by the farm owner, manager, supervisor or landowner, and you may also supervise casual staff. You will often need technical agricultural knowledge to understand the tasks you carry out. Most jobs involve working outdoors in all weather conditions. Farm work can be dirty and dusty and may not suit people who suffer from allergies such as hay fever.

What can you earn?

Rates of pay may vary, depending on the employer and where people live, however there is a minimum wage for those working in England and Wales (set by the Agricultural Wages Board).

Farm workers usually earn at least £7239 a year at age 16, and £9795 a year at age 19. Those over 19 years of age usually earn at least £14,986 a year, and experienced farm workers may earn up to £19,000 a year. Individual employers may pay more depending on skills and experience. Many farm workers can be given free or low rent accommodation, or a lodging allowance. Overtime may also be available.

Entry requirements

You do not need any particular qualifications for starting in this job, but it helps to have an interest in farming. It would also help you if you have experience of working on a farm, either through work experience or a weekend or holiday job.

You may be able to start this work through an Apprenticeship scheme. You will need to check which schemes are available in your area. To find out more, see the Apprenticeships website.

You could also take short courses, such as on how to operate a particular piece of agricultural equipment, tractor driving or fork lift operation.

If your job involves tasks such as operating chainsaws and using pesticides, you will need to have relevant certificates of competence as a legal requirement. These are awarded by City & Guilds Land-based Services and by Lantra Awards. See their websites for more information.

More information

Lantra Awards
www.lantra-awards.co.uk

Lantra
Lantra House
Stoneleigh Park
Nr Coventry
Warwickshire
CV8 2LG
Tel: 0845 707 8007
www.lantra.co.uk

City & Guilds
1 Giltspur Street
London
EC1A 9DD
Tel: 0844 543 0000
www.cityandguilds.com

Department for Environment, Food & Rural Affairs (DEFRA)
www.defra.gov.uk

COUNTRYSIDE RANGER

The nature of the work
As a countryside ranger, your work could include:

- planning and creating habitats to conserve plants and animals
- tree planting, pond management and other practical tasks
- making sure that footpaths, bridleways and waterways meet health and safety recommendations
- carrying out field surveys to detect changes in the environment
- patrolling sites to help visitors and to discourage poaching or damage to the environment
- giving talks
- managing exhibitions and resource centres
- leading guided walks
- taking part in community projects
- working with local landowners and businesses whose activities may affect the environment
- keeping records and writing reports.

You could specialise in a particular area such as habitat management, fieldwork or education, or in certain types of habitat such as waterways, coasts or moorlands.

What can you earn?

In local authorities, rangers can earn from around £18,000 to over £25,000 a year. Senior Rangers can earn over £30,000 a year. Salaries with other employers vary considerably.

Entry requirements

Before starting work as a countryside ranger you will usually need a relevant qualification and work experience. A good way to get experience is by volunteering with organisations such as:

- a Wildlife Trust
- the National Trust
- BTCV
- the Forestry Commission
- Groundwork UK.

See organisations' websites for details. Some run training courses for their volunteers.

The qualifications you need before starting a paid job will vary depending on the employer and the amount of experience you have. Relevant qualifications include:

- BTEC Level 3 Certificate/Diploma in Countryside Management
- BTEC HNC/HND in Environmental Conservation
- Diploma in Work-Based Environmental Conservation
- Environmental Conservation Apprenticeship
- foundation degrees in subjects such as countryside management and conservation
- degrees in subjects such as countryside management, rural environmental management, conservation and environment, or environmental studies.

For all courses you should check entry requirements with individual colleges or universities.

To search for foundation degree, HND and degree courses, see the UCAS (Universities and Colleges Admissions Service) website.

You may be able to start this job through an Apprenticeship scheme. You will need to check which schemes are available in your area. To find out more, see the Apprenticeships website.

More information

LGcareers (local government careers)
www.lgcareers.com

Lantra
Lantra House
Stoneleigh Park
Nr Coventry
Warwickshire
CV8 2LG
Tel: 0845 707 8007
www.lantra.co.uk

Wildlife Trusts
www.wildlifetrusts.org

National Trust
www.nationaltrust.org.uk

Groundwork UK
www.groundwork.org.uk

BTCV
Sedum House
Mallard Way
Potteric Carr
Doncaster
DNL 8DB
Tel: 01302 388883
www.btcv.org.uk

Forestry Commission
www.forestry.gov.uk

Countryside Management Association (CMA)
Writtle College
Lordship Road
Writtle
Chelmsford
Essex
CM1 3RR
Tel: 01245 424116
www.countrysidemanagement.org.uk

FOREST OFFICER

The nature of the work

A forest officer may have progressed from a working role in the woodland into this more managerial position. Where several woodlands are owned, or managed, a forest officer may be responsible for each individual woodland, with a head forester overseeing the work in all of the woodlands.

Working in private woodland or for the Forestry Commission will often require a wider range of skills and knowledge including land management skills. The forest officer will also usually have to control a budget and follow a business plan developed for the sites they manage. They will be answerable in the first instance to the head forester, who will oversee the forestry work on a number of different locations.

Their main tasks may include planning the work to be carried out by staff and contractors, managing the maintenance of machinery and equipment, maintaining records of work and ensuring that heath and safety policies are observed.

They will also be required to survey and inspect trees and sites, selecting and marking up timber to be harvested as well as planning, monitoring and evaluating habitat management work.

Forest officers are also known as foresters, forest managers, woodland managers and assistant head foresters.

What can you earn?

Salaries can range from around £19,000 to around £30,000 a year.

Entry requirements

Individuals entering at this level will have significant experience in forestry and will usually have completed a higher level qualification in forestry or related subjects. They may also have completed the relevant certificates of competence for their work area. These might include chainsaw use, chipper use and operation of specialist equipment such as a forwarder or harvester.

More information

Lantra
Lantra House
Stoneleigh Park
Nr Coventry
Warwickshire
CV8 2LG
Tel: 0845 707 8007
www.lantra.co.uk

Royal Forestry Society (RFS)
www.rfs.org.uk

Forestry Commission
www.forestry.gov.uk

Institute of Chartered Foresters
59 George Street
Edinburgh
EH2 2JG
Tel: 0131 240 1425
www.charteredforesters.org

BTCV
Sedum House
Mallard Way
Potteric Carr
Doncaster
DNL 8DB
Tel: 01302 388883
www.btcv.org.uk

The Arboricultural Association
Ullenwood Court
Ullenwood
Cheltenham
Gloucestershire
GL53 9QS
Tel 01242 522152
www.trees.org.uk

GAMEKEEPER

The nature of the work
Your work would vary according to the season, but your main tasks would include:

- organising shoots and fishing parties
- hiring and supervising staff such as beaters (who flush out birds during shoots)
- keeping records of what is shot or caught and arranging the sale of game
- training gun dogs and working with them
- breeding game birds for release in the wild
- controlling predators such as foxes, crows and rats by shooting and trapping
- protecting game from poachers by patrolling the beat area at night
- repairing equipment, buildings and game pens and cleaning guns

- clearing woodland and burning heather
- liaising with the police to deal with crime such as badger digging and hare coursing.

As a keeper protecting and managing rivers and streams as habitats for trout and salmon you would be known as a river keeper or ghillie.

What can you earn?

Gamekeepers can earn from £11,000 to around £18,000 a year.
Employers often provide free or cheap accommodation and a vehicle.
Figures are intended as a guideline only.

Entry requirements

You would usually start your career as a gamekeeper by working as an assistant or under-keeper, working with an experienced keeper.

Competition for vacancies is strong, so it will be useful if you have some paid or unpaid experience, perhaps as part of a beating team, or in a related area such as forestry or farming. Practical skills such as carpentry would also be useful. You would need a driving licence for most jobs.

You could prepare for work as a gamekeeper by doing a relevant full-time course before looking for work, although this is not essential. Courses include:
- BTEC (Edexcel) Level 3 Certificate or Diploma in Countryside Management.
- SQA National Certificate Introduction to Gamekeeping (in Scotland)
- SQA Higher National Certificate in Gamekeeping and Wildlife Management (in Scotland).

You should check with individual colleges for their entry requirements. See the 'Links' section of the National Gamekeepers Organisation Educational Trust website for a list of some of the colleges running gamekeeping courses.
You may be able to get into this job through an Apprenticeship scheme. The range of Apprenticeships available in your area will depend on the local jobs market and the types of skills employers need from their workers. For more information, visit the Apprenticeships website.

More information

National Gamekeepers Organisation
www.nationalgamekeepers.org.uk

Scottish Gamekeepers Association
www.scottishgamekeepers.co.uk

GROUNDS PERSON OR GREEN KEEPER

The nature of the work
Your main responsibility would be to manage the soil and grass to make sure the turf is always in top condition. Your duties would typically include:
- preparing land for turf laying
- applying nutrients
- rolling and mowing the turf
- identifying and controlling weeds
- setting out and marking lines on surfaces
- installing and maintaining equipment like nets, posts and protective covers
- ensuring irrigation and drainage systems are maintained
- looking after surrounding areas - decorative displays, concrete or tarmac
- operating equipment like hedge cutters, strimmers and ride-on mowers
- painting, removing rubbish and carrying out general duties
- maintaining good communication with your customers

Your tasks would vary according to the season and weather conditions.

What can you earn?

Salary scales for this work can be:
Groundsperson: £14,985 to £18,310 a year
Skilled groundsperson: £18,700 to £22,850
Head groundsperson: £24,445 to £31,795.

There may be bonuses and payment for overtime, and accommodation is sometimes provided.

Entry requirements

If you have experience in horticulture, you could find work as an unskilled groundsperson without relevant qualifications. You may then be able to progress to skilled level by gaining experience and working towards qualifications.

Alternatively, you could start by doing a course that would help you develop the skills needed for the job. Relevant courses include:

- Certificate/Diploma in Horticulture at levels 2 and 3
- Certificate/Diploma in Sports and Amenity Turf Maintenance at Level 2.
- Entry requirements for courses vary, so you should check directly with colleges.
- A driving licence will be useful for some jobs.
- You may be able to get into this job through an Apprenticeship scheme. The range of Apprenticeships available in your area will depend on the local jobs market and the types of skills employers need from their workers.

More information

Lantra
Lantra House
Stoneleigh Park
Nr Coventry
Warwickshire
CV8 2LG
Tel: 0845 707 8007
www.lantra.co.uk

Institute of Groundsmanship (IOG)
28 Stratford Office Village
Wolverton Mill East
Milton Keynes

MK12 5TW
Tel: 01908 312511
www.iog.org

British and International Golf Greenkeepers Association Limited (BIGGA)
BIGGA HOUSE
Aldwark
Alne
York
YO61 1UF
Tel:+44(0)1347 833800
Fax:+44(0)1347 833801
Email:info@bigga.co.uk
www.bigga.org.uk

HORSE GROOM

The nature of the work
As a groom, you would:
- provide food and water for horses
- replace bedding
- clean equipment such as saddles and bridles ('tack')
- clean, brush and sometimes clip, horses' coats
- muck out stables
- check for changes in the condition of horses and report problems
- treat minor wounds, change dressings and give medication
- follow instructions from vets when treatment is needed.

You may also be responsible for exercising the horses each day.
If you work with show jumpers or race horses, you will prepare them for events, and may accompany them. In studs and breeding yards you will work with stallions, mares and foals, and may help vets to deliver foals. In riding schools you may greet clients, lead riders out on foot, and accompany them on horseback.

What can you earn?

Grooms can start at around £12,500 a year
Experienced grooms can earn around £16,000
Head lads/girls in a racing yard can earn £20,000 or more.
Some employers provide accommodation, food, free stabling for your own horse and riding lessons.

Entry requirements

You must be at least 16, and there may be weight restrictions for some jobs. Although you may not need qualifications, employers may prefer you to have experience, and some may ask for a nationally-recognised qualification such as:

- BTEC Level 2 Certificate and Diploma in Horse Care
- BTEC Level 3 Diploma in Horse Management
- British Horse Society (BHS) Stage 1 in Horse Knowledge and Care
- Association of British Riding Schools (ABRS) Preliminary Horse Care and Riding Certificate.

For BHS or ABRS qualifications you must be at least 16, and would usually need experience of handling and riding horses. Visit the BHS and ABRS websites for details.

You could get practical experience as a volunteer, for example helping out at a local stable. This could give you an advantage when looking for paid work.

You can train in race-horse care at the British Racing School in Newmarket and the Northern Racing College in Doncaster. You will not need riding experience to start, as there is a non-rider option up to NVQ level 2. However, most trainees do ride.
If you are interested in the horse breeding industry, you can train at the National Stud in Newmarket or at other training centres. See the Thoroughbred Breeders' Association website for details.

You may be able to get into this job through an Apprenticeship scheme. The range of Apprenticeships available in your area will depend on the local jobs market and the types of skills employers need from their workers. To find out more, visit the Apprenticeships website.

Visit the British Horse Racing Board careers website for full details of careers in horse-racing and breeding.

More information
Lantra
Lantra House
Stoneleigh Park
Nr Coventry
Warwickshire
CV8 2LG
Tel: 0845 707 8007
www.lantra.co.uk

British Racing School (BRS)
Snailwell Road
Newmarket
Suffolk
CB8 7NU
Tel: 01638 665103
www.brs.org.uk

Northern Racing College (NRC)
The Stables
Rossington Hall
Great North Road
Doncaster
South Yorkshire
DN11 0HN
Tel: 01302 861000
www.northernracingcollege.co.uk

Association of British Riding Schools (ABRS)
Queens Chambers
38-40 Queen Street
Penzance

Cornwall
TR18 4BH
Tel: 01736 369440
www.abrs-info.org

British Horseracing Authority
www.britishhorseracing.com

British Horse Society (BHS)
Stoneleigh Deer Park
Kenilworth
Warwickshire
CV8 2XZ
Tel: 0844 848 1666
www.bhs.co.uk

HORTICULTURAL MANAGER

The nature of the work

As a horticultural manager you would oversee the development and growth of plants for one of the following purposes:

- Production / commercial horticulture - producing food crops and ornamental plants for sale to wholesalers, retailers, nurseries, garden centres and the public
- garden centres - producing plants for sale to the public along with products such as tools and garden furniture
- Parks and Gardens - designing, constructing, managing and maintaining areas such as parks, gardens (historic or botanic) and public green spaces.

Your day-to-day tasks would vary depending on your particular job, but could include:

- managing, and possibly helping with, all aspects of cultivation
- preparing and modifying operational and business plans

- keeping records and handling budgets and accounts
- analysing procurement costs
- developing new products and markets and negotiating with suppliers
- designing layouts and developing planting programmes
- scheduling the planting and harvesting of crops
- managing the implementation of health and safety regulations and procedures
- recruiting and managing staff
- maintaining a skilled and trained workforce

What can you earn?

Horticultural managers can earn from around £16,000 to over £30,000 a year.
Senior managers can earn around £40,000.
Figures are intended as a guideline only.

Entry requirements

You may be able to work your way up to management by starting in a more basic position and gaining experience and qualifications.

To start directly as a manager, you would usually need a higher education qualification and practical experience. Relevant qualifications include:

- degrees in subjects such as horticulture and commercial horticulture
- BTEC HNCs/HNDs and foundation degrees in subjects like horticulture, horticultural management and professional horticulture.

You should check with colleges and universities for their exact entry requirements as these can vary.
You can also complete Royal Horticultural Society (RHS) qualifications:
See the RHS website for details of qualifications and a list of course providers.

Examples of the ways you can gain practical experience include:

- work placements
- RHS voluntary internships

- Management Development Services graduate training – a paid programme of job placements and formal training for the food and produce industry.

See the Management Development Service website for details of their graduate training.

If you have not gained experience before, during or after a course you may need to begin at a more basic level before being considered for a management position. You could move into horticultural management if you have appropriate experience in a related area, such as farming, forestry, retailing or marketing.

More information
Management Development Services Ltd
www.mds-ltd.co.uk

National Trust
www.nationaltrust.org.uk

Royal Horticultural Society (RHS)
www.rhs.org.uk

Lantra
Lantra House
Stoneleigh Park
Nr Coventry
Warwickshire
CV8 2LG
Tel: 0845 707 8007
www.lantra.co.uk

Grow Careers
www.growcareers.info

Institute of Horticulture
www.horticulture.org.uk
hs.org.uk

10. THE HEALTH SERVICE

The health sector is a large and diverse area. the job opportunities are very varied and are within the private and public sectors, mainly the NHS. In this section we cover mainly NHS opportunities as follows:

- Adult Nurse
- Ambulance Paramedic
- Anesthetist
- Clinical Support Worker
- Health Visitor
- Health Service manager
- Hospital Doctor
- Hospital Porter
- Mental Health Nurse
- Occupational Therapist
- Pharmacist
- Physiotherapist
- School Nurse
- Speech and Language Therapy Assistant
- Radiographer
- Surgeon
- Psychiatrist

For further details about the wide variety of jobs in the health sector (NHS) you should go to:

NHS Careers
PO Box 2311
Bristol
BS2 2ZX
Tel: 0345 60 60 655
www.nhscareers.nhs.uk

ADULT NURSE

The nature of the work

Adult nurses check patients' progress and decide with doctors what care to give. They may also advise and support patients and their relatives.

As an adult nurse, the practical care you give could include:

- checking temperatures
- measuring blood pressure and breathing rates
- helping doctors with physical examinations
- giving drugs and injections
- cleaning and dressing wounds
- giving blood transfusions
- using high technology (high-tech) medical equipment.

You could specialise in an area such as accident and emergency, cardiac rehabilitation, outpatients, neonatal nursing, and operating theatre work. As well as hospitals, you could also work in the community, health centres, clinics or prisons.

What can you earn?

Nurses can earn between £21,176 and £27,534 a year. Nurse team leaders and managers can earn around £30,460 to £40,157 a year. Nurse consultants can earn up to £55,945 a year. Extra allowances may be paid to those living in or around London.

Entry requirements

To work as an adult nurse, you need a Nursing and Midwifery Council (NMC)-approved degree or Diploma of Higher Education in Nursing (adult branch). Please note: The final opportunity to start the nursing diploma will be Spring 2013. From September 2013, students will only be able to qualify as a nurse by studying for a degree.

To do an approved course, you need:

- proof of your English and maths skills, good health and good character

- evidence of recent successful study (especially if you have been out of education for a number of years)
- Criminal Records Bureau (CRB) clearance.

Course providers can also set their own academic entry requirements, which can include:

- for a nursing diploma – five GCSEs (A-C) preferably in English, maths and/or a science-based subject
- for a nursing degree – the same GCSEs as the diploma, plus two or three A levels, possibly including a biological science or an equivalent qualification.

Some course providers offer Advanced Diplomas in Adult Nursing. This qualification and the entry requirements lie between diploma and degree level.

Check with universities for exact entry requirements, as other qualifications, such as an Access to Higher Education course, may also be accepted. For a list of degree and diploma course providers and application advice, visit the Universities and Colleges Admissions Service (UCAS) website.

You may be able to become an adult nurse through an Apprenticeship scheme. You will need to check which schemes are available in your area.

Professional registration

As a qualified nurse you must renew your professional registration with the NMC every three years. To renew, you need to have worked a minimum of 450 hours and completed at least five study days of professional development every three years. Check with the NMC for details.

Return to practice

If you are a former registered nurse wanting to return to the profession, you can take a return-to-practice course. Contact your local NHS Trust for details.

More information

Nursing and Midwifery Council (NMC)
23 Portland Place
London
W1B 1PZ
Tel: 020 7333 9333
www.nmc-uk.org

Queens University of Belfast
School of Nursing and Midwifery
Medical Biology Centre
97 Lisburn Road
Belfast
BT9 7BL
Tel: 028 9097 2233
www.qub.ac.uk

University of Ulster at Jordanstown
School of Nursing
Shore Road
Newtownabbey
Co Antrim
BT37 0QB
Tel: 08700 400 700
www.ulster.ac.uk

Health Learning and Skills Advice Line
Tel: 08000 150850

National Leadership and Innovation Agency for Healthcare
Innovation House
Bridgend Road
Llanharan
CF72 9RP
Tel: 01443 233 333
www.nliah.wales.nhs.uk/

NHS Careers
PO Box 2311
Bristol

BS2 2ZX
Tel: 0345 60 60 655
www.nhscareers.nhs.uk

Skills for Health
Goldsmiths House
Broad Plain
Bristol
BS2 0JP
Tel: 0117 922 1155
www.skillsforhealth.org.uk

AMBULANCE PARAMEDIC

The nature of the work

As a paramedic, you could deal with a range of situations, from minor wounds to serious injuries caused by a major road or rail accident. Your job would be to provide immediate care or treatment.

When responding to a call, you would check a patient's condition and decide what action to take. Your work may also include:

- making quick decisions about moving the patient
- using advanced life support techniques, such as electric shocks, to resuscitate patients
- carrying out surgical procedures, such as inserting a breathing tube
- using advanced devices to keep people breathing
- providing drug and fluid therapy
- giving medicines and injections
- putting on dressings for wounds and supports for broken bones.

Daily tasks include keeping accurate records and checking equipment.

You could work on a traditional ambulance or alone using a car, motorbike or bicycle. With experience you could work in a helicopter ambulance team.

What can you earn?

Student paramedics may be paid around £15,500 to £18,600 a year.

Qualified paramedics can earn around £21,200 to £27,500 a year.

Emergency care practitioners (ECPs) and team leaders can earn up to £34,200 a year, and area managers may earn around £40,200 a year.

Additional allowances may be paid to staff in certain parts of the country and to those working on standby or in shift patterns.

Entry requirements

You need to be registered with the Health Professions Council before you can work unsupervised as a paramedic. To join the register, you need to complete a Health Professions Council (HPC) approved qualification that includes clinical placements with an ambulance service and various other health providers.

There are two ways that you can work towards HPC registration:

- by taking a Foundation Degree, Diploma of Higher Education (DipHE), or degree in paramedic emergency care (other subject titles may also be used)
- by getting a student paramedic job with an Ambulance Trust and studying whilst learning on the job (see the NHS Jobs website for vacancies).

To do a course, you will usually need five GCSEs (A-C) including English, maths and science, and between one and three A levels, often including a science. Check with course providers for exact requirements as other qualifications, such as an Access to Higher Education course, may also be accepted. Course providers are listed on the HPC website.

For a student paramedic job, requirements can vary but in general you will need:

- four or five GCSEs (A-C) including English, maths and science
- **or** around 12 months' experience as an ambulance care assistant, technician or emergency care assistant, plus evidence that you can study at higher education level. Some employers prefer those with Open University 'Openings' course credits, which cover research and study skills.

For further advice, contact your local ambulance service. These are listed on the NHS Choices website.

More information

Health Professions Council
Park House
184 Kennington Park Road
London
SE11 4BU
Tel: 020 7582 0866
www.hpc-uk.org

NHS Careers
PO Box 2311
Bristol
BS2 2ZX
Tel: 0345 60 60 655
www.nhscareers.nhs.uk

College of Paramedics
The Exchange
Express Park
Bristol Road
Bridgewater
TA6 4RR
Tel: 01278 420 014
www.collegeofparamedics.co.uk

Health Learning and Skills Advice Line
Tel: 08000 150850

ANESTHETIST

The nature of the work
Anesthetists are qualified medical doctors who specialise in pain management, anesthesia for surgery and intensive care. They often deal with emergency situations by providing advanced life support, the ability to breathe and resuscitation to the heart and lungs.

- As an anesthetist, your work could include:

- preparing patients for surgery and giving anesthesia
- relieving pain during childbirth
- easing pain after an operation
- managing acute and chronic pain
- helping psychiatric patients receiving electric shock therapy
- providing sedation and anesthesia to patients having radiology and radio-therapy.

You would use a range of techniques, including local anesthetics such as epidurals and other nerve blocks. During an operation, you would observe your patient, monitor their progress and respond to any changes. You would work closely with other healthcare professionals to provide the most appropriate and complete treatment plan for your patients.

You could work in areas ranging from high dependency units to cardiac arrest teams. As a senior doctor, you could lead a team and train junior doctors, undergraduate medical students, nurses and paramedics.

What can you earn?
Foundation house officers (junior doctors) can earn between £33,300 and £41,300 a year.

Doctors in specialist training can earn up to £69,400, and consultants can earn between £74,500 and £180,000 a year.

The salaries given for doctors in training include an additional amount based on average hours of overtime worked, time spent covering unsocial hours and workload.

Consultants working in private hospitals may be paid higher fees.

Entry requirements

To become a doctor specialising in anesthetics you will need to complete:

- a degree in medicine, recognised by the General Medical Council (GMC)
- a two-year foundation programme of general training
- three years of core training, including acute care
- higher specialty training in anesthesia, intensive care medicine and pain management.

To do a five-year degree in medicine you will usually need at least five GCSEs (A-C) including English, maths and science, plus three A levels at grades AAB in subjects such as chemistry, biology and either physics or maths. See the GMC website for details of recognised courses.

If you do not have qualifications in science, you may be able to do a six-year degree course in medicine that includes a one-year pre-medical or foundation course. You will need to check with individual universities.

If you already have an honours degree in a science subject (minimum 2:1) you may be able to join a four-year graduate entry programme to medicine. Some universities will also accept non-science graduates. See the Medical Schools Council website for details of course providers.

When you apply for a degree in medicine, you may be asked to take the UK Clinical Aptitude Test (UKCAT). Universities use this test to help them select students with the personal qualities and mental abilities needed for a career in medicine. Your university will tell you if you need to take the test.

If you trained as a doctor overseas, contact the GMC for details about registering and practising in the UK.

More information

Royal College of Anesthetists (RCA)
Churchill House
35 Red Lion Square
London
WC1R 4SG
Tel: 020 7092 1500
www.rcoa.ac.uk

UKCAT (UK Clinical Aptitude Test)
www.ukcat.ac.uk

British Medical Association (BMA)
Tavistock Square
London
WC1H 9JP
Tel: 020 7387 4499
www.bma.org.uk

General Medical Council (GMC)
Regent's Place
350 Euston Road
London
NW1 3JN
Tel: 0845 357 3456
www.gmc-uk.org

CLINICAL SUPPORT WORKER

The nature of the work

As a clinical support worker, your duties could include a range of lab skills such as:

- labelling, sorting and storing specimens
- assisting with the analysis of tissue and fluid samples
- putting together chemical solutions
- loading and operating machines
- using a computer to input and analyse data
- disposing of hazardous waste
- sterilising equipment
- maintaining stock levels.

Part of your work may also include responding to telephone enquiries as well as the keeping and filing of records.

You could work closely with scientists in a range of areas:

- biochemistry: studying chemical reactions in the body like kidney failure
- histopathology: examining the structure of diseased tissue
- virology: analysing viruses, the diseases they cause, and vaccines
- cytology: studying the structure and function of cells, and screening for cancers
- haematology: analysing diseases of the blood and blood forming tissues
- immunology: examining how the immune system works, for example with allergies

- transfusion science: transferring blood and blood products from one person to another.

You could combine your role with working in a closely related area of work such as phlebotomy.

Please see the phlebotomy job profile for more information.

What can you earn?
Clinical support workers can earn around £13,600 to £16,700 a year. With experience this can rise to around £18,500.

Entry requirements

You may not need any qualifications to start as a clinical support worker. Some employers will prefer you to have GCSEs (A-C) including English, maths and science, and basic IT and word processing skills. It would be an advantage to have experience in the NHS (especially in a lab setting) and an understanding of medical terminology.

You could contact the personnel or biomedical sciences department at your local hospital for further information on their specific entry requirements. See the NHS Choices website for details of local NHS Trusts.

Joining a professional body, such as the Association of Medical Laboratory Assistants (AMLA), could also be useful in giving you access to education and training opportunities and helping you keep your skills up to date.

More information

NHS Careers
PO Box 2311
Bristol
BS2 2ZX
Tel: 0345 60 60 655
www.nhscareers.nhs.uk

Institute of Biomedical Science
12 Coldbath Square
London
EC1R 5HL

Tel: 020 7713 0214
www.ibms.org

Health Learning and Skills Advice Line
Tel: 08000 150850

HEALTH VISITOR

The nature of the work

As a health visitor you would provide information, practical care and support to help your clients cope with any difficulties they are experiencing. You would work with a broad section of people in the community and your duties would often include:

- advising older people on health related issues
- giving advice to new mothers about their baby – for example hygiene, safety, feeding and sleeping
- counselling people on issues such as post-natal depression, bereavement or being diagnosed HIV positive
- coordinating child immunisation programmes
- organising special clinics or drop-in centres.

You would work closely with other agencies such as social services and local housing departments.

What can you earn?

Health visitors can earn between £24,800 and £33,500 a year. Team managers can earn up to £39,300.

Extra allowances may be given for additional responsibilities, location and length of service.

Entry requirements

You will usually need around two years' experience as a qualified midwife or nurse (any branch) before you can begin an approved health visitor training programme and work as a health visitor.

To qualify as a registered nurse or midwife you will need to complete a Nursing and Midwifery Council (NMC) approved degree or Diploma of Higher Education.

More information

Nursing and Midwifery Council (NMC)
23 Portland Place
London
W1B 1PZ
Tel: 020 7333 9333
www.nmc-uk.org

Queens University of Belfast
School of Nursing and Midwifery
Medical Biology Centre
97 Lisburn Road
Belfast
BT9 7BL
Tel: 028 9097 2233
www.qub.ac.uk

University of Ulster at Jordanstown
School of Nursing
Shore Road
Newtownabbey
Co Antrim
BT37 0QB
Tel: 08700 400 700
www.ulster.ac.uk

NHS Careers
PO Box 2311
Bristol
BS2 2ZX
Tel: 0345 60 60 655
www.nhscareers.nhs.uk

Community Practitioners' and Health Visitors' Association
33-37 Moreland Street

London
EC1V 8HA
Tel: 020 7505 3000
www.amicustheunion.org/cphva

Health Learning and Skills Advice Line
Tel: 08000 150850

National Leadership and Innovation Agency for Healthcare
Innovation House
Bridgend Road
Llanharan
CF72 9RP
Tel: 01443 233 333
www.nliah.wales.nhs.uk

HEALTH SERVICE MANAGER

The nature of the work
As a health service manager, your duties could include:

- supervising staff and taking responsibility for the work they do
- dealing with day-to-day operational matters
- using statistical information to monitor performance and help with long term planning
- setting and maintaining budgets
- creating and carrying out the company objectives
- implementing the policies of the board, making sure government guidelines are followed
- working with clinical staff and other professionals
- managing contracts.

Your role could range from chief executive of a large hospital to manager of a GP surgery. You could also be a manager within the ambulance service, community health service (Primary Care Trust) or a strategic health authority (local NHS headquarters, monitoring service and performance of local NHS Trusts). Alternatively, you could specialise in an area such as personnel and finance, or clinical, therapeutic or technical support.

What can you earn?

On completion of a graduate scheme, you can earn between £27,000 to £37,000 a year. Directors and chief executives can earn between £90,000 and £100,000.

Entry requirements

There are a number of ways you could get into health service management. The most direct route is through one of the NHS Graduate Management Training Schemes. To get on to a scheme, you will need a degree (minimum grade 2:2) or an equivalent qualification in a health or management related subject. Check the training and development section below for more information.

Alternative routes into health service management include:

working your way up from an administrative post by taking in-service training courses such as those run by the Institute of Healthcare Management (IHM) – to start as an administrator you are likely to need four or five GCSEs (grade A-C) and possibly A levels

- applying directly to the NHS for a junior management position – for this you will usually need a degree plus management experience
- taking an in-service training programme leading to a Certificate or Diploma in Managing Health and Social Care – for this you will usually need to be working within the NHS in a clinical role (or a profession related to health).

You can also check the IHM and NHS Careers websites for more details of schemes, training programmes and alternative entry qualifications.

More information

NHS Graduate Training Schemes
www.nhsgraduates.co.uk/About-the-NHS

NHS Careers ⊡
PO Box 2311
Bristol
BS2 2ZX

Tel: 0345 60 60 655
www.nhscareers.nhs.uk

Health Learning and Skills Advice Line
Tel: 08000 150850

Institute of Healthcare Management (IHM)
21 Morley Street
London
SE1 7QZ
Tel: 020 7620 1030
www.ihm.org.uk

HOSPITAL DOCTOR

The nature of the work
If you're interested in science and want a career in medicine, this job could be ideal for you. Hospital doctors treat illness, disease and infection in patients admitted to hospital.

To become a hospital doctor you will need a degree in medicine. And you'll also need to complete a two-year foundation programme of general training.

As a hospital doctor, you would examine and treat patients referred to you by GPs and other health professionals. You could work in one of about 60 specialist fields within four main categories: medicine, surgery, pathology and psychiatry.

Medicine – general medical conditions, emergencies, and specialisms like paediatrics, cardiology, dermatology, ophthalmology, geriatrics and neurology.

Surgery – caring for patients before, during and after an operation. You could work within one of nine areas including cardiothoracic, neurosurgery or plastic surgery.

Pathology – investigating the cause of disease and the effect on patients. You could specialise in subjects such as histopathology (diagnosing disease from changes in tissue structure), chemical pathology (examining biochemical changes relating to medical conditions) or molecular genetics (identifying abnormalities in DNA and chromosomes).

Psychiatry – working with patients experiencing mental health problems, ranging from depression and anxiety to personality disorders and addictions. Your work could include psychotherapy, counselling, psychiatric tests and prescribing medication.

You could also work in areas such as anaesthetics, obstetrics, gynaecology, radiology and oncology.

Please see the anaesthetist job profile for more information.

Your duties may include leading a team or managing a department, and teaching and supervising trainee doctors. You would keep accurate and up to date patient records, write reports, go to meetings or conferences, and keep GPs informed about the diagnosis and care of their patients.

What can you earn?
Junior hospital doctors can earn between £33,300 and £41,300 a year.

Hospital doctors in specialist training can earn up to £69,400 a year, and consultants can earn between £74,500 and £176,300 a year.

The salaries given for hospital doctors in training include an additional amount based on the average overtime worked, cover during unsocial hours and workload.

Consultants working in private hospitals may negotiate higher fees.

Entry requirements

To become a hospital doctor you need to complete:

- a degree in medicine, recognised by the General Medical Council (GMC)
- a two-year foundation programme of general training (see training and development section below)
- specialist training in your chosen area of medicine (see section below).

To do a five-year degree in medicine you will usually need at least five GCSEs (A-C) including English, maths and science, plus three A levels at grades AAB in subjects such as chemistry, biology and either physics or maths. Check the GMC website for a list of degree courses.

If you do not have qualifications in science, you may be able to join a six-year degree course in medicine. This includes a one-year pre-medical or foundation year. If you already have a degree in a science subject (minimum 2:1) you could take a four-year graduate entry programme into medicine. Some universities will also accept non-science graduates. See the British Medical Association (BMA) website for details.

When you apply for a course, you may be asked to take the UK Clinical Aptitude Test to check your suitability for a career in medicine. This tests your mental abilities and behaviour characteristics, rather than your academic achievements. If you trained as a doctor overseas, contact the GMC for details about registering and practising in the UK.

It could be an advantage to have some relevant paid or voluntary experience, for example as a care assistant in a hospital, nursing or residential home. For paid opportunities, you could approach care homes directly or check the NHS jobs website. For voluntary work, or to arrange time watching a doctor at work, contact the voluntary services coordinator or manager at your local NHS Trust.

More information

NHS Careers
PO Box 2311
Bristol
BS2 2ZX
Tel: 0345 60 60 655
www.nhscareers.nhs.uk

Royal College of Surgeons of England
35-43 Lincoln's Inn Fields
London
WC2A 3PE
Tel: 020 7405 3474
www.rcseng.ac.uk

British Medical Association (BMA)
Tavistock Square
London
WC1H 9JP
Tel: 020 7387 4499
www.bma.org.uk

General Medical Council (GMC)
Regent's Place
350 Euston Road
London
NW1 3JN
Tel: 0845 357 3456
www.gmc-uk.org

Health Learning and Skills Advice Line
Tel: 08000 150850

HOSPITAL PORTER

The nature of the work
As a hospital porter your work could take you anywhere on the hospital site. In some hospitals you would help with security, which could involve working on the reception desk.

You could also carry out other duties such as:

- taking meals to patients
- transferring clean linen to wards from the laundry
- moving furniture and vital equipment safely
- disposing of waste, which may be hazardous
- delivering post, files and specimens, such as blood samples, to different parts of the hospital.

What can you earn?
Starting salaries can be around £13,600 a year. With experience this can rise to around £16,700 a year. Senior porters or team leaders can earn around £18,500 a year.

There are additional payments for working overtime and shifts. Salaries in private hospitals are based on those in the NHS.

Entry requirements

You do not usually need any qualifications to become a hospital porter, however you will need good written and spoken communication skills. It could help you if you have a manual handling, or health and safety qualification.

Some employers will test your physical fitness when you apply for a job, which may include a medical check. Larger hospitals or NHS Trusts may prefer you to have a driving licence so that you can work at a number of different sites during a working day.

Experience of working with the public, especially in a caring role, would be particularly helpful. If you do not have relevant experience, you could learn about this role by volunteering in a hospital, helping the porter with duties. Contact the voluntary services coordinator or manager at your local NHS Trust for further advice.

You could go on to work towards NVQ Level 2 in Support Services in Health Care.

More information

NHS Careers
PO Box 2311
Bristol
BS2 2ZX
Tel: 0345 60 60 655
www.nhscareers.nhs.uk

Health Learning and Skills Advice Line
Tel: 08000 150850

MENTAL HEALTH NURSE

The nature of the work
As a mental health nurse, you would support people who have conditions such as:

- anxiety
- depression
- stress-related illnesses
- personality disorders
- eating disorders
- drug and alcohol addiction.

You could work with a variety of clients, or specialise and work with a particular group, like adolescents or offenders. Your duties could involve:

- assessing and supporting patients
- encouraging patients to take part in role play, art, drama and discussion as therapies
- physical care, if the patient is too old or ill to look after themselves
- giving medication to patients.

You would work closely with support workers, psychiatrists, clinical psychologists and health visitors. You may also help clients if they need to deal with social workers, the police, relevant charities, local government and housing officials.

What can you earn?

Nurses can earn between £21,176 and £27,534 a year.

Team leaders and managers can earn between £30,460 and £40,157 a year, and nurse consultants can earn up to £55,945 a year.

Extra allowances may be paid to those living in or around London.

Entry requirements

To work as a mental health nurse, you will need to complete a Nursing and Midwifery Council (NMC) approved degree, or a Diploma of Higher Education in Nursing (mental health branch).

Please note: from September 2013, students will only be able to qualify as a nurse by doing a degree. Until this date, you could complete either a diploma or a degree, however the final chance to start the nursing diploma is Spring 2013.

To do an approved course, you will need:

- proof of your English and maths skills, good health and good character
- evidence of recent successful study experience (especially if you have been out of education for some time).

You must also agree to a Criminal Records Bureau (CRB) check.

You will probably need to have previous experience (paid or voluntary) of working with people. This could include those who use mental health services. If you want to gain experience like this, contact the voluntary services coordinator or manager at your local NHS Trust for details of opportunities.

Course providers can set their own academic entry requirements, which can include:

- for a nursing diploma – five GCSEs (A-C) preferably in English, maths and/or a science-based subject
- for an Advanced Diploma in Mental Health Nursing – this qualification and the entry requirements for it are between diploma and degree level
- for a nursing degree – usually the same GCSEs as the diploma, plus two or three A levels, possibly including a biological science.

Check with universities for exact entry details as other qualifications, such as an Access to Higher Education diploma, may be accepted. For a list of degree and diploma course providers and application advice, see the Universities and Colleges Admissions Service (UCAS) website.

If you are interested in social work as well, you could take a degree in, for example Mental Health Studies (Nursing and Social Work) accredited by the NMC and the General Social Care Council. After gaining your degree, you could do a variety of jobs including mental health nurse, and social worker specialising in an area such as child and adolescent mental health or substance misuse.

Funding

Nursing students starting to study in 2011 on the nursing diploma and degree courses may get non-repayable bursaries to cover living expenses. Those starting their studies on an approved nursing course from September 2012 will receive a non means-tested grant of £1,000, an additional means tested bursary of £4,395 per year (£5,460 for students in London) and a reduced rate non-means tested loan.

For more information on NHS student bursaries and for eligibility, see the NHS Business Services Authority website.

Other entry routes

You could prepare for a nursing course by doing a two-year Cadet Scheme or Apprenticeship. Schemes vary between NHS Trusts, but will usually include clinical placements and working towards a QCF/ NVQ Level 3 in Health. To find out more about Apprenticeships, visit the Apprenticeships website. Contact your local NHS Trust for details of Apprenticeships and cadet scheme opportunities.

If you are a healthcare assistant with an NVQ or QCF qualification at Level 3 in Health and you have financial support from your employer, you may be able to complete part-time nurse training by applying for a secondment. You would receive a salary while you study. Once you qualify, you may need to commit to working with the NHS Trust that funded you for a minimum period.

If you have a first or second class honours degree in a subject related to health or nursing, you could qualify as a nurse by taking an accelerated programme for graduates. You can search for courses on the NHS Careers Course Finder facility.

If you are a nurse who trained outside the UK and European Economic Area (EEA), you may need to complete the Overseas Nurses Programme before you begin work. Occasionally, EEA trained nurses may be required to take an aptitude test (or similar) in order to prove professional competence. See the NMC website for details.

More information

Nursing and Midwifery Council (NMC)
23 Portland Place
London

W1B 1PZ
Tel: 020 7333 9333
www.nmc-uk.org

Queens University of Belfast
School of Nursing and Midwifery
Medical Biology Centre
97 Lisburn Road
Belfast
BT9 7BL
Tel: 028 9097 2233
www.qub.ac.uk

University of Ulster at Jordanstown
School of Nursing
Shore Road
Newtownabbey
Co Antrim
BT37 0QB
Tel: 08700 400 700
www.ulster.ac.uk

Health Learning and Skills Advice Line
Tel: 08000 150850

National Leadership and Innovation Agency for Healthcare
Innovation House
Bridgend Road
Llanharan
CF72 9RP
Tel: 01443 233 333
www.nliah.wales.nhs.uk/

NHS Careers
PO Box 2311
Bristol
BS2 2ZX
Tel: 0345 60 60 655
www.nhscareers.nhs.uk

Skills for Health
Goldsmiths House
Broad Plain
Bristol
BS2 0JP
Tel: 0117 922 1155
www.skillsforhealth.org.uk

OCCUPATIONAL THERAPIST

The nature of the work

As an occupational therapist, you would often work with clients on a one-to-one basis and adapt treatment programmes to suit each person's needs and lifestyle. Your work could include things like:

- teaching an older patient recovering from a stroke how to dress themselves
- encouraging someone suffering with depression to take up a hobby or activity
- suggesting ways to adapt an office so that an employee injured in a car accident can return to work
- helping clients adjust to permanent disabilities.

You would also keep notes about clients' progress, and advise and support clients and their families and carers.

Some patients may have conditions such as motor neurone disease or multiple sclerosis, which means that they gradually become less mobile and more disabled. You would work with these clients to encourage a positive attitude, which can help them keep active for as long as possible.

With experience, you could specialise in an area such as:

- burns or plastic surgery
- cardiac or stroke rehabilitation
- paediatrics
- orthopaedics (spinal injury)
- community disability services
- mental health.

You could work with patients for several months or just for a few sessions. You would often work as part of a team of professionals, including physiotherapists, nurses and social workers.

What can you earn?
Starting salaries can be between £21,200 and £27,500 a year. With experience and extra responsibilities, this can rise to around £40,000 a year.

Entry requirements

To become a registered occupational therapist you will need to have a degree, or have completed a postgraduate course, in occupational therapy that is approved by the Health Professions Council (HPC). See the HPC website for approved courses and course providers.

Before you apply for a course, it is a good idea to gain some relevant experience or knowledge of the profession. You could contact the occupational therapy unit at your local hospital, nursing home or other health centre where therapists practice, to ask how you could get involved.

To do a degree in occupational therapy, you will usually need:

- five GCSEs (A-C)
- three A levels, often including at least one science subject (biology may be preferred).

Check with individual universities for exact entry details as other qualifications, such as an Access to Higher Education course, may be accepted.

To do a postgraduate course you will usually need an honours degree in a related area plus previous healthcare experience. Course providers will be able to tell you which degree subjects they accept.

You can join the British Association of Occupational Therapists (BAOT) and the World Federation of Occupational Therapists (WFOT) as a student or graduate. The BAOT website also includes details of course providers.

Another option is to start as occupational therapy support worker. With backing from your employer, you could work towards qualifying as an occupational therapist by completing a four-year in-service course leading to state registration.

You will need to agree to a Criminal Records Bureau check when you apply for a course and before you can register with the HPC. See the Criminal Records Bureau for details.

More information

Health Professions Council
Park House
184 Kennington Park Road
London
SE11 4BU
Tel: 020 7582 0866
www.hpc-uk.org

NHS Careers
PO Box 2311
Bristol
BS2 2ZX
Tel: 0345 60 60 655
www.nhscareers.nhs.uk

British Association of Occupational Therapists
106-114 Borough High Street
Southwark
London
SE1 1LB
Tel: 020 7450 2332 (Careers Info)
www.cot.co.uk

Health Learning and Skills Advice Line
Tel: 08000 150850

PHARMACIST

The nature of the work
Pharmacists provide expert advice on the use and supply of drugs and medicines. This could include checking prescriptions and making sure that laws controlling medicines are followed.

You would usually be based at a retail location (where you would be known as a community pharmacist) or at a hospital pharmacy.

As a community pharmacist in a retail location your work could include:
- giving healthcare advice and help to the public
- delivering medication to people who are unable to leave home
- visiting care homes to advise on the use and storage of medication
- preparing medicines bought at the counter
- giving advice on how to use medicines correctly, including the amount to use (dosage) and any risks selling a range of products
- ordering and controlling stock
- running or helping to run a business, including supervising and training staff.

In a hospital setting, your duties could include:
- giving advice on dosage and the most suitable form of medicine (such as a tablet, inhaler or injection)
- producing medicines (for example, creating a treatment or solution when ready made ones are not available)
- visiting wards, giving advice about medicines to colleagues and providing them with current information
- buying, quality testing and distributing medicines throughout the hospital
- supervising trainees and junior pharmacists.

Another option is to work as a pharmacist with a local primary care trust. This could involve giving advice to GPs on prescribing, running clinics at a GP practice and training local prescribers on issues related to managing and prescribing medicines.

You could also work in education or in industry, carrying out research into new medicines and running clinical trials.

What can you earn?

Pharmacists can earn between around £22,000 and £34,200 a year.

Pharmacy consultants or team managers can earn between £45,300 and £80,810 a year.

Entry requirements

Before you can work as a pharmacist, you need to complete:

- a four-year Master of Pharmacy (MPharm) degree
- a one-year pre-registration training course in a pharmacy
- a registration exam.

Your degree and training must be approved by the Royal Pharmaceutical Society of Great Britain (RPSGB), the professional body for pharmacists. See the RPSGB's Careers in Pharmacy website pages for links to a list of approved degree courses.

To do a degree, you will usually need five GCSEs (A-C) including maths and English, plus three A levels, usually in chemistry and two other science-based subjects such as biology, maths or physics. Check with course providers for exact entry requirements as other qualifications may be accepted.

When you have finished your degree, you can apply for the one-year pre-registration programme. This includes spending at least six months in a community or hospital pharmacy, and leads to a final registration exam. For details of pre-registration training vacancies, check the NHS Hospital Pharmacy Pre-registration Training website.

Once you have completed all three stages of training you can apply for state registration and membership of the RPSGB.

Pharmacy regulation

The General Pharmaceutical Council (GPhC) is the regulator for pharmacists, pharmacy technicians and pharmacy premises. For more information, see the GPhC website.

More information

General Pharmaceutical Council
129 Lambeth Rd
London
SE1 7BT

Tel: 020 3365 3400
www.pharmacyregulation.org

Pharmaceutical Society of Northern Ireland
73 University Street
Belfast
BT7 1HL
Tel: 028 9032 6927
http://www.psni.org.uk/

Royal Pharmaceutical Society of Great Britain
1 Lambeth High Street
London
SE1 7JN
Tel: 020 7735 9141
www.rpsgb.org.uk

NHS Careers
PO Box 2311
Bristol
BS2 2ZX
Tel: 0345 60 60 655
www.nhscareers.nhs.uk

Association of the British Pharmaceutical Industry (ABPI) Careers
12 Whitehall London
SW1A 2DY
Tel: 020 7930 3477
http://careers.abpi.org.uk

Health Learning and Skills Advice Line
Tel: 08000 150850

PHYSIOTHERAPIST

The nature of the work
As a physiotherapist your work could include:

- helping patients with spine and joint problems, especially after an operation

- helping patients recovering from accidents, sports injuries and strokes
- working with children who have mental or physical disabilities
- helping older people with physical problems become more mobile.

You could work in various areas and departments, such as paediatrics, outpatients, intensive care, women's health and occupational health. You could use a variety of treatments and techniques including:

- physical manipulation
- massage
- therapeutic exercise
- electrotherapy
- ultrasound
- acupuncture
- hydrotherapy.

You would keep accurate records of patients' treatment and progress, and you would often work closely with other health professionals. These could be occupational therapists, health visitors and social workers.

What can you earn?

Starting salaries for physiotherapists in the NHS are between £21,200 and £27,500 a year. Specialist physiotherapists can earn around £34,200 a year. Team managers and advanced physiotherapists can earn up to £40,200 a year.

Salaries in the private sector are usually similar to those in the NHS.

Entry requirements

To become a chartered (qualified) physiotherapist you need a physiotherapy degree approved by the Health Professions Council (HPC). This will make you eligible for state registration and membership of the Chartered Society of Physiotherapy (CSP). Check the HPC and CSP websites for a list of course providers.

To do a degree in physiotherapy, you will usually need:

- at least five GCSEs (A-C) including maths, English and a range of science subjects
- four AS levels at grade B or above (including a biological science)

- three A2 level subjects at grade C or above (including a biological science).

Check with universities for exact entry requirements as other qualifications, such as an Access to Higher Education course, may also be accepted.

It would help you if you also had some relevant experience, for example as a volunteer. Contact the voluntary services coordinator or manager at your local NHS Trust for details.

When you apply for a course you will have a Criminal Records Bureau (CRB) check, however a criminal conviction does not automatically prevent you from working in the NHS. The admissions tutor for your course can give you details.

Alternative entry routes

Cadet or apprenticeship scheme

You may be able to prepare for a career in physiotherapy through a two-year Cadet/Apprenticeship Scheme. This involves clinical placements and working towards a qualification such as an NVQ Level 3 in Health, and may meet the entry requirements for a physiotherapy degree. Check with your local NHS Trust or NHS Careers for details.

Physiotherapy assistant

As an assistant you may be able to take a part-time degree in physiotherapy whilst you are working. The CSP website has details of part-time, work-based degree course providers. The HPC website also includes a list of approved courses.

Accelerated postgraduate courses

If you have a first class or upper second class honours degree in a relevant subject (such as a biological science, psychology or sports science) you could qualify as a physiotherapist by taking a fast-track postgraduate course. Contact the CSP for details.

More information

Health Professions Council
Park House
184 Kennington Park Road
London
SE11 4BU
Tel: 020 7582 0866

NHS Careers
PO Box 2311
Bristol
BS2 2ZX
Tel: 0345 60 60 655

Chartered Society of Physiotherapy
14 Bedford Row
London
WC1R 4ED
Tel: 020 7306 6666

Health Learning and Skills Advice Line
Tel: 08000 150850

SCHOOL NURSE

The nature of the work

School nurses work with pupils, teachers and parents to promote good health and wellbeing in school age children.

As a school nurse, your duties could include:

- raising awareness of issues that can have a negative effect on student health (such as smoking and drug abuse)
- promoting healthy living, including safe-sex education
- administering immunisations and vaccinations
- carrying out developmental screening
- contributing to social education and citizenship classes
- supporting children with medical needs such as asthma, diabetes, epilepsy or mental health problems.

You may also give training to teachers about the health care needs of individual children.

You could work for a single school or cover a number of schools. If your role involves visiting a range of schools, you will probably be based at a GP practice or health centre.

You could also work in a private boarding school, which may involve living on school premises and being on 24-hour call (in case of emergency).

What can you earn?

Nurses can earn between £20,700 and £26,800 a year. Nurse specialists, such as school nurses, may earn around £33,500. With experience and managerial responsibilities, this can rise to around £39,300.

Extra allowances may be paid to those living in or around London.

Entry requirements

You will usually need around two years' professional experience as a qualified nurse (any branch) before you can begin training or working as a school nurse.

To qualify as a nurse you need a Nursing and Midwifery Council (NMC) approved degree or Diploma of Higher Education. For more information about becoming a nurse, check the relevant Nurse job profiles.

You could start work as a school nurse without further training or qualifications, especially if you have relevant experience. However, some employers will prefer you to have completed a (shortened) degree or postgraduate course leading to registration as a Specialist Community Public Health Nurse (School Nursing).

Courses are available on a one-year full-time or two-year part-time basis. You could fund yourself or you may be able to find a vacancy, for example on the NHS Jobs website, that includes working under supervision and studying for the specialist qualification. Check the NMC website for details of course providers.

You could have an advantage (when looking for work or applying for a course) if you have experience in health promotion or working with children in the community. Knowledge of child protection and an understanding of family planning issues and the health needs of school children would also be helpful.

You are likely to need a driving licence for this job.

More information

Nursing and Midwifery Council (NMC)
23 Portland Place
London
W1B 1PZ
Tel: 020 7333 9333
www.nmc-uk.org

Queens University of Belfast
School of Nursing and Midwifery
Medical Biology Centre
97 Lisburn Road
Belfast
BT9 7BL
Tel: 028 9097 2233
www.qub.ac.uk

University of Ulster at Jordanstown
School of Nursing
Shore Road
Newtownabbey
Co Antrim
BT37 0QB
Tel: 08700 400 700
www.ulster.ac.u

NHS Careers
PO Box 2311
Bristol
BS2 2ZX
Tel: 0345 60 60 655
www.nhscareers.nhs.uk

Community Practitioners and Health Visitors Association
33-37 Moreland Street

London
EC1V 8HA
Tel: 020 7505 3000
www.amicustheunion.org/cphva

Health Learning and Skills Advice Line
Tel: 08000 150850

National Leadership and Innovation Agency for Healthcare
Innovation House
Bridgend Road
Llanharan
CF72 9RP
Tel: 01443 233 333
www.nliah.wales.nhs.uk/

SPEECH AND LANGUAGE THERAPY ASSISTANT

The nature of the work
If you are interested in communication problems and you want to help others, this job could be ideal for you.

As a speech and language therapy assistant, you would support registered speech and language therapists during their assessment and treatment of people with communication, eating, drinking and swallowing problems.

You could work with a range of client groups, including:

- children
- adults with physical disabilities, mental health issues or learning difficulties
- people recovering from medical conditions, such as a stroke
- older people.

Your duties would usually involve:

- working with clients on a one-to-one basis
- liaising with the therapist about adjustments to a client's therapy
- group work and activities
- preparing therapy rooms and equipment

- supporting clients with any personal needs, for example, mobility issues.

You may also carry out general administrative tasks.

What can you earn?

Speech and language therapy assistants can earn between £13,600 and £18,500 a year. With experience and relevant qualifications, this could rise to around £21,800.

Entry requirements

Each employer can set their own entry requirements – some NHS Trusts may not ask for any academic qualifications whereas others will prefer a good standard of general education (possibly including four or five GCSEs grades A–C). For some jobs it may be desirable, possibly essential, to have the ability to speak a second community-based language, knowledge of British Sign Language and an awareness of other cultures.

Qualifications in childcare (such as the Council for Awards in Care, Health and Education (CACHE) Certificate/Diploma in Child Care and Education) or an NVQ Level 2 in Health or Health and Social Care would be useful, though not essential.

It could be an advantage to have paid or unpaid experience of working with older people, children or people with physical disabilities, mental health problems or learning difficulties. Contact the voluntary services coordinator or manager at your local NHS Trust for further advice.

Another way to get experience would be through a Cadet Scheme or Apprenticeship (in many parts of the country, cadet schemes have been replaced with Apprenticeships). Schemes vary between NHS Trusts, but will usually include clinical placements and working towards a qualification such as the new Level 3 Diploma in Clinical Healthcare Support (title subject to change). To find out more, visit the Apprenticeships website.

You could also contact your local NHS Trust for details of both Cadet and Apprenticeship schemes in your area.

More information

Royal College of Speech and Language Therapists
2 White Hart Yard
London
SE1 1NX
Tel: 020 7378 1200
www.rcslt.org

NHS Careers
PO Box 2311
Bristol
BS2 2ZX
Tel: 0345 60 60 655
www.nhscareers.nhs.uk

Health Learning and Skills Advice Line
Tel: 08000 150850

RADIOGRAPHER

The nature of the work
There are two types of radiography – diagnostic and therapeutic.

As a diagnostic radiographer, your work would involve:

- producing and interpreting high quality images of the body to identify and diagnose injury and disease
- screening for abnormalities
- taking part in surgical procedures, such as biopsies (examining tissues to find the cause of disease).

As a therapeutic radiographer, your duties would include:

- planning and delivering treatment using x-rays and other radioactive sources
- working closely with medical specialists to plan and treat malignant tumours or tissue defects
- assessing and monitoring patients throughout treatment and follow up.

Both areas of radiography involve working as part of a team alongside radiologists, clinical oncologists, physicists, radiology nurses and other health care professionals.

You would usually wear a uniform, and if you specialise in diagnostic radiography, you would sometimes wear protective clothing. This work can be physically and emotionally demanding.

What can you earn?
Newly qualified radiographers can earn between £21,200 and £27,500 a year. With experience, this can rise to about £34,200 a year.

Senior radiographers or team leaders can earn about £40,200 a year, and consultant radiographers can earn up to about £67,200 a year.

Entry requirements

To work as a radiographer you will need a degree approved by the Health Professions Council (HPC). Before you apply, you will need to decide whether you want to work in diagnostic radiography or therapeutic radiography. Visiting a radiography department or radiotherapy centre may help you decide. You will need to contact your local NHS Trust to arrange this.

To do a degree in diagnostic or therapeutic radiography you will usually need five GCSEs (A-C), plus three A levels, including a science. Check exact entry requirements with course providers as other qualifications, such as an Access to Higher Education course, may be accepted.

If you are a health professional or a graduate with a relevant first degree, you may be able to qualify in radiography by completing a pre-registration postgraduate diploma or Masters qualification. See the Health Professions Council website for details of all approved courses.

Most places on approved courses are funded by the NHS. Check the NHS Business Services Authority website for details.

Another route into radiography is to start as a radiography assistant and work your way up to assistant practitioner. At practitioner level, your employer may give you the opportunity to work and study part-time for a degree and professional qualification as a radiographer.

Once you are on a radiography degree, you will combine theoretical study with clinical placements in local hospitals and therapy/diagnostic units. Courses usually take three years full-time or the part-time equivalent.

More information

NHS Careers
PO Box 2311
Bristol
BS2 2ZX
Tel: 0345 60 60 655
www.nhscareers.nhs.uk

Society and College of Radiographers
207 Providence Square
Mill Street
London
SE1 2EW
Tel: 020 7740 7200
www.sor.org

Health Learning and Skills Advice Line
Tel: 08000 150850

Health Professions Council
Park House
184 Kennington Park Road
London
SE11 4BU
Tel: 020 7582 0866
www.hpc-uk.org

SURGEON

The nature of the work
To become a surgeon, you will need to complete a degree in medicine, recognised by the General Medical Council. You will also have to do further training that would last another ten years.

A surgeon needs to put people at their ease and inspire trust and confidence. They also need to work under pressure and make quick, accurate decisions.

Surgeons specialise in caring for patients who may need an operation. This could be, for example, if the patient has been injured, has a disease or has a condition that is getting worse.

As a surgeon you would use your in-depth knowledge of physiology, biochemistry, pathology and anatomy to work in one of nine surgical specialities. These are: cardiothoracic surgery; general surgery; plastic surgery; ENT; paediatric surgery; trauma and orthopaedic surgery; urology; neurosurgery; and oral and maxillofacial surgery.

Patients would be referred to you by other hospital doctors and GPs, and through admission to accident and emergency. Your key duties would involve:

- making a diagnosis
- deciding on the most appropriate course of action
- operating on patients
- monitoring patients after an operation.

You would also be responsible for training and supervising junior doctors and other healthcare professionals in the hospital. In addition, you may carry out research and write papers for publication.

As a senior or consultant surgeon, you would see patients in outpatient clinics, lead a team during surgery, and see patients on wards before and after an operation. You would keep patient records and write to GPs about their patients' condition and treatment.

What can you earn?

Foundation house officers (junior doctors) can earn between £33,300 and £41,300 a year. Doctors in specialist training can earn up to £69,400 a year, and consultants can earn between £74,500 and £180,000 a year.

Salaries for doctors in training include an additional amount based on the average hours of overtime worked, time spent covering unsocial hours, and workload.

Surgeons working in private sector hospitals may obtain higher fees.

Entry requirements

To become a surgeon, you will need to complete:

- a degree in medicine, recognised by the General Medical Council (five years)
- a foundation programme of general training (two years)
- core training (two years)
- specialty training (five to six years).

Each medical school has an individual approach, so it is important that you research each one and choose a course that will best prepare you for a career in surgery. See the Royal College of Surgeons of England website for advice, and check the General Medical Council (GMC) website for a list of degree courses.

To do a degree in medicine, you will usually need:

- at least five GCSEs (A-C) including English, maths and science
- plus three A levels at grades AAB in subjects such as chemistry, biology and either physics or maths.

If you do not have qualifications in science, you may be able to do a six-year degree course in medicine that includes a one-year pre-medical or foundation year. You will need to check with individual universities.

If you already have an honours degree in a science subject (minimum 2:1) you may be able to get on to a four-year graduate entry course. Some universities will accept non-science graduates. See the Medical Schools Council website for details of course providers.

When you apply for a course in medicine, you may be asked to take the UK Clinical Aptitude Test (UKCAT). This is used to check your suitability for a career in medicine by testing your mental abilities and behavioural characteristics, rather than your academic achievements. For details see the UKCAT website.

If you trained as a doctor overseas, you will need to contact the GMC to find out about registering and practising in the UK.

When you are awarded the CCT, you will be eligible to join the General Medical Council (GMC) Specialist Register and apply for a licence to practise. For more information on licensing and a new system of revalidation, check the GMC website.

This is the most direct route through surgical training and covers most specialties. For help with choosing your specialism, see the NHS Medical Careers website. Throughout your career you will be expected to continue learning and developing your surgical skills. The Royal College of Surgeons' website has information on all aspects of training and continuing medical education for practising surgeons.

More information

Royal College of Surgeons of England
35-43 Lincoln's Inn Fields
London
WC2A 3PE
Tel: 020 7405 3474
www.rcseng.ac.uk

UKCAT, UK Clinical Aptitude Test
www.ukcat.ac.uk

Health Learning and Skills Advice Line
Tel: 08000 150850

British Medical Association (BMA)
Tavistock Square
London
WC1H 9JP
Tel: 020 7387 4499
www.bma.org.uk

General Medical Council(GMC)
Regent's Place
350 Euston Road
London
NW1 3JN
Tel: 0845 357 3456
www.gmc-uk.org

PSYCHOLGIST

The nature of the work

If you are interested in how people behave and in helping them to deal with challenges, this career could be perfect for you.

Psychologists study people's behaviour, motivations, thoughts and feelings and help them overcome or control their problems.

Psychologists usually specialise in one of the following areas. They may be referred to by their specialism or as a chartered or practitioner psychologist.

- educational psychology – helping children and young people to overcome difficulties and further their educational and psychological development
- occupational psychology (also known as organisational psychology) – helping businesses improve their performance and increase employees' job satisfaction
- health psychology – promoting healthy attitudes and behaviour, and helping patients and their families to cope with illness
- counselling psychology – helping people resolve their problems and make decisions, particularly at stressful times in their lives
- neuropsychology – helping patients with brain injuries and neuropsychological diseases to recover or improve their quality of life
- forensic or criminological psychology – using psychological theory to help investigate crimes, rehabilitate offenders and support prison staff
- clinical psychology
- sports psychology.

Some areas of psychology have no direct training route. For example, to become a child psychologist you might first train as a clinical or counselling psychologist and then specialise in working with children. Or you could train in educational psychology and work with children in education.

What can you earn?

Assistant psychologists can earn around £15,000 to £23,000 a year. With experience, this can rise to between £30,000 and £40,000 a year.

Managers and consultants can earn up to around £80,000.

Entry requirements

To work as a chartered or practitioner psychologist, you need to complete training in psychology approved by the Health Professions Council (HPC).

Your training would begin with a British Psychological Society (BPS) accredited degree in psychology leading to the Graduate Basis for Chartered Membership (GBC). To undertake a degree course you will usually need five GCSEs (A-C), plus three A levels. Check with course providers for exact entry requirements.

If you already have a degree in a subject other than psychology, you may be able to achieve GBC by completing a BPS-approved conversion course.

Once you have completed your BPS-accredited course/exam and are eligible for registration with the HPC, you will need to achieve the following depending on your specialism:

- educational psychology - a Doctorate in Educational Psychology (in England, Northern Ireland and Wales)
- occupational psychology - the BPS Qualification in Occupational Psychology, which usually consists of an accredited MSc in Occupational Psychology plus two years' supervised practice
- health psychology - an MSc in Health Psychology and two years' supervised experience
- counselling psychology - the BPS Qualification in Counselling Psychology or a BPS accredited Doctorate in Counselling Psychology
- neuropsychology - training in either clinical or educational

- psychology, plus two years' supervised practice and an accredited course in neuropsychology
- forensic psychology - an MSc in Forensic Psychology plus two years' supervised practical experience.
- clinical psychology - a three-year, full time, NHS funded Doctorate in Clinical Psychology.
- sport and exercise psychology - an accredited MSc in Sport and Exercise Psychology plus two years' supervised work experience.

Competition for postgraduate training is strong. Entry requirements will often include a first or upper second class honours degree, evidence of your research skills, plus relevant work experience. Whichever specialist area you want to go in to, it is important to check that your postgraduate programme is approved by the HPC. See the Register of Approved Programmes page on the HPC website.

More information

NHS Careers
PO Box 2311
Bristol
BS2 2ZX
Tel: 0345 60 60 655
www.nhscareers.nhs.uk

British Psychological Society
St Andrew's House
48 Princess Road East
Leicester
LE1 7DR
Tel: 0116 254 9568
www.bps.org.uk

11. INFORMATION TECHNOLOGY

The world of information technology is now very broad, having expanded over the years to cover many roles. In this chapter we look at the following:

- Computer service and repair technician
- Database administrator
- software developer
- Systems analyst
- Web content manager
- Web designer

For more details of careers in information technology go to:

Skills Framework for the Information Age
www.sfia.
org.uk

COMPUTER SERVICE AND REPAIR TECHNICIAN

The nature of the work

As a computer service and repair technician you would install, maintain and repair computer systems and equipment.

You could work as a member of an IT support team in a large organisation, on commercial contracts for an IT servicing company, or as a field technician for a computer manufacturer. You might also run your own PC repair and upgrade business.

Your day-to-day tasks would include:

- installing new IT systems
- upgrading existing hardware and software
- visiting home users to set up their PCs or fix faulty equipment
- testing systems to make sure that they are working properly

- servicing printers, scanners and other office equipment (known as peripherals)
- preparing cost estimates for new installations
- carrying out routine administration, like organising staff rotas.

In a larger organisation, you may also be responsible for training staff to use equipment correctly and safely.

What can you earn?
Starting salaries are between £14,000 and £17,000 a year.

Experienced staff can earn between £18,000 and £25,000 a year, and senior staff with management responsibility can earn up to £30,000 a year.

Entry requirements

You could start without formal qualifications if you have a good enough working knowledge of computer systems and software. However, you may improve your chances of finding work by taking a computer maintenance qualification at college, for example:

- BTEC National Certificate and Diploma for IT Practitioners (Systems Support) Level 3
- City & Guilds IT Practitioners Diploma Level 2
- OCR Certificate and Diploma for IT Practitioners levels 1 and 2
- CompTIA A+ Certification.

You may be able to start this job through an apprenticeship scheme with an IT company or a technical support team in a larger company. You will need to check which schemes are available in your area. For more information, visit the Apprenticeships website.

For more information about careers and qualifications in IT, see the e-skills UK website.

More information

Microsoft UK
www.microsoft.com/uk

Skills Framework for the Information Age (SFIA)
www.sfia.org.uk

UK Resource Centre for Women in Science, Engineering and Technology
(UKRC)
Listerhills Park of Science and Commerce
40-42 Campus Road
Bradford
BD7 1HR
Tel: 01274 436485
www.theukrc.org

DATABASE ADMINISTRATOR

The nature of the work
As a DBA you could work on a variety of databases, from banks' customer account networks to hospital patient record systems. Your tasks could range from upgrading an existing database to creating a completely new system.

On a new system, you would work with an organisation to:

- establish what the database is for, who will use it and what other systems it will link to (for example telephony)
- plan the structure of the database, working out how to organise, find and display the data
- build a test version and check the results to iron out any technical problems (bugs)
- fill (populate) the database with new information or transfer existing data into it

- plan how to update information, create back-up copies and report errors
- put in security measures.

You may have extra duties, like supervising technical support staff, training users and producing performance reports for IT managers.

Increasingly, you could be working with web-based technologies and would need to understand how databases fit in with these systems. Database security is another area of growing importance.

In a senior position you would normally be responsible for strategic planning, information policy, budgets and managing client relationships.

You would work on projects with other IT professionals, such as analysts, programmers and IT project managers.

What can you earn?

Starting salaries are between £18,000 and £22,000 a year.

Experienced staff can earn between £23,000 and £35,000 a year, and senior DBAs can earn over £45,000 a year.

Rates for short and medium-term contract jobs may be significantly higher than those listed above, particularly at senior levels.

Entry requirements

For most database administrator jobs, you would need to know how to use structured query language (SQL) and database management systems (DBMS), which include:

- DBMS (relational database management systems)
- OODBMS (object-oriented database management systems)
- XML database management systems.

Employers often look for previous experience in computing such as IT support, programming or web development.

You could study for a qualification such as a BTEC HNC/HND or degree, then join a company's graduate training scheme straight from college or university. Relevant subjects include:

If you do not have an IT-related degree, you may still be able to get a place on a graduate training scheme, as larger employers tend to accept graduates from any discipline. You could study for a postgraduate IT conversion qualification, although this is not essential.

More information

Skills Framework for the Information Age (SFIA)
www.sfia.org.uk

e-skills UK
1 Castle Lane
London
SW1E 6DR
020 7963 8920
www.e-skills.com

BCS – the Chartered Institute for IT
Block D
North Star House
North Star Avenue
Swindon
Wiltshire
SN2 1FA
www.bcs.org.uk

Institute for the Management of Information Systems
5 Kingfisher House
New Mill Road
Orpington

Kent
BR5 3QG
Tel: 0700 002 3456
www.imis.org.uk

Computer Technology Industry Association (CompTIA)
www.comptia.org

e-skills UK
1 Castle Lane
London
SW1E 6DR
0207 963 8920
www.e-skills.com

SOFTWARE DEVELOPER

The nature of the work

Software developers (also known as programmers) design and build computer programs that help organisations and equipment work effectively.

As a software developer, your work could involve:

- designing computer controls for industrial and manufacturing machinery
- building administrative and financial databases
- developing software for home entertainment equipment (known as embedded controls).

You would work closely with senior programmers and business analysts, and create technical plans to meet the needs of the client.

You may write computer programs from the beginning, or amend existing programs to meet the needs of the project.

You could work with a range of web-based technologies, and you would need to understand how databases integrate with these systems.

What can you earn?

Starting salaries for graduates can be between £20,000 and £26,000 a year.

Experienced developers can earn between £28,000 and £40,000, and software developers with management responsibilities can earn over £50,000 a year.

Entry requirements

You will normally need a degree, foundation degree or BTEC HNC/HND to become a software developer. You could choose from a variety of subjects, including:

- computer science/studies
- information technology
- software development
- software engineering
- business information systems.

If you do not have an IT-related degree, you may still be able to find a place on a graduate trainee scheme, as larger employers often accept graduates in any subject. You could study for a postgraduate IT conversion qualification, although this is not essential.

Several universities are now offering the Information Technology Management for Business (ITMB) degree. The degree, which was developed by e-skills UK and major employers, combines both IT and business skills, such as project management and business thinking.

Experience in IT or a related area can be useful. You can gain experience through work placements, internships or a year in industry.

You will also need a working knowledge of the main programming languages and operating systems used, for example:

- SQL, Java, C++, XML, Smalltalk and Visual Basic
- Oracle, UML (Unified Modelling Language), Linux and Delphi
- .NET frameworks (such as C# (C-sharp), ASP and VB).

Visit the developer.com website for information and links to resources relating to programming languages.

More information

Skills Framework for the Information Age (SFIA)
www.sfia.org.uk

e-skills UK ⌑
1 Castle Lane
London
SW1E 6DR
0207 963 8920
www.e-skills.com

British Computer Society
Block D
North Star House
North Star Avenue
Swindon
Wiltshire
SN2 1FA
www.bcs.org.uk

Institution of Analysts and Programmers
Charles House
36 Culmington Road
London
W13 9NH
Tel: 020 8567 2118
www.iap.org.uk

Institute for the Management of Information Systems
5 Kingfisher House
New Mill Road
Orpington
Kent

BR5 3QG

Tel: 0700 002 3456

www.imis.org.uk

National Skills Academy for IT

www.itskillsacademy.ac.uk/

SYSTEMS ANALYST

The nature of the work

Your work could range from integrating the telephone and computer networks in a call centre, to re-structuring a bank's customer account databases to make them more secure.

Your work would involve:

- identifying the client organisation's needs
- drawing up plans for a modified or replacement IT system
- carrying out feasibility studies of proposals and making recommendations
- working closely with programmers and software developers to build the system
- overseeing installation and testing correcting problems ('bugs') before the final version is released
- providing staff training and instruction manuals for the new or upgraded system.

An important part of your job would be to make sure that your designs are flexible enough to adapt as the organisation or business grows (known as 'future-proofing'). You would use various computer assisted software engineering (CASE) tools and programming methods in your job.

What can you earn?

Salaries can range from around £20,000 and £45,000 a year depending on experience. Senior analysts can earn significantly more.

Entry requirements

To work as a systems analyst you normally need a BTEC HNC/HND or degree, backed up with industry experience. Relevant subjects include:

- computer science/studies
- information management systems
- business information systems
- maths and operational research.

Alternatively, you could take the Information Technology Management for Business (ITMB) degree. The degree has been developed by e-skills and employers to meet specific industry skills shortages, for example in project management and business awareness. For more details, see the e-skills UK website.

If you have a non-IT related degree, you could take a postgraduate IT 'conversion' course, although companies may still ask for relevant work experience. Employers recommend that you look for a course which focuses on business skills as well as technical knowledge.

You would be expected to have a working knowledge of programming skills and analysis methods. Some of the most common are:

- SQL
- Visual Basic, C++ and Java
- Unified Modelling Language (UML)
- SAP business software applications.

See the websites for e-skills UK, British Computer Society (BCS), the Institute for the Management of Information Systems (IMIS) and the Institution of Analysts and Programmers (IAP) for more details about careers in this field.

For more information about professional development options, see the Skills Framework for the Information Age (SFIA) website. This website has been developed by professional bodies and employers and allows you to identify your current skills and work out career development options.

More information

Institute for the Management of Information Systems
5 Kingfisher House
New Mill Road
Orpington
Kent
BR5 3QG
Tel: 0700 002 3456
www.imis.org.uk

Institute of Analysts and Programmers
Charles House
36 Culmington Road
London
W13 9NH
Tel: 020 8567 2118
www.iap.org.uk

Skills Framework for the Information Age (SFIA)
www.sfia.org.uk

British Computer Society
Block D
North Star House
North Star Avenue
Swindon
Wiltshire
SN2 1FA
www.bcs.org.uk

e-skills UK
1 Castle Lane
London

WEB CONTENT MANAGER

The nature of the work

As a web content manager, you could work on sites that are open to the public on the world wide web, or sites for staff use only on a company's intranet.

Your duties could include:

- taking a lead role in maintenance and development of the site
- meeting with editing, marketing and design teams to plan and develop site content, style and appearance
- using web content management systems to analyse website usage statistics
- writing reports for senior managers, clients and partnership organisations
- setting permissions for site users
- promoting information about the website to target customers and partners
- carrying out quality assurance checks on content
- reporting technical problems to IT support staff
- dealing with legal issues, such as copyright and data protection.

In larger companies, you may manage an editorial team who research and produce material – text, images and multimedia – for publication on the website. In smaller organisations, you might have a more 'hands on' role in content production and writing.

What can you earn?

Web content managers' salaries fall between £24,000 and £50,000 a year, depending on the level of experience.

Entry requirements

There is no set entry route into this career. You may have a background in journalism, marketing or IT, or you might move into the role after gaining experience in another area of a business.

Whatever your background, you would normally need previous experience of writing content in some form, although not necessarily online. A useful way to show employers your skills is to build up a collection of your published work.

You could take a course that would teach you some of the skills needed for producing web content. Relevant subjects include journalism, publishing, media, and communications, PR and marketing. Contact your local colleges for course details and entry requirements.

You do not need specific IT skills for a management position, although knowledge of web design, desktop publishing and photo imaging would broaden your options, as many jobs combine management with writing or web design.

An understanding of web content management systems and how they work could be useful, but you would be given training in specific packages once you start working.

More information

Society for Editors and Proofreaders (SfEP)
Apsley House
176 Upper Richmond Road
Putney
London
SW15 2SH
Tel: 020 8785 6155
www.sfep.org.uk

National Union of Journalists (NUJ)
www.nuj.org.uk

SW1E 6DR
0207 963 8920
www.e-skills.com

BCS Professional Certification
http://certifications.bcs.org

National Skills Academy for IT
www.itskillsacademy.ac.uk

WEB DESIGNER

The nature of the work

As a web designer, you could work on any kind of website, from an interactive education site to one offering online shopping. Your main tasks would include:

- meeting clients to discuss what they want their site to do and who will use it
- preparing a design plan, showing the site structure and how the different parts link together
- deciding which text, colours and backgrounds to use
- laying out pages and positioning buttons, links and pictures using design software
- adding multimedia features like sound, animation and video
- testing and improving the design and site until everything works as planned
- uploading the site to a server for publication online.

Depending on the project, you could also be asked to manage your client's website once it is up and running.

What can you earn?

Starting salaries can be between £15,000 and £22,000 a year. The average salary is £30,000. Experienced designers can earn up to £37,500 a year, and senior designers and those with specialist skills can earn over £40,000 a year.

Self-employed web designers set their own rates.

Entry requirements

You do not usually need qualifications to become a web designer. However, most designers have experience in other types of design, or have done training in web design, either through college or by teaching themselves.

You will need to show evidence of your creative and technical skills, usually in the form of a CD, DVD or 'live' websites you have worked on. You could gain this evidence from college, paid work or volunteering.

You will need a good working knowledge of HTML, and experience of writing web pages in a combination of codes. It could be useful if you a working knowledge of the following programs:

- Dreamweaver
- Photoshop
- Flash and Fireworks
- CSS
- Javascript
- .Net

Colleges offer courses on these programs. You can also find many online tutorials, which are often free to use.

You could take one of the following qualifications, which provide good basic training in web design, interactivity and internet technology:

- BTEC Interactive use of Media levels 1 to 3
- OCR ITQ levels 1 to 3
- OCR Creative iMedia levels 1 to 3
- City & Guilds E-Quals IT Users awards (7266) – Level 2 (Diploma) and Level 3 (Advanced Diploma).

You could also take a higher level course, such as a foundation degree, BTEC HNC/HND, or degree in a design or multimedia subject. Relevant subjects include:

- web design and development
- multimedia design

- digital media development
- interactive computing.

To search for colleges and universities offering foundation degrees, HNC/HNDs and degrees, visit the Universities and Colleges Admissions Service (UCAS) website.

To find out more about careers in web design, visit the E-skills UK, British Computer Society and Big Ambition websites.

More information

UK Web Design Association
www.ukwda.org

World Wide Web Consortium (W3C)
www.w3.org

Big Ambition
www.bigambition.co.uk

British Computer Society
Block D
North Star House
North Star Avenue
Swindon
Wiltshire
SN2 1FA
www.bcs.org.uk

Certified Internet Web Professional (CIW)
www.ciwcertified.com

12. JOURNALISM AND PRINTING

The world of journalism offers many exciting opportunities. However, like ever other career, you need to gain a toehold. There are a number of ways to enter this profession. Printing is also a fascinating career choice and there are a number of opportunities available. In this section, we cover:

- Newspaper journalism
- Magazine Journalism
- Advertising copywriting
- Proof reading
- Sub-editing
- Bookbinding and print finisher
- Printing administrator
- Machine printing

For details of all career opportunities in these fields go to:

National Council for the Training of Journalists
The New Granary
Station Road
Saffron Walden
Essex
CB11 3PL
Tel: 01799 544014
www.nctj.com

British Printing Industries Federation (BPIF)
Farringdon Point
29/35 Farringdon Road
London
EC1M 3JF
www.britishprint.com

NEWPAPER JOURNALIST

The nature of the work

Newspaper journalists cover any event of interest to their specific audience, ranging from reporting on council meetings and school fetes for a local paper, to general elections and world events for the national press.

As a newspaper journalist, your work would typically include:

- investigating a story as soon as it breaks
- following up potential leads
- developing new contacts
- interviewing people, both face-to-face and over the phone
- attending press conferences
- recording meetings and interviews using recording equipment or shorthand
- coming up with ideas for new stories and features
- writing up articles in a style that will appeal to the intended audience.

You could choose to specialise in a specific subject such as sport, politics or entertainment. Because most newspapers have an online edition, you may also write stories for the web. Newspaper journalists sometimes work as sub-editors, preparing reporters' writing ('copy') for printing.

What can you earn?

Trainees earn around £15,000 a year on local newspapers
Experienced journalists can earn from £15,000 a year to over £40,000
The highest paid journalists and national newspaper editors can earn up to £100,000.
Freelance journalists negotiate a set fee for each piece of work they do. Fees can be negotiated individually or from guidance provided by the NUJ.

Entry requirements

You can become a newspaper journalist by training at college or university (known as pre-entry) or by joining a local or regional newspaper and training on the job (known as direct entry).

For both types of entry you will be at an advantage if you have relevant experience. To build up your experience you can:

- volunteer for student and community newspapers
- submit articles to websites or keep an online journal or blog
- work for local or student radio stations
- submit articles and reviews to local, free or specialist papers.

It is a good idea to keep cuttings and printouts of your published work to show to potential employers, especially if these include your name (known as a 'byline').

Training before starting work

This is the most common way to enter journalism. It involves completing a journalism course, then finding work as a trainee.

It is advisable to choose a course that is accredited by the National Council for the Training of Journalists (NCTJ). Some courses accept five GCSEs (including English) and two A levels, or similar qualifications, whilst others will expect you to have a degree. If you have a degree, you may be able to do an 18-20 week Fast Track course. See the NCTJ website for details of courses and training providers.

As part of any journalism course, you will take the NCTJ preliminary exams, which you need to pass before being taken on as a trainee.

You may be able do the NCTJ self-study programme, and enter yourself for the preliminary exams. To follow this route you would need to arrange work experience so that you can practise your skills. See the NCTJ website for details.

On-the-job training

To become a journalist by direct entry you need to apply to the editors of local and regional newspapers to be taken on as a trainee. You can find contact details on the Newspaper Society website.

You will need a minimum of five GCSEs (A-C), including English, or equivalent qualifications. However, it is increasingly rare for applicants to be accepted at this level. More than 60% of recruits have degrees, and most others have at least two A levels or the equivalent.

You can find advice and information on starting or developing your career in journalism on the NCTJ and National Union of Journalists (NUJ) websites.

More information

NUJ Training
www.nujtraining.org.uk

Creative Skillset
Focus Point
21 Caledonian Road
London
N1 9GB
www.creativeskillset.org

Creative Skillset Careers
Tel: 08080 300 900 (England and Northern Ireland)
Tel: 0845 850 2502(Scotland)
Tel: 08000 121 815 (Wales)
www.creativeskillset.org/careers

National Council for the Training of Journalists
The New Granary
Station Road
Saffron Walden
Essex
CB11 3PL
Tel: 01799 544014
www.nctj.com
National Union of Journalists (NUJ)
www.nuj.org.uk

Newspaper Society
www.newspapersoc.org.uk

MAGAZINE JOURNALIST

The nature of the work
Types of magazine include:
- consumer magazines – for the general public
- specialist consumer magazines – for people with interests in a particular subject, such as travel, arts and crafts, or cars
- professional magazines – for those working in a particular career such as human resources or management
- business and trade magazines
- in-house (internal) company magazines.

You would usually have specialist knowledge of the subject covered by the publication you write for.

As a magazine journalist, your work would vary depending on the type of magazine you are writing for, but would normally include:

- going to meetings to plan the content of the magazine
- suggesting ideas for articles that would interest the magazine's readers
- interviewing and researching to collect information for articles
- writing articles to suit the magazine's style
- keeping up to date with developments and trends in the magazine's subject area.

You might also produce versions of your articles for the magazine's website.

As a freelance (self-employed) journalist, you could write for both magazines and newspapers.

What can you earn?
Starting salaries can be between £18,000 and around £25,000 a year. With experience earnings can be up to £35,000 or more a year.

Entry requirements

There are no set qualifications for becoming a magazine journalist, although most people applying for this role have a degree.

A common starting point is to work as an editorial assistant for a magazine publishing house. This allows you to develop your skills and make contacts in the industry. Making contacts is important, as many journalist vacancies are not advertised.

You could gain a journalism qualification or degree before looking for work. Although this is not essential, doing this would help you learn about the magazine industry and develop the skills you would need as a journalist. Qualifications that are recognised by the industry are accredited by:

Periodicals Training Council - courses are delivered by the Professional Publishers Association (PPA)

National Council for the Training of Journalists (NCTJ)

See the PPA and NCTJ websites for details.

The NCTJ also runs distance learning courses, including Writing for the Periodical Press, which gives a basic understanding of the magazine industry.

Whether or not you have journalism qualifications, you will have to be proactive and persistent in order to start in magazine journalism. The key to getting into the industry is to gain practical experience and build up examples of your published work. Ways to do this include:

- contacting magazines to ask about opportunities for unpaid work experience
- contacting editors with ideas for articles relevant to their magazine
- writing reviews of films, plays or products
- volunteering to work on newsletters run by not-for-profit organisations.

Visit the PPA website for advice on finding work experience and applying for jobs.

Competition for jobs is strong, especially with the better-known magazines. It may be easier to get started on a specialist, trade or business publication, especially if you have knowledge of the area it covers. The more specialist the magazine, the more likely you are to need appropriate knowledge or experience.

More information
NUJ Training
www.nujtraining.org.uk

Newspaper Society
www.newspapersoc.org.uk

Periodicals Publishers Association (PPA)
Queens House
28 Kingsway
London
WC2B 6JR
Tel: 020 7404 4166
www.ppa.co.uk

Creative Skillset Careers
Tel: 08080 300 900 (England and Northern Ireland)
Tel: 0845 850 2502(Scotland)
Tel: 08000 121 815 (Wales)
www.creativeskillset.org/careers

Creative Skillset
Focus Point
21 Caledonian Road
London
N1 9GB
www.creativeskillset.org

National Union of Journalists (NUJ)
www.nuj.org.uk

Broadcast Journalism Training Council
18 Miller's Close
Rippingale
near Bourne
Lincolnshire
PE10 0TH
Tel: 01778 440025
www.bjtc.org.uk

Association of British Science Writers
www.absw.org.uk

European Medical Writers Association
www.emwa.org

National Council for the Training of Journalists (NCTJ)
The New Granary
Station Road
Saffron Walden
Essex
CB11 3PL
Tel: 01799 544014
www.nctj.com

ADVERTISING COPYWRITER

The nature of the work

As a copywriter, you would work as a team with an art director, who would provide the visual images to go with your words. Your job would begin with a briefing about the client, their product, the target audience and the advertising message to be put across. Your work could then involve:

- creating original ideas that fit the brief (working closely with the art director)
- presenting ideas to the agency's creative director and account team
- helping to present ideas to the client

- making any changes that the client asks for
- writing clear and persuasive copy
- making sure that ads meet the codes of advertising practice
- proofreading copy to check spelling, grammar and facts
- casting actors for TV and radio advertisements
- liaising with photographers, designers, production companies and printers.

What can you earn?

Starting salaries can be around £18,000 to £25,000 a year. With experience this rises to between £25,000 and £50,000 a year. Senior creatives in leading agencies can earn up to £100,000 or more.

Entry requirements
Employers will usually be more interested in your creativity, writing skills and business sense than your formal qualifications.

However, advertising is a very competitive industry to join, so you may have an advantage with a qualification that includes some copywriting, such as:
- a foundation degree, BTEC HND or degree in advertising
- Communication, Advertising and Marketing Education Foundation (CAM) Diploma in Marketing Communications.
- Other useful courses include BTEC HNDs or degrees in journalism, English, media studies and marketing.

Most people get their first copywriting job as a result of work experience. This can give you the chance to make industry contacts and impress potential employers.

You could contact agencies directly to ask about placements, and make industry contacts through relevant groups on social networking sites. See the Work Experience section of the Institute of Practitioners in Advertising (IPA) website for more information and a list of member agencies. The IPA also runs a Graduate Recruitment Agency, and D&AD runs a Graduate Placement Scheme.

When looking for jobs, you will need to show a portfolio of your work (known as a 'book') to potential employers, as you will be employed on the strength of your creative ideas, versatility and writing ability.

It's a good idea to team up with a would-be art director and work together on campaign ideas for your portfolio, as this can help prove your ability to fulfil a client's 'brief'. See D&AD's website for details of their advertising workshops, aimed at helping people build a portfolio and make contacts in the advertising industry.

If you join the IPA, you can also showcase the best of your portfolio online on their All Our Best Work website.

Visit the Diagonal Thinking website to find out if you have what it takes for a career in advertising.

More information

D&AD
9 Graphite Square
Vauxhall Walk
London
SE11 5EE
Tel: 020 7840 1111
www.dandad.org

Institute of Practitioners in Advertising (IPA)
44 Belgrave Square
London
SW1X 8QS
Tel: 020 7235 7020
www.ipa.co.uk

Communication Advertising and Marketing Education Foundation Limited (CAM)
Tel: 01628 427120
www.camfoundation.com

Creative Skillset
Focus Point
21 Caledonian Road
London
N1 9GB
www.creativeskillset.org

Creative Skillset Careers
Tel: 08080 300 900 (England and Northern Ireland)
Tel: 0845 850 2502(Scotland)
Tel: 08000 121 815 (Wales)
www.creativeskillset.org/careers

PROOFREADER

The nature of the work

As a proofreader, you would carefully check the 'proofs' (which show how the final pages will be laid out), using either a printed ('hard') copy or an on-screen version. Your main tasks would include making sure that:

- there are no errors such as letters in the wrong order
- all the material is included and is in the right place
- page numbers are in the right order
- the document follows the 'house style'
- chapter titles match the list of contents
- there are no confusing word, column or page breaks
- illustrations have the right captions and relate to the text
- the layout is logical and attractive.

You would mark any necessary changes using British Standards Institution symbols, which are internationally recognised. When working directly on computer, you may use specialist software to mark up the document. If necessary, you would also produce a separate list of any queries which need to be resolved.

Before marking any changes that could result in unacceptable costs or delay, you would discuss them with your client.

What can you earn?

Freelance proofreaders are usually paid by the page or the hour. The minimum rate suggested by the Society for Editors and Proofreaders (SfEP) from March 2012 is £20.75 an hour. Visit the SfEP website for the latest figures.

Rates of pay depend on experience, with new proofreaders often being paid a lower rate.

Entry requirements

You do not need any particular qualifications to be a proofreader. Employers will usually be more interested in your experience than your qualifications, and many proofreaders have worked in publishing, journalism or other related areas.

However, proofreaders are often graduates, so it could be an advantage if you have a degree, perhaps in English or in a subject which could become your specialist area for proofreading. For example, a science degree would be useful for proofreading scientific textbooks or manuals.

You can gain proofreading skills by completing short courses through the Society for Editors and Proofreaders (SfEP) and the Publishing Training Centre. Courses are also offered by private training providers. You can study the Publishing Training Centre Basic Proofreading course by distance learning. When you have completed the SfEP courses, you can get support in establishing your career by joining the SfEP mentoring scheme.

See the SfEP and the Publishing Training Centre websites for more details.

More information

Creative Skillset Careers
Tel: 08080 300 900 (England and Northern Ireland)

Tel: 0845 850 2502(Scotland)
Tel: 08000 121 815 (Wales)
www.creativeskillset.org/careers

Society for Editors and Proofreaders (SfEP)
Apsley House
176 Upper Richmond Road
Putney
London
SW15 2SH
Tel: 020 8785 6155
www.sfep.org.uk

Women in Publishing
www.wipub.org.uk

Publishers Association
29b Montague Street
London
WC1B 5BW
Tel: 020 7691 9191
www.publishers.org.uk

Publishing Training Centre at Book House
45 East Hill
Wandsworth
London
SW18 2QZ
Tel: 020 8874 2718
www.train4publishing.co.uk Job profiles

SUB EDITOR

The nature of the work
As a sub-editor, your work would typically include:

- making sure articles are accurate and do not break laws such as libel and copyright
- checking any queries with the reporter or journalist
- re-writing articles if necessary to make them clearer or shorter
- making sure articles follow the publication's house style
- writing headlines, captions, short paragraphs (known as 'standfirsts') which lead in to articles, and 'panels' which break up the text
- making sure articles are in the right place on each page
- using page layout and image editing software like Quark Express, InDesign and Photoshop
- sending completed pages to the printers.

You would work closely with reporters, editors, designers, production staff and printers.

What can you earn?

Starting salaries can range from £15,000 to £23,000 a year, depending on the type of publication. Experienced and senior sub-editors can earn from £25,000 a year to over £40,000.

Entry requirements

For newspaper sub-editing you would need a journalism qualification or experience. Industry-recognised qualifications are accredited by the National Council for the Training of Journalists (NCTJ).

It is common to move into sub-editing after gaining experience as a reporter. However, you can train specifically in sub-editing by completing a 12-week Diploma in Production Journalism at Brighton Journalist Works in Brighton – at present this is the only NCTJ-accredited sub-editing course available.

There are also several NCTJ-accredited newspaper courses which offer an additional certificate in sub-editing, which involves completing a subbing exam at the end of the course, as well as the reporters' exam. See the NCTJ website for details.

There are no set qualifications for becoming a magazine journalist, although most people applying for this sort of work have a degree. A common starting point is to work as an editorial assistant for a magazine publishing house. This route allows you to develop your skills and make contacts in the industry, which is important as many vacancies are not advertised.

Alternatively, you could prepare for a magazine sub-editing job by:
- completing the Diploma in Production Journalism mentioned above
- completing an industry-recognised journalism qualification accredited by the NCTJ or the Periodical Publishers Association (PPA).

See the NCTJ and PPA websites for full details of journalism careers and qualifications.

The NCTJ distance learning course, Basics of Sub-Editing, will help you to develop sub-editing skills, but does not lead to a qualification.

For many sub-editing jobs you will need to be able to use QuarkXpress. InDesign and Photoshop skills could also be useful. Courses in these are available at many colleges and private training providers.

More information

Creative Skillset Careers
Tel: 08080 300 900 (England and Northern Ireland)
Tel: 0845 850 2502(Scotland)
Tel: 08000 121 815 (Wales)
www.creativeskillset.org/careers

Society for Editors and Proofreaders (SfEP)
Apsley House
176 Upper Richmond Road
Putney
London
SW15 2SH
Tel: 020 8785 6155
www.sfep.org.uk

Creative Skillset
Focus Point

21 Caledonian Road
London
N1 9GB
www.creativeskillset.org

National Council for the Training of Journalists (NCTJ)
The New Granary
Station Road
Saffron Walden
Essex
CB11 3PL
Tel: 01799 544014
www.nctj.com

Periodicals Publishers Association (PPA)
Queens House
28 Kingsway
London
WC2B 6JR
Tel: 020 7404 4166
www.ppa.co.uk

Creative Skillset
Focus Point
21 Caledonian Road
London
N1 9GB
www.creativeskillset.org

BOOKBINDER OR PRINT FINISHER

The nature of the work
As a print finisher or machine bookbinder, your tasks would include:

- setting up machinery
- feeding the machinery with paper
- reporting machine breakdowns

- taking away and stacking the finished products.

As a craft or hand bookbinder, you would work on a much smaller scale. Your tasks would typically include:

- hand binding small numbers of books, such as family histories or books for libraries and museums
- using specialist hand tools to make bindings for books and to sew pages
- adding decoration such as gold lettering and edging, or marbled end-papers.

You could also restore and repair antique books, cleaning discoloured pages or using leathers and papers to match those originally used.

What can you earn?

Starting salaries can be around £14,000 a year.
Experienced binders and finishers can earn between £16,000 and £35,000.
Earnings for self-employed craft bookbinders vary widely depending on the amount of work they have.

Entry requirements
You may not need formal qualifications to be a print finisher or machine bookbinder and you would usually receive on-the-job training. However, some employers may prefer you to have GCSEs or equivalent qualifications, including English and maths.

You may be able to get into this type of work through an Apprenticeship scheme. The range of Apprenticeships available in your area will depend on the local jobs market and the types of skills employers need. To find out more, visit the Apprenticeships website.

To be a craft bookbinder, you would need to gain skills before starting work. You can attend part-time or short courses in bookbinding at many colleges. You can also complete higher education courses, including BTEC HNCs/HNDs and degrees in craft bookbinding at specialist colleges. Visit the Society of Bookbinders (SoB) website for details of courses.

The Designer Bookbinders (DB) website also lists courses offered by colleges and private providers, as well as joint SOB/DB courses and DB lectures.

More information
Proskills UK
www.proskills.co.uk

Society of Bookbinders
www.societyofbookbinders.com

Designer Bookbinders
www.designerbookbinders.org.uk

British Printing Industries Federation (BPIF)
Farringdon Point
29/35 Farringdon Road
London
EC1M 3JF
www.britishprint.com

City & Guilds
London
EC1A 9DD
Tel: 0844 543 0000
www.cityandguilds.com

PRINTING ADMINISTRATOR
The nature of the work

You could be involved in various areas of print production, such as planning, estimating, buying, sales and overall management. Your duties would include:

- supervising print orders through the pre-press, printing and finishing stages
- coordinating different print runs by planning the most efficient way to use machinery and staff

- solving problems in the production process
- using software packages to help put together quotations for jobs
- negotiating with suppliers, stocktaking and purchasing materials
- developing new business opportunities and looking after existing clients.

If you manage a print workshop or department, you would organise workloads, supervise staff and plan schedules. You would also meet with customers and take overall responsibility for making sure print runs are cost-effective, meet deadlines and achieve quality standards.

What can you earn?

Starting salaries range from £14,000 to £17,000 a year. Experienced print administrators earn between £18,000 and £25,000. Senior administrators with management responsibilities can earn around £30,000 a year.
The re additional payments for overtime and shiftwork.

Entry requirements

You would usually need previous experience in the industry to work as a print administrator. Supervisory, management or sales experience gained from other industries would also give you an advantage when looking for work. Employers may ask for GCSE or A level passes in maths, English, art and IT, or equivalent qualifications.

Alternatively, you could complete a print-related qualification before looking for work, such as:

- City & Guilds Certificate in Printing and Graphic Communications levels 2 and 3
- BTEC Certificate, Diploma and Award in Graphics levels 1, 2 and 3
- ABC Diploma in Digital Origination at Level 3.
- Higher level options include a foundation degree, BTEC HNC/HND or degree in print media, digital media, graphics or graphic design. See the Universities and Colleges Admissions Service (UCAS) website for colleges and universities offering these qualifications.

217

Alternatively, you may be able to get into this career through a printing Apprenticeship, working your way up to an administration role. The range of Apprenticeships available in your area will depend on the local jobs market and the types of skills employers need from their workers. To find out more, visit the Apprenticeships website.

See the British Printing Industry Federation (BPIF) and the PrintIT! websites for more details on printing careers and training providers.

More information

PrintIT!
www.printit.org.uk

Proskills UK
www.proskills.co.uk

British Printing Industries Federation (BPIF)
Farringdon Point
29/35 Farringdon Road
London
EC1M 3JF
www.britishprint.com

Institute of Paper, Printing and Publishing
www.ip3.org.uk

MACHINE PRINTERS
The nature of the work

Machine printers, also known as print minders, operate and maintain printing presses. Their work involves taking instructions from the pre-press operator and setting up the press with the right materials for the production run.

As a machine printer, your work would involve:

- matching colours to the pre-press proofs
- restocking ink levels
- feeding the print materials into the presses
- putting job data into computerised control units
- carrying out quality checks during the print run
- identifying problems and fixing faults
- cleaning presses after a print run has finished (either by hand or using automatic cleaning systems)
- carrying out basic machine maintenance.

You would usually work on a particular type of press, but you would train in a variety of printing techniques. These could include:

- flexigraphic (relief process) – commonly used to print onto items like shopping bags and food packaging
- screen printing (stencilling) – for printing onto clothing, posters or display signs
- gravure (intaglio process) – used for high quality work on catalogues, fabrics and wallpapers
- digital printing – using inkjet and laser printing methods
- lithographic (planographic process) – the most widely used method and often used for large print runs such as catalogues, newspapers and magazines.

On large presses, you might work in a team, but on smaller ones you could be responsible for all the tasks on the print run.

What can you earn?

Starting salaries for qualified printers are between £16,000 and £19,000 a year. Experienced machine printers can earn up to £40,000 a year. Additional payments are made for shift allowances, specific responsibilities and overtime.

Entry requirements

Most employers expect a good standard of general education, such as GCSEs in English and maths, science subjects and IT. You would also be expected to have good colour vision.

You may be able to get into this career through an Apprenticeship scheme with a printing company. To get on to a scheme, you are likely to need four or five GCSEs (A-C) including maths and English, or equivalent qualifications. The range of Apprenticeships available in your area will depend on the local jobs market and the types of skills employers need from their workers. To find out more, visit the Apprenticeships website.

You could learn some of the skills needed for this job by taking a college printing course, such as:

- ABC Diploma in Print Media at Level 3 covers various processes including digital printing and print finishing
- City & Guilds (5261) Certificate in Printing and Graphic Communications – covers all the main print processes.

General art and design courses may offer you options in techniques like screen printing. Contact your local colleges to find out what is available.

For more details about careers in printing and training providers, visit the British Printing Industries Federation (BPIF) website and the PrintIT! website.

More information

Proskills UK
www.proskills.co.uk

PrintIT!
www.printit.org.uk

British Printing Industries Federation (BPIF)
Farringdon Point
29/35 Farringdon Road
London
EC1M 3JF
www.britishprint.com

City & Guilds
London
EC1A 9DD
Tel: 0844 543 0000
www.cityandguilds.com

****

13. THE LEGAL PROFESSION

The legal profession is very diverse and can be a very rewarding career. the training is long and arduous and not always that glamorous. However, for the right person the rewards can be many. In this chapter we cover:

- Solicitor
- Barrister
- Barristers clerk
- Legal secretary
- Licensed conveyancer

For details of other roles in the legal profession you should go to:

Law Careers
www.lawcareers.net

All About Law - The Law Careers Website
www.allaboutlaw.co.uk

SOLICITOR

The nature of the work
You could work as a solicitor in a range of settings, including:

- private practice - providing legal services such as conveyancing, probate, civil and family law, litigation, personal injury and criminal law
- commercial practice - advising and acting for businesses in areas including contract law, tax, employment law and company sales and mergers
- in-house legal advice for companies, the government or local authorities

- Crown Prosecution Service - examining evidence to decide whether to bring cases to court.
- You would often choose to specialise in a particular area of law.

Your duties would vary according to the setting you worked in, but might typically include:

- advising clients about legal matters
- representing clients in court, or instructing barristers or advocates to act for your clients
- drafting letters, contracts and documents
- researching similar cases to guide your current work
- keeping financial records
- attending meetings and negotiations
- preparing papers for court.

What can you earn?

The minimum salary for trainee solicitors is £18,590 a year in London, and £16,650 in the rest of England and Wales.

Once qualified, salaries can rise to between £25,000 and £70,000 a year, depending on experience and the type of employer. Salaries for partners in large firms or heads of in-house legal departments can reach £100,000 a year or more.

Entry requirements

To become a solicitor, you must first meet certain academic standards, and then you must complete vocational training.

In England and Wales, you can meet the academic standards in one of the following three ways:

- by gaining a qualifying law degree

- by gaining a degree in any other subject, then taking a postgraduate law conversion course – either the Common Professional Examination (CPE) or Graduate Diploma in Law (GDL)
- by qualifying as a Fellow of the Institute of Legal Executives (ILEX)

To do a law degree, you will generally need at least five GCSEs (A-C) and two A levels with good grades, or alternatives such as an Access to Higher Education qualification. Some universities may ask you to pass the National Admissions Test for Law (LNAT) before accepting you for a law degree. You should check exact entry requirements with course providers.

You can find lists of qualifying law degrees and postgraduate law conversion courses at the Solicitors' Regulation Authority (SRA) website.

In Northern Ireland, you can meet the academic stage by either:

- gaining an approved law degree, or having a degree in another subject and proving that you have a satisfactory level of legal knowledge
- having substantial experience of relevant legal work.

After this you must complete an apprenticeship of between two and four years with a solicitor. This will include a year's study at the Institute of Professional Legal Studies in Belfast or the University of Ulster in Londonderry. Contact the Law Society of Northern Ireland for more details.

More information

Law Society
113 Chancery Lane
London
WC2A 1PL
Tel: 0870 606 2555
www.lawsociety.org.uk

Law Society of Northern Ireland
Law Society House

40 Linenhall Street
Belfast
BT2 8BA
Tel: 028 9023 1614
www.lawsoc-ni.org

National Admissions Test for Law (LNAT)
www.lnat.ac.uk

Law Careers
www.lawcareers.net

All About Law - The Law Careers Website
www.allaboutlaw.co.uk

BARRISTER

The nature of the work

If you are interested in a career in law and want to specialise, this could be perfect for you.

Barristers give specialist legal advice to professional and non-professional clients, and represent individuals and organisations in court, at tribunals and at public enquiries.

As a barrister, your work could include:

- taking on cases (known as briefs)
- advising on the law and how strong your client's legal case is
- researching points of law from previous similar cases
- providing written legal opinions to advise on cases
- having meetings with clients to discuss their case and offer legal advice
- getting cases ready for court by reading witness statements and reports, and preparing legal arguments
- representing clients in court – presenting the case to the judge and jury, cross-examining witnesses and summing up

- negotiating settlements for clients.

You would specialise in one particular area of law, which would determine the amount of time you spend in court. For example, as a criminal law specialist working in private practice or for the Crown Prosecution Service, you would spend most of your time preparing for cases and presenting in court.

In other areas of law, such as civil law (family law, property and tort) or chancery law (company law, tax, wills, trusts, and estates), you would mainly do office-based advisory work.

What can you earn?

Salaries during pupillage are at least £12,000 a year (pupillage is the final stage of training to be a barrister). In the first few years of practice, earnings can be anywhere between £25,000 and £200,000 a year, depending on specialism and reputation.

Salaries in the Crown Prosecution Service are between £28,000 and £60,000 a year.

Top earnings in private practice can reach £750,000 a year or more.

Entry requirements

To become a barrister, you must first complete an academic stage of training, followed by a vocational stage and a practical pupillage.

You can complete the academic stage by gaining:

- either an approved law degree (known as a qualifying law degree) at class 2:2 or above
- or a degree at 2:2 or above in any other subject, followed by a postgraduate Common Professional Examination (CPE) or Graduate Diploma in Law (GDL).

Many Chambers require that applicants for pupillage have a minimum 2:1 degree, and the proportion accepted with a lower second class degree is very low.

See the Education and Training section of the Bar Standards Board website for details of qualifying law degrees and postgraduate law courses.

To do a qualifying law degree, you normally need three A levels with good grades, plus at least five GCSEs (A-C). Other qualifications, such as an Access to Higher Education course, may be accepted. At some universities, you may also need to pass the National Admissions Test for Law (LNAT). Check exact entry requirements with individual course providers.

Most barristers begin vocational training straight after getting their law degree or postgraduate law qualification, but this is not essential. Others work for a number of years in related fields first, and some transfer from other professions. For information about the vocational stage and pupillage, see the Training and Development section below.

Competition is extremely strong for all stages of barrister training, so any relevant work experience can improve your chances. In particular, you should try to undertake at least three mini pupillages - a short period of work experience shadowing a barrister in Chambers. Information on mini pupillages and how to apply is available on individual Chambers' websites.

BARRISTERS CLERK

The nature of the work
Your day-to-day duties could include:

- preparing papers and taking books, documents and robes to and from court
- messenger work (collecting and delivering documents by hand)
- photocopying, filing and dealing with letters, e-mails and phone calls
- handling accounts, invoices and petty cash

- collecting fees
- organising the law library
- managing each barrister's daily diary and keeping their case information up to date
- liaising between solicitors, clients and their barristers=
- reorganising barristers' schedules when necessary.

With experience, you might become a senior barristers' clerk (which may also be known as chambers director or practice manager). In this key role you would also be responsible for:

- recruiting, training and supervising junior clerks
- bringing business into chambers
- allocating cases to barristers
- negotiating fees
- financial management of the chambers.

What can you earn?

Entry requirements

Most chambers will expect you to have at least four GCSEs (A-C), including maths and English, although many barristers' clerks have higher qualifications such as A levels or degrees.

It would be useful to have some experience in court administration, legal secretarial work, accounts or management.

Some chambers offer work experience to potential applicants, which may give you an advantage when applying for jobs.

More information

Institute of Barristers' Clerks (IBC)
289-293 High Holborn
London
WC1 7HZ

Tel: 020 7831 7144
www.ibc.org.uk

LEGAL SECRETARY

The nature of the work

As a legal secretary, you would provide administrative support for lawyers and legal executives, and help with the day-to-day tasks involved in running a legal firm.

Your tasks would be varied and depending on what department you work in your duties could include:

If you worked in a small local law firm, you would develop experience in a wide range of legal matters, whilst in larger firms you would tend to specialise in a particular area of law.

What can you earn?

Starting salaries can be between £12,000 and £20,000 a year depending on your location. This can rise with experience.

Entry requirements

Employers will expect a good standard of literacy, and you may have an advantage with a GCSE (A-C) in English, or a similar level of qualification.

You will usually need experience of office work, plus accurate typing skills. You would also have an advantage if you had audio transcription skills. Temporary office work (known as 'temping') is a good way of getting relevant experience. Full- and part-time courses in computer and secretarial skills are widely available at local colleges and through training companies.

You may find it useful to take a recognised legal secretarial course before you look for work. However, this is not always essential if you have good general administrative skills and a knowledge of law.

You may be able to get into secretarial work through an Apprenticeship scheme. The range of Apprenticeships available in your area will depend on the local jobs market and the types of skills employers need from their workers. For more information, visit the Apprenticeships website.

More information

Chartered Institute of Legal Executives
Kempston Manor
Kempston
Bedfordshire
MK42 7AB 01234 841000
www.ilex.org.uk

Institute of Legal Secretaries and PAs
308 Canterbury Court
Kennington Business Park
1-3 Brixton Road
London
Tel: 0845 643 4974 / 0207 1009210
Fax: 0203 384 4976
e-mail: info@institutelegalsecretaries.com
www.institutelegalsecretaries.com

City & Guilds
1 Giltspur Street
London
EC1A 9DD
Tel: 0844 543 0000
www.cityandguilds.com

LICENSED CONVEYANCER

The nature of the work
Conveyancing is the legal process of transferring a house or flat, commercial property or piece of land from one owner to another. Licensed or qualified

conveyancers are specialist property lawyers who deal with the paperwork and finances involved in buying and selling property in England and Wales.

As a conveyancer, your main duties would include:

- advising clients on the buying and selling process
- researching who legally owns the property being bought
- conducting 'searches' – asking local authorities about any plans that might affect the property in the future
- drafting contracts with details of the sale
- liaising with mortgage lenders, estate agents and solicitors
- paying taxes such as stamp duty
- preparing leases and transfer documents
- keeping records of payments
- checking that contracts are signed and exchanged.

What can you earn?

Starting salaries can be between £14,000 and £20,000 a year. After qualifying, earnings can be between £20,000 and £50,000

Entry requirements

To become a licensed conveyancer you must pass the Council for Licensed Conveyancers (CLC) exams. To begin CLC training, you will usually need at least four GCSEs (A-C) including English, or equivalent qualifications. However, if you have relevant work experience from a solicitor's or licensed conveyancer's office, you may be accepted without the minimum qualifications. Contact CLC for advice. In practice, people often start with higher qualifications, for example law degrees, LPC or Institute of Legal Executives (ILEX) qualifications. You do not need to be working in the legal profession to start studying for the CLC exams.

Some solicitors specialise in conveyancing. If you are already a qualified solicitor, you don't need to pass any further exams but you must apply to the CLC for a licence to practise as a conveyancer.

More information

Council for Licenced Conveyancers
16 Glebe Road
Chelmsford
Essex
CM1 1QG
Tel: 01245 349599
www.clc-uk.org

****

14. MARKETING

Marketing is a very important field of work, and calls for creative dynamic people. The rewards can be significant for the right candidates. In this section we cover key jobs in the field:

- Marketing Executive
- Marketing manager
- Marketing Research Data Analyst
- Market research Interviewer

For further details of careers in the field of marketing go to:

Chartered Institute of Marketing (CIM)
Moor Hall
Cookham
Maidenhead
Berkshire
SL6 9QH
Tel: 01628 427120
www.cim.co.uk

MARKETING EXECUTIVE

The nature of the work
Your work would involve:
- researching the market, consumer attitudes and competitors
- coming up with ideas for marketing campaigns
- arranging for advertisements to go into newspapers, magazines, the trade press, TV or radio
- organising the production of posters, flyers and brochures
- writing and distributing press releases and mailshots
- maintaining a database of customers
- arranging sponsorship

- organising and attending events and exhibitions
- making sure that all parts of a campaign run smoothly
- reporting on the campaign's progress to managers
- networking with clients, suppliers and the media.

In some jobs you may be known as a marketing officer, brand executive or account executive.

What can you earn?

Starting salaries can be between £18,000 and £22,000 a year
With experience, this can rise to between £25,000 and £40,000
Marketing directors can earn £50,000 a year or more.

Entry requirements

You could get into marketing with various levels of experience, but generally the more experience and skills you have, the higher up the career ladder you can start.

Many marketing executives have a degree or BTEC HNC/HND in marketing or another business-related subject. With a degree, you could join one of the graduate training schemes that larger employers often run for new recruits. Most degree subjects are acceptable, but you may have an advantage with one of the following:

- marketing (especially if the course included work placements)
- communications
- advertising
- business and management
- psychology.

A degree is not always essential if you have business and marketing skills gained from previous jobs such as sales, customer service or public relations work. You could also join a company's marketing department as an administrator or assistant (perhaps as a temp), and work your way up to marketing executive with experience.

Taking a professional qualification from the Chartered Institute of Marketing (CIM) could help your promotion prospects or increase your chances of finding your first marketing job. Some CIM qualifications are suitable if you don't already have a marketing-related degree or relevant work experience:

- Introductory Certificate in Marketing – an entry-level qualification open to anybody
- Professional Certificate in Marketing – for anyone educated to A level standard, or with a little marketing experience.

CIM qualifications are available full- or part-time at many colleges, and by distance learning – see the Training and Qualifications section of the CIM website for more information.

More information

Chartered Institute of Marketing (CIM)
Moor Hall
Cookham
Maidenhead
Berkshire
SL6 9QH
Tel: 01628 427120
www.cim.co.uk

Institute of Direct and Digital Marketing (IDM)
1 Park Road
Teddington
Middlesex
TW11 0AR
Tel: 020 8614 0277
www.urthebrand.co.uk
www.theidm.com

Communication Advertising and Marketing Education Foundation Limited (CAM)
Tel: 01628 427120
www.camfoundation.com

Arts Marketing Association
Tel: 01223 578078
www.a-m-a.co.uk

Focus Point
21 Caledonian Road
London
N1 9GB
www.creativeskillset.org

Creative Skillset Careers
Tel: 08080 300 900 (England and Northern Ireland)
Tel: 0845 850 2502(Scotland)
Tel: 08000 121 815 (Wales)
www.creativeskillset.org/careers

MARKETING MANAGER

The nature of the work

You would use various marketing strategies (such as media advertising, direct mail, websites and promotional events) to communicate with customers. Your typical tasks would include:

- researching and analysing market trends
- identifying target markets and how best to reach them
- coming up with marketing strategies
- planning campaigns and managing budgets
- organising the production of posters, brochures and websites
- attending trade shows, conferences and sales meetings
- making sure that campaigns run to deadline and on budget
- monitoring and reporting on the effectiveness of strategies and campaigns
- managing a team of marketing executives and assistants.

You would often specialise in certain types of product or market, such as fashion, fast moving consumer goods (FMCG) or financial services. In some companies you might be known as a brand or account manager.

What can you earn?

- Management salaries are usually between £25,000 and £40,000 a year.
- Senior managers and marketing directors can earn £50,000 a year or more.

Entry requirements

You will usually need solid experience as a marketing executive before you progress into management.

For jobs at management level, employers are likely to be more interested in your skills, track record and industry knowledge than your formal qualifications.

If an employer does ask for qualifications, they will generally prefer you to have a marketing or business-related degree, or a professional marketing qualification such as:

- Chartered Institute of Marketing (CIM) Professional Diploma in Marketing
- Institute of Direct and Digital Marketing (IDM) Diploma in Direct and Interactive Marketing.

You could also move into marketing management if you have a strong background in a related area such as sales management or public relations.

More information

Chartered Institute of Marketing (CIM)
Moor Hall
Cookham
Maidenhead

Berkshire
SL6 9QH
Tel: 01628 427120
www.cim.co.uk

Communication Advertising and Marketing Education Foundation Limited
(CAM)
Tel: 01628 427120
www.camfoundation.com

Institute of Direct and Digital Marketing (IDM)
1 Park Road
Teddington
Middlesex
TW11 0AR theidm.com

Arts Marketing Association
Tel: 01223 578078
www.a-m-a.co.uk

MARKETING RESEARCH DATA ANALYST

The nature of the work

As a market research analyst, it would be your job to analyse statistics that
have been collected through market research surveys. This could be consumer,
industrial or social and political research commissioned by all types of client
in industry, business and government.

Your work would involve:

- writing proposals describing how you will carry out the research
- advising researchers about survey methodology and design
- checking that the data that has been collected
- analysing the data using statistical software programmes and
  techniques

- presenting the findings through talks, written reports, graphs and tables
- explaining the results to research executives (who may not have specialist mathematical or statistical knowledge)
- helping research executives present the findings in a way that the client can understand and use.

Job titles can vary, for example you might be known as a data analyst, statistician or insight professional.

What can you earn?

Graduate starting salaries are around £22,000 a year. With experience, earnings can rise to between £25,000 and £35,000. Salaries for senior posts can range from £40,000 to £55,000.

Entry requirements

You will need a degree in statistics or a related subject that involves statistics, such as maths, business studies or economics. The most useful courses focus on the practical applications of statistics. To get onto a statistics degree you will usually need at least five GCSEs (A-C) plus three A levels including a good grade in maths, or equivalent qualifications. You should contact universities to find out about their exact entry requirements.

Many market research data analysts also have a Masters degree (MSc) or PhD in statistics or applied statistics. You may find it particularly useful to take an MSc if you want to specialise in an area like medical or social science statistics. See the Education and Qualifications section of the Royal Statistical Society (RSS) website for a list of degrees and Masters degrees that they accredit.

You will find it useful to have work experience in research, advertising, data analysis, or as a market research interviewer.

When looking for your first graduate job, you could start as a junior statistician/analyst, perhaps on a structured graduate training scheme offered by some of the larger companies. Alternatively you could start as a research assistant, and move into statistical work after gaining more experience.

More information

Market Research Society (MRS)
15 Northburgh Street
London
EC1V 0JR
Tel: 020 7490 4911
www.mrs.org.uk

Royal Statistical Society (RSS)
12 Errol Street
London
EC1Y 8LX
Tel: 020 7638 8998
www.rss.org.uk

Association for Qualitative Research (AQR)
Davey House
31 St Neots Road
Eaton Ford
St Neots
Cambridgeshire
PE19 7BA
Tel: 01480 407227
www.aqr.org.uk

MARKET RESEARCH INTERVIEWER

The nature of the work

As a market research interviewer, you would gather information on people's attitudes and opinions by asking them questions from pre-prepared surveys. The research that you carried out could be commissioned by a wide range of organisations, including:

- advertising agencies

- businesses of all kinds
- government
- opinion polls
- charities.

The market research process starts when the commissioning organisation briefs a research agency about what they want to find out. The agency then prepares questionnaires to use with the target audience, and recruits interviewers to carry out the surveys.

As part of a market research interviewing team, you would:

- attend an agency briefing about the research project
- approach interviewees in the street, phone them or call on them at home
- explain about the research and how it will be used
- ask a series of scripted questions from the questionnaire
- record people's answers on paper forms, a hand-held computer or video
- carry out a set number of interviews to meet a quota
- collate the results and pass them back to the market research organisation.

What can you earn?

- Earnings are usually £50 to £65 a day or £5.75 to £8.50 an hour, plus expenses.
- This is the equivalent of around £11,000 to £16,000 a year in a permanent full-time job.
- Field supervisors or research assistants can earn £18,000 to £22,000 a year.

Entry requirements

You don't need any qualifications to become a market research interviewer. Employers will be more interested in your personality, enthusiasm and communication skills.

You will find it useful to have experience of dealing with the public, in any kind of customer service job.

Employers may prefer you to have a driving licence and your own transport.

More information

Market Research Society
15 Northburgh Street
London
EC1V 0JR
Tel: 020 7490 4911
www.mrs.org.uk

Association for Qualitative Research (AQR)
Davey House
31 St Neots Road
Eaton Ford
St Neots
Cambridgeshire
PE19 7BA
Tel: 01480 407227
www.aqr.org.uk

****

15. MUSIC RADIO AND TV

Without a doubt, this is one of the most competitive and difficult areas of work to gain a foothold in. However, for those who persist the rewards are great. This chapter covers a cross section of jobs, as follows:

- Pop Musician
- Roadie
- Studio Sound Engineer
- Radio Broadcast Engineer
- Screen Writer
- TV or Film Assistant Director
- TV or Film Camera Operator
- TV or Film Director
- TV or Film producer
- TV or Film production Assistant
- TV or Film Sound Technician
- Wardrobe Assistant
- Make Up Artist

As can be appreciated the number of opportunities in these areas are numerous. For more details you should go to the various websites listed below each job.

POP MUSICIAN

The nature of the work
If you've got musical talent and you enjoy performing in front of an audience, being a pop musician might be ideal for you.

You would spend your time:

- practising and rehearsing
- playing in front of an audience

- composing songs and music to perform (or learning 'covers' of other artists' music)
- taking part in recording sessions (as an individual performer, with your own band or by providing backing or vocals at recording sessions)
- promoting your act in various ways, such as contacting agents and record companies, setting up a website and making 'demos'
- arranging gigs and tours (or dealing with a manager or agent who arranges this for you).

You would often combine music with other types of work, particularly at the start of your career.

What can you earn?

Your annual income would vary according to how successful you were and how much work you could get.

See the Musicians' Union, Equity (the performers' union) and the Incorporated Society of Musicians (ISM) websites for recommended rates of pay for session musicians and live performers.

Entry requirements

You will need a good level of musical ability as a singer or on your chosen instrument. It's not essential that you know how to read music, but it can be an advantage, especially if you want to work as a session musician.

Many musicians start learning an instrument from an early age, and you can take part-time classes at many colleges, adult education centres, private music teachers and performing arts schools. Some of these may offer qualifications such as Rockschool popular music graded exams in:

- guitar
- bass
- drums
- popular piano
- vocals.

You could take a college or university course in popular music or music technology, although this is not essential. Relevant qualifications include BTEC National Certificates/Diplomas, or foundation, undergraduate and postgraduate degrees. Check with colleges for exact entry requirements, as you may need to pass an audition to get onto some courses.

The most important thing, however, is to gain plenty of practical experience by performing and doing gigs. Many record companies send Artists and Repertoire (A&R) staff to small clubs, pubs and other venues to scout for emerging talent.

When trying to break into the music business, you can approach record companies with a 'demo' CD or MP3 of your music. Companies receive thousands of demos so yours will need to stand out immediately: if it does not attract the listeners attention after 30 seconds or so, they are likely to discard it. See the BPI and Showcase websites for record company contact details.

It is common for bands and solo artists to showcase their music on networking websites. You could also get yourself noticed by entering talent competitions.

More information

Creative and Cultural Skills
Lafone House
The Leathermarket
Weston Street
London
SE1 3HN
www.creative-choices.co.uk

Incorporated Society of Musicians (ISM)
10 Stratford Place
London
W1C 1AA
Tel: 020 7629 4413
www.ism.org

BPI - The British Recorded Music Industry
Riverside Building
County Hall
Westminster Bridge Road
London
SE1 7JA
Tel: 020 7803 1300
www.bpi.co.uk

Rockschool
Evergreen House
2-4 King Street
Twickenham
Middlesex
TW1 3RZ
Tel: 0845 460 4747
www.rockschool.co.uk

Equity
Guild House
Upper St Martin's Lane
London
WC2H 9EG
Tel: 020 7379 6000
www.equity.org.uk

Musicians Union
Tel: 020 7582 5566
www.musiciansunion.org.uk

RADIO BROADCAST ASSISTANT

The nature of the work
Broadcast assistants (often known in the radio industry as 'BAs') support producers and presenters in making radio programmes. As a broadcast assistant, it would be your job to handle the administration, help to plan

programmes and provide technical support in the studio. Becoming a BA is a common starting point for a career in radio.

The work can vary widely from one station to the next and even from one programme to the next. The main differences are between speech and music radio, and between live and pre-recorded radio. However, your administrative duties would generally include:

- typing scripts
- keeping track of costs
- researching programmes
- booking guests, preparing their contracts and arranging payment
- producing programme logs and running orders
- archiving programme material
- arranging and sending out competition prizes
- booking studio time and equipment
- updating the programme or station website.
- Studio production work can include:
- managing phone lines for phone-ins and competitions
- timing shows
- operating recording, editing and mixing equipment on pre-recorded or live programmes (often known as 'driving the desk')
- recording and editing programme trailers
- offering creative input, such as writing links or devising quiz questions.

With experience, you may also take on some of the more high-profile tasks, such as contributing programme ideas, interviewing guests or presenting part of a programme. In speech or news radio, you would often be asked to go out and collect short interviews (known as 'vox pops') from the general public.

What can you earn?

Starting salaries are often between £13,000 and £18,000 a year
With experience, this could rise to around £25,000 a year.
If you work freelance, you will usually negotiate a fee for each contract. Rates can vary, and there may be gaps between contracts.

Figures are intended as a guideline only.

Entry requirements

The key to becoming a broadcast assistant is to get plenty of practical experience in radio (paid or unpaid), and to prove your initiative, enthusiasm and flexibility to employers.

You can gain useful experience through:

- community, hospital or student radio – see the Community Media Association website for a list of local stations, and the Hospital Broadcasting Association for a list of hospital stations
- work placements – for details of possible opportunities, see BBC Work Experience Placements or the RadioCentre (for commercial radio).

As your experience grows, it's a good idea to develop a 'demo' or 'showreel' CD or MP3 of productions you have worked on to send to potential employers.

You may also find it helpful to take a course in radio or media production. Look for courses that include practical skills training and work placements. Several colleges, community media schemes and universities offer relevant full-time, part-time and short courses including:

- ABC Level 3 Awards in Broadcast Media (Talk Radio Broadcast Skills and Radio Production Skills)
- NCFE Certificates and Diplomas in Radio Production at levels 1 and 2
- City & Guilds (7501) Diploma in Media Techniques (will be the Level 1, 2 and 3 Award, Certificate and Diploma in Media Techniques (7601) from September 2010)
- BTEC National Certificate/Diploma in Media Production (BTEC Level 3 Certificate/Diploma in Creative Media Production from September 2010)
- BTEC HNDs, Foundation Degrees, degrees and postgraduate courses in radio or media production.

Check with course providers for entry requirements.

For news-based and factual radio, you may have an advantage with a background in journalism or research.

More information
Creative Skillset
Focus Point
21 Caledonian Road
London
N1 9GB
www.creativeskillset.org

Creative Skillset Careers
Tel: 08080 300 900 (England and Northern Ireland)
Tel: 0845 850 2502(Scotland)
Tel: 08000 121 815 (Wales)
www.creativeskillset.org/careers

The RadioCentre
4th Floor
5 Golden Square
London
W1F 9BS
Tel: 020 3206 7800
www.radiocentre.org

Radio Academy
2nd Floor
5 Golden Square
London
W1F 9BS
Tel: 020 3174 1180
www.radioacademy.org

Broadcast Journalism Training Council
18 Miller's Close
Rippingale

near Bourne
Lincolnshire
PE10 0TH
Tel: 01778 440025
www.bjtc.org.uk

Community Media Association
15 Paternoster Row
Sheffield
S1 2BX
Tel: 0114 279 5219
www.commedia.org.uk

Hospital Broadcasting Association
www.hbauk.com

ROADIE

The nature of the work
Roadies, sometimes called technical support staff or crew, help to stage music concerts and other events. You would set up before a gig, look after the instruments during the show, and pack away afterwards.

You might work alone or as part of large crew, doing some or all of the following duties:

- lifting and carrying equipment and sets
- driving, loading and unloading vans, trailers and buses
- acting as security for equipment and band members
- setting up and looking after sound equipment
- setting up video equipment and screens
- rigging up wiring and lighting
- setting up pyrotechnics (fireworks) and laser displays
- tuning the instruments during the show.

You could also be responsible for other tour management duties like booking travel and caterers or issuing backstage passes.

What can you earn?

Unskilled roadies working full-time can earn around £12,000 a year. With technical skills, earnings could be £20,000 to £30,000 a year or more. You may also be paid living expenses when on tour.

Entry requirements

You would often start by working for free for local bands – many people get their first job through making contacts in this way. You can also get relevant experience through things like:

- working backstage in college or amateur theatre productions
- casual work at local concert venues and gigs
- working for equipment hire and supply companies.

It would be helpful to have a driving licence. You may have an advantage if you have a Large Goods Vehicle (LGV) licence or Passenger Carrying Vehicle (PCV) licence, which would allow you to drive tour buses and lorries.

You don't need formal qualifications to work as a roadie, but you may have an advantage with experience and qualifications in electronics, electrical work, sound production, music technology or lighting. The more skills you have, the more employable you will be. See the related profiles for more information on these jobs.

More information

Roadie
www.roadie.net

Association of British Theatre Technicians
55 Farringdon Road
London
EC1M 3JB
Tel: 020 7242 9200
www.abtt.org.uk

Production Services Association
PO Box 2709
Bath
BA1 3YS
Tel:01225 332668
www.psa.org.uk

Broadcasting Entertainment Cinematograph and Theatre Union (BECTU)
373-377 Clapham Road
London
SW9 9BT
Tel: 0845 850 2502
www.bectu.org.uk

SCREENWRITER

The nature of the work
Screenwriters create ideas and bring stories to life in scripts for feature films, TV comedy and drama, animation, children's programmes and computer games.

As a screenwriter, you might develop your own original ideas and sell them to producers. Alternatively, producers may commission you to create a screenplay from an idea or true story, or to adapt an existing piece such as a novel, play or comic book.

Your work would typically involve:

- coming up with themes and ideas
- researching background material
- developing believable plots and characters
- laying out the screenplay to an agreed format
- preparing short summaries of your ideas and selling (known as 'pitching') them to producers or development executives
- getting feedback about the first draft of your work from producers or script editors

- rewriting the script if necessary (you may need to do this several times before arriving at the final agreed version).

You might also spend time networking with agents and producers, and handling your own tax and accounts. You would often combine writing with other work such as teaching, lecturing or editing.

What can you earn?

As a freelance writer, you or your agent would negotiate a fee for each piece of work. You might be partly paid in advance. Depending on your contract, you might also receive a percentage of the profits from a feature film.

See the Writers' Guild of Great Britain website for recommended minimum pay rates for writers in film, TV and theatre.

Entry requirements

You will need imagination, writing talent and creativity rather than formal qualifications. However, when starting out you may find it useful to take a course that helps you develop your skills and understand dramatic structure.

Courses in creative writing and scriptwriting for all levels from beginner to advanced are widely available at colleges, adult education centres and universities.

Some screenwriters have degrees or postgraduate qualifications in creative writing, English or journalism, but this is not essential. You may have an advantage if you have writing and storytelling experience from another field such as journalism, advertising copywriting or acting.

You would normally start by coming up with your own screenplays and ideas, and trying to sell them to agents and producers. Once you have had some work accepted and started to build a professional reputation, producers might then commission you to produce scripts for them.

As a new writer, you could get yourself noticed by entering screenwriting competitions, which broadcasters and regional screen agencies sometimes hold to discover new talent. Contact Creative Skillset Careers for more information. You can also find advice about submitting your work to the BBC at the BBC Writers' Room website.

More information

Creative Skillset
Focus Point
21 Caledonian Road
London
N1 9GB
www.creativeskillset.org

Creative Skillset Careers
Tel: 08080 300 900 (England and Northern Ireland)
Tel: 0845 850 2502(Scotland)
Tel: 08000 121 815 (Wales)
www.creativeskillset.org/careers

The Script Factory
Welbeck House
66/67 Wells Street
London
W1T 3PY
Tel: 020 7323 1414
www.scriptfactory.co.uk

Writers Guild of Great Britain
49 Roseberry Avenue
London
EC1R 4RX
Tel: 020 7833 0777
www.writersguild.org.uk

BBC Writers Room
www.bbc.co.uk/writersroom

STUDIO SOUND ENGINEER

The nature of the work

As a sound engineer in a recording studio, you would make high quality recordings of music, speech and sound effects for use in different media, from music recordings to commercials.

In this job you would need good hearing. You would also need a good appreciation of pitch, timing and rhythm.

You would use complex electronic equipment to record sound for many different uses, such as:

- commercial music recordings
- radio, TV, film and commercials
- corporate videos
- websites
- computer games and other types of interactive media.

Your work would involve:

- planning recording sessions with producers and artists
- setting up microphones and equipment in the studio
- setting the right sound levels and dynamics
- operating equipment for recording, mixing, mastering, sequencing and sampling
- recording each instrument or item onto a separate track
- monitoring and balancing sound levels
- mixing tracks to produce a final 'master' track
- logging tapes and other details of the session in the studio archive.

With experience, you might also act as studio manager.

What can you earn?

Starting salaries can be from £13,000 a year full-time equivalent. With experience, salaries can rise to between £20,000 and £40,000. Freelance earnings can be higher or lower, depending on reputation and how much work is available.

Entry requirements

You will need a good knowledge of music and recording technology, and you'll also find it useful to understand physics and electronics. Many sound engineers start by taking a music technology course at college or university, to develop skills before looking for work in a studio.

Music technology courses are available at various levels, such as:

- City & Guilds Level 1, 2 and 3 Award, Certificate and Diploma in Sound and Music Techniques (7603)
- BTEC National Certificate/Diploma in Music Technology
- foundation degrees, BTEC HNCs/HNDs or degrees in sound engineering, audio technology, music technology or music production.

Check with colleges or universities for course entry requirements. See the Association of Professional Recording Services (APRS) JAMES website for information on industry-approved courses.

Alternatively, instead of taking a music technology course before looking for work, you could start as an assistant or 'runner' in a recording studio. Here you would carry out basic routine jobs, but you would also get the chance to learn how to use studio equipment and assist on sessions.

When looking for your first job, you'll find it helpful to have practical experience of using studio equipment. Taking a music technology course can help with this, and you could also build up your experience through:

- community music or DJ projects
- hospital or community radio
- mixing and recording music in a home studio.

Customer service experience and good 'people skills' such as teamwork and communication are also important, as you would often be working in close contact with clients and artists.

More information
Creative Skillset Careers
Tel: 08080 300 900 (England and Northern Ireland)
Tel: 0845 850 2502(Scotland)
Tel: 08000 121 815 (Wales)
www.creativeskillset.org/careers

PLASA
Redoubt House
1 Edward Road
Eastbourne
BN23 8AS
Tel: 01323 524120
www.plasa.org

Association of Professional Recording Services
PO Box 22
Totnes
Devon
TQ9 7YZ
Tel: 01803 868600
www.aprs.co.uk

BPI - The British Recorded Music Industry
Riverside Building
County Hall
Westminster Bridge Road
London
SE1 7JA
Tel: 020 7803 1300
www.bpi.co.uk
Institute of Sound and Communications Engineers
PO Box 7966
Reading

RG6 7BP
www.isce.org.uk
Tomorrow's Engineers ⌷
www.tomorrowsengineers.org.uk

TV or FILM ASSISTANT DIRECTOR

The nature of the work

Assistant directors (known in the industry as 'ADs') support film directors by organising and planning everything on set. Most productions use a team of assistant directors, with a 1st AD, at least one 2nd AD and possibly one or more 3rd ADs, each with different tasks.

1st ADs have the most important supporting role to the director. In this job you would do much of the planning before production begins, and you would manage the set during filming to leave the director free to concentrate on the creative side. Your responsibilities would include:

- working with the director to break the script down into a shot-by-shot 'storyboard' and decide the order of shooting
- planning a filming schedule, taking into account the director's ideas and the available budget
- overseeing the hire of locations, props and equipment
- recruiting the cast and crew
- making sure that filming stays on schedule
- supervising a team of 2nd and 3rd ADs and runners
- motivating the cast and crew
- responsible for health and safety on set.

2nd ADs support the 1st AD and make sure that their orders are carried out on set. As a 2nd AD you would:

- produce each day's 'call sheet' (a list of timings and logistics for the following day's shoot)
- be the link between the set and the production office

- distribute call sheets, so that the cast and crew know exactly when they are needed on set
- deal with paperwork
- organise transport and hotels
- make sure that cast members are in make-up, wardrobe or on set at the right time
- find and supervise extras on productions where there is no 3rd AD.

3rd ADs assist 2nd ADs, 1st ADs and location managers on set. As a 3rd AD your main job would be to make sure any extras were on set at the right time and place. You would brief the extras and give them their cues, and you might direct the action in background crowd scenes. You would also act as a messenger on set.

What can you earn?

Freelance assistant directors are usually paid a fee for each individual contract or project. Rates can vary widely, and may be based on the budget available and your track record.

Contact the Broadcasting Entertainment Cinematograph and Theatre Union (BECTU) for current pay guidelines.

People working on films may agree to work for little or no pay on the understanding that they will share in any profit that the film makes. You should check the exact terms before going ahead with this type of contract or agreement.

Entry requirements

The key to becoming an assistant director is to get practical experience of the production process, and also to develop a network of contacts in the industry. Employers are usually more interested in your experience and your enthusiasm and initiative than your formal qualifications.

You would often start as runner or production assistant on set, and work your way up to 3rd or 2nd AD and beyond. To get a job as a runner, you will need to show your commitment by finding work experience and being involved in activities like student or community film or TV. It can take several years to move from Runner through to First AD.

It is not essential to have studied film, video or media production before you look for work, although it can be helpful as the most useful courses include practical skills and work placements. Several colleges and universities offer relevant courses, including:

- City & Guilds (7501) Diploma in Media Techniques (will be Level 1, 2 and 3 Award, Certificate and Diploma in Media Techniques (7601) from September 2010)
- BTEC National Certificate/Diploma in Media Production (will be BTEC Level 3 Certificates and Diplomas in Creative Media Production from September 2010)
- BTEC HNDs, degrees and postgraduate courses.

Check with course providers for entry requirements, and see Creative Skillset's website for details of industry-endorsed Film and TV production courses.

More information

Creative Skillset Careers
Tel: 08080 300 900 (England and Northern Ireland)
Tel: 0845 850 2502(Scotland)
Tel: 08000 121 815 (Wales)
www.creativeskillset.org/careers

Creative Skillset
Focus Point
21 Caledonian Road
London
N1 9GB
www.creativeskillset.org

Broadcasting Entertainment Cinematograph and Theatre Union (BECTU)
373-377 Clapham Road
London

SW9 9BT
Tel: 0845 850 2502
www.bectu.org.uk

TV or FILM CAMERA OPERATOR

The nature of the work

As a camera operator, it would be your job to record moving images for film, television, commercials, music videos or corporate productions. You would operate film, videotape or digital video cameras, usually under instructions from the Director or Director of Photography.

Your work could involve:

- setting up and positioning camera equipment
- planning and rehearsing shots
- following a camera script and taking cues from the director or floor manager (in TV studio recording)
- choosing the most suitable lenses and camera angles
- solving practical or technical problems such as lighting
- working closely with other technical departments such as lighting and sound.

You may be the only camera operator and use a portable single camera, or you could be part of a TV studio camera team. On feature films and TV drama productions you may be part of a large crew with a specific role, such as:

- second assistant camera (clapper loader) – loading and unloading film, counting the takes and helping the camera crew
- first assistant camera (focus puller) – judging and adjusting the focus on each shot
- grip – building and operating any cranes and pulleys needed to move a camera during shooting.

You would usually specialise in either film or television work, as the equipment and techniques can differ, however with the advent of digital cameras and HD technology, camera professionals are finding it easier to work across all sectors ensuring more stable employment.

What can you earn?

Freelance camera operators are usually paid a fee for each contract.

Rates can vary widely. You could negotiate fees based on the type of production and your own track record. Contact BECTU for current pay guidelines.

Entry requirements

Employers will be more interested in your technical skills and practical experience than your formal qualifications. In practice, many camera operators take a college or university course to develop the necessary skills before looking for work. Relevant courses include:

- City & Guilds Diploma (7501) in Media Techniques (Level 1, 2 and 3 Award, Certificate and Diploma in Media Techniques (7601) from September 2010)
- BTEC National Certificate or Diploma in Media Production
- BTEC HNC/HND in Media (Moving Image)
- degrees in media production, media technology or photography
- trainee courses run by the GBCT (camera guild).

The most useful courses offer practical experience and may include work placements. Please check with colleges or universities for exact entry requirements.

As well as gaining technical skills, you should also build practical experience and make contacts in the industry. Courses can help you with this, but you can also get useful experience from:

- getting involved in community film projects
- working for a camera equipment hire company
- finding work experience as a runner or camera assistant with a production company.

You may also find it useful to have skills in stills photography and basic electronics.

You should also make a 'showreel' DVD of productions that you have worked on, to demonstrate your skills to employers when you are looking for work.

More information

Creative Skillset
Focus Point
21 Caledonian Road
London
N1 9GB
www.creativeskillset.org

Creative Skillset Careers
Tel: 08080 300 900 (England and Northern Ireland)
Tel: 0845 850 2502 (Scotland)
Tel: 08000 121 815 (Wales)
www.creativeskillset.org/careers

Creative Skillset Craft and Technical Skills Academy
Easling, Hammersmith and West London College
The Green
Ealing
London
W5 5EW
info@craftandtech.org
www.craftandtech.org

Guild of Television Cameramen
www.gtc.org.uk

Guild of British Camera Technicians
c/o Panavision UK
Metropolitan Centre
Bristol Road
Greenford

Middlesex
UB6 8GD
Tel: 020 8813 1999
www.gbct.org

TV or FILM DIRECTOR

The nature of the work

Directors have overall responsibility for the way films or television programmes are made. As a director, you would use your creativity, organisational skills and technical knowledge to manage the whole production process.

You might lead a small team or a large cast and crew, to direct full-length feature films, short films, live or recorded television programmes, commercials, music videos or corporate videos. Your main purpose would be to make the creative decisions that guide the rest of the crew.

Your work could include:

- meeting producers
- commissioning a script or an idea for a documentary
- interpreting scripts and developing storyboards
- deciding on how the production should look and where it should be filmed
- planning the shooting schedule and logistics
- hiring the cast and crew
- guiding the technical crew
- directing the actors (or the contributors to a documentary)
- supervising the editing to produce the final 'cut'.

In some cases you might write your own scripts and raise finance for projects. On some productions you might also operate camera or sound equipment – this is particularly common with documentaries or productions with a small budget.

What can you earn?

Freelance directors are usually paid a fee for each individual contract or project. Rates can vary widely, and may be based on the budget available and your track record.

Contact the Broadcasting Entertainment Cinematograph and Theatre Union (BECTU) for current pay guidelines.

People working on films may agree to work for little or no pay on the understanding that they will share in any profit that the film makes. You should check the exact terms before going ahead with this type of contract or agreement.

Entry requirements

You could take various routes to becoming a director. The most important requirements are to have substantial experience in TV or film, in-depth understanding of the production process, and a network of contacts in the industry.

Many successful directors start as runners and work their way up through other jobs like 3rd and 2nd assistant director or floor manager. Others move into directing after experience in camera work or acting.

To get a job as a runner, you will need to show your commitment to working in the media. You could do this through taking part in activities like student or community film or TV, and finding work experience placements.

You may find it helpful to take a filmmaking or media production course that helps you to build practical skills and make contacts. Several universities and colleges offer relevant BTEC HNDs, degrees and postgraduate courses, and some private film schools offer intensive directing and filmmaking courses. See Creative Skillset's website for details of industry-endorsed courses.

Another way of breaking into film directing is to make your own short films (known as 'shorts'), which you could market to agents or enter into film festivals and competitions such as those run by the BBC and Channel 4. To make your own films, you will need access to equipment, crew and actors. Getting involved in community film projects can help you with this.

More information

Creative Skillset
Focus Point
21 Caledonian Road
London
N1 9GB
www.creativeskillset.org

Creative Skillset Careers
Tel: 08080 300 900 (England and Northern Ireland)
Tel: 0845 850 2502(Scotland)
Tel: 08000 121 815 (Wales)
www.creativeskillset.org/careers

Broadcasting Entertainment Cinematograph and Theatre Union (BECTU)
373-377 Clapham Road
London
SW9 9BT
Tel: 0845 850 2502
www.bectu.org.uk

Directors Guild of Great Britain
4 Windmill Street
London
W1T 2HZ
Tel: 020 7580 9131
www.dggb.org

Shooting People 🖵
www.shootingpeople.org

TV or FILM PRODUCER

The nature of the work

Producers play an important role in the film, television and video industries. As a producer, your main purpose would be to deal with the practical and business side of a project, so that the director and crew could concentrate on the creative side. Film Producers are instrumental in obtaining funding for a film while in TV, programmes are usually (but not always) commissioned and therefore funding is not a major part of the job.

You would manage the production process from start to finish, organising all the resources needed and often coming up with the initial idea for a project. Your work might include:

- deciding which projects to produce, or creating programme ideas yourself
- reading scripts
- securing the rights for books or screenplays, or getting writers to produce new screenplays
- raising finance for projects
- pitching to television broadcasters to commission your programme
- identifying sources of film funding and pitching projects to investors
- assessing what resources will be needed
- planning the schedule
- hiring all the necessary technical resources and support services
- recruiting key production staff and crew, and being involved with casting performers
- editing scripts
- managing cash flow
- making sure that the entire production stays on schedule and within budget
- overall responsibility for the quality of the production.

On feature film and large-scale TV productions, you would be part of a team of producers and may be responsible for just some of these duties. On a smaller production such as a documentary, you would often do all of these tasks and may also direct the project.

What can you earn?

Freelance producers are usually paid a fee for each individual contract or project.

Rates can vary widely and you could negotiate fees based on the type of production, the budget available and your track record. Contact the Broadcasting Entertainment Cinematograph and Theatre Union (BECTU) for current pay guidelines.

Depending on your contract, you may also receive a percentage of the profits from a feature film.

Entry requirements

You will need substantial experience in both the creative and business sides of film or programme making. You will also need an in-depth understanding of the production process, and a network of contacts in the industry.

You could work your way up through the industry in various ways. In TV, you could start as a runner or production assistant. Producers of factual programmes often start as programme researchers or journalists. Alternatively, you could progress through production office roles, from production secretary to assistant production coordinator and beyond.

In film, you would usually start as a runner. You could then work your way up to production coordinator, line producer and production manager, or alternatively progress through the roles of 3rd, 2nd and 1st assistant director.

Before finding an entry-level job in film or TV, you will be expected to build as much practical experience as you can. You can do this through activities like student film/TV, work experience placements, or hospital or community radio. It is not essential to have studied film, video or media production before you look for work. However, you may find it helpful to take a course that includes practical skills, work placements and the chance to make contacts. Many colleges and universities offer relevant courses. See Creative Skillset's website for details of industry-endorsed courses.

More information

Creative Skillset
Focus Point
21 Caledonian Road
London
N1 9GB
www.creativeskillset.org

Creative Skillset Careers
Tel: 08080 300 900 (England and Northern Ireland)
Tel: 0845 850 2502(Scotland)
Tel: 08000 121 815 (Wales)
www.creativeskillset.org/careers

Production Guild
Tel: 01753 651767
www.productionguild.com

Broadcasting Entertainment Cinematograph and Theatre Union (BECTU)
373-377 Clapham Road
London
SW9 9BT
Tel: 0845 850 2502
www.bectu.org.uk

Indie Training Fund (ITF)
www.indietrainingfund.com

TV or FILM PRODUCTION ASSISTANT

The nature of the work

As a production assistant, you would give practical support to the director and production team during the making of films and television programmes. It would be your job to handle administrative and organisational tasks so that the production ran smoothly and on time.

269

You would be involved in a wide range of tasks before, during and after filming, which would often include:

- hiring studio facilities and equipment
- booking hotels and making travel arrangements
- attending production meetings
- copying and distributing scripts
- typing and distributing schedules ('call sheets') and daily reports
- getting permission to use copyrighted music or film clips
- dealing with accounts and expenses.

In television, you might also carry out production duties such as:

- timing the show in the studio gallery
- calling camera shots
- cueing pre-recorded material
- keeping records (known as 'logging') of shots taken
- keeping continuity.

You would work as part of a wider production team, including producers, researchers, and technical staff like camera crew and editors.

What can you earn?

Freelance production assistants are usually paid a fee for each contract.

Freelance rates can vary widely, and may be negotiated based on the type of production and your track record. Contact the Broadcasting Entertainment Cinematograph and Theatre Union (BECTU) for current pay guidelines.

Entry requirements

You will need good office IT skills and plenty of initiative, enthusiasm and common sense. You should also build as much practical experience as you can. Although many production assistants are graduates, this is not essential as most employers will be more interested in your experience and personal qualities than your qualifications.

You can build useful experience through activities such as:

- student or community film/TV projects
- community or student radio
- work experience placements (often unpaid).

Creative Skillset Careers offers advice on finding work experience – visit their website to find out more.

It isn't essential to have studied film, video or media production, although you might find it helpful to take a course that includes practical skills, work placements and the chance to make contacts. Several colleges and universities offer relevant courses, including:

- Level 1, 2 and 3 Award, Certificate and Diploma in Media Techniques (7601)
- BTEC Level 3 Certificates and Diplomas in Creative Media Production
- BTEC HNDs, degrees and postgraduate courses.

Check with course providers for entry requirements, and see Creative Skillset's website for details of industry-endorsed courses.

Your first paid job would often be as a runner or a junior assistant or secretary in the production office, and you would work your way up the production ladder as you gained experience.

More information

Creative Skillset
Focus Point
21 Caledonian Road
London
N1 9GB
www.creativeskillset.org

Creative Skillset Careers
Tel: 08080 300 900 (England and Northern Ireland)

Tel: 0845 850 2502(Scotland)
Tel: 08000 121 815 (Wales)
www.creativeskillset.org/careers

Broadcasting Entertainment Cinematograph and Theatre Union (BECTU)
373-377 Clapham Road
London
SW9 9BT
Tel: 0845 850 2502
www.bectu.org.uk

TV or FILM SOUND TECHNICIAN

The nature of the work
As a sound technician, you would record, mix and check the sound for live and recorded film and television productions. You would use microphones, recording equipment and editing software to record sound and produce a clear, high-quality soundtrack. You could specialise in one of the following:

- production sound – recording sound on set or location
- post-production – putting the final soundtrack together in an editing studio.
- On a production sound team you could work as sound recordist (also known as production mixer), a boom operator or a sound assistant. Depending on your job role, your duties may include:
- setting up equipment to suit the acoustics and the sound designer's instructions
- selecting and placing fixed microphones
- operating the boom (positioning the moving microphones around the performers for the best sound)
- monitoring sound quality
- recording onto digital audio tape
- servicing and repairing equipment
- playing music or sound effects into a live programme.

- Post-production teams can include a re-recording (dubbing) mixer, dialogue editor/mixer, foley artist and foley editor. Post-production sound work can involve:
- following a sound designer or sound supervisor's instructions
- mixing and balancing speech, effects and background music
- editing speech to fit the action on screen
- creating extra sound effects and adding them into the soundtrack (known as the 'foley').

What can you earn?

Starting salaries can be around £18,000 to £25,000 a year for ongoing full-time work (although it is common to work for less at the start of your career). Experienced freelance rates can be between £800 and £1600 a week (before tax). Freelance rates can vary widely. You could negotiate fees based on the type of production and your own track record. Contact BECTU for current pay guidelines.

Entry requirements

You will need a good knowledge of sound technology and equipment, and you will find it useful to understand basic electronics and the physics of sound.

You may increase your chances of getting into the industry by taking a relevant course to develop your knowledge and skills before you look for work. Courses include:

- City & Guilds 7503 Certificate/Diploma in Sound and Music Technology (will be the City & Guilds Award, Certificate and Diploma in Sound and Music Techniques (7603) at levels 1-3 from September 2010)
- BTEC National Certificate/Diploma in Media Production (Sound Recording) or Music Technology (BTEC Level 3 Certificates and Diplomas in Creative Media Production (Sound Recording) or Music Technology (Production) from September 2010)

- BTEC HNC/HND in Media (Audio) (will become BTEC Level 4 and 5 HND Diplomas in Creative Media Production or Music (Production) from September 2010)
- foundation degrees or degrees in sound engineering, music technology, media technology or technical theatre.
- Check with colleges or universities for entry requirements.

When looking for your first job, you will find it useful to have practical experience of using sound equipment. Taking a relevant course can help with this, and you can also build experience in the following ways:

- working on student or community film or radio projects
- setting up ('rigging') sound equipment for amateur theatre or local bands
- working for a sound equipment manufacturer or hire company
- assisting in a recording or editing studio.

Contact Creative Skillset Careers for more advice about finding work experience.

More information

Creative Skillset
Focus Point
21 Caledonian Road
London
N1 9GB
www.creativeskillset.org

Creative Skillset Careers
Tel: 08080 300 900 (England and Northern Ireland)
Tel: 0845 850 2502(Scotland)
Tel: 08000 121 815 (Wales)
www.creativeskillset.org/careers

Association of Professional Recording Services
PO Box 22

Totnes
Devon
TQ9 7YZ
Tel: 01803 868600
www.aprs.co.uk

Broadcasting Entertainment Cinematograph and Theatre Union (BECTU)
373-377 Clapham Road
London
SW9 9BT
Tel: 0845 850 2502
www.bectu.org.uk

WARDROBE ASSISTANT

The nature of the work

Wardrobe assistants help to make, find and look after the clothing and costumes used in theatre, film and television productions. In this job you will need to have good sewing skills. You will also need to have an eye for design and style.

As a wardrobe assistant, you would work under the direction of a costume supervisor or wardrobe master/mistress. Your work might include:

- helping to buy and hire costume items
- looking after the costumes between takes or scenes
- mending and altering items
- packing and unpacking costumes and accessories
- cleaning and ironing
- helping to make pieces and put costumes together
- fitting the performers
- making sure that all items are available when needed
- keeping an accurate record of all items needed
- storing costumes and returning hired items (known as 'breaking down' costumes).

In theatre, you might also act as a 'dresser', helping performers with costume changes during the show.

What can you earn?

Wardrobe assistants tend to work on a freelance basis. Freelance rates can vary widely. You could negotiate your fees based on the type of production and your own track record. Contact BECTU for current pay guidelines for film and TV.

Entry requirements

You will need practical skills in hand and machine sewing, pattern cutting and dressmaking. You don't always need formal qualifications, but you could build useful skills on college courses such as:

- City & Guilds Certificates and Diplomas at levels 1, 2 and 3 in Creative Techniques – part-time courses, with options including for theatre costume and pattern cutting.
- BTEC Level 2 Certificate/Diploma in Fashion and Clothing or Level 3 Certificate/Diploma in Production Arts (Costume) – courses may be full-time or part-time.
- You may have an advantage with a BTEC HND, degree or postgraduate qualification in costume design, fashion or textiles, especially if you want to eventually become a costume designer. You should check entry requirements with course providers.

The key to finding paid work is to get practical experience, which you can get from:

- student theatre and film productions
- amateur or community theatre
- dressmaking
- work for a theatrical costume hire company
- casual work as a costume 'daily' (temporary helper) on film and TV sets.

Contact Creative Skillset Careers for advice about work experience in film and television.

More information

Creative and Cultural Skills
Lafone House
The Leathermarket
Weston Street
London
SE1 3HN
www.creative-choices.co.uk

Creative Skillset
Focus Point
21 Caledonian Road
London
N1 9GB
www.creativeskillset.org

Creative Skillset Careers
Tel: 08080 300 900 (England and Northern Ireland)
Tel: 0845 850 2502(Scotland)
Tel: 08000 121 815 (Wales)
www.creativeskillset.org/careers

Get Into Theatre
www.getintotheatre.org

Association of British Theatre Technicians
55 Farringdon Road
London
EC1M 3JB
Tel: 020 7242 9200
www.abtt.org.uk

Broadcasting Entertainment Cinematograph and Theatre Union (BECTU)
373-377 Clapham Road
London
SW9 9BT

Tel: 0845 850 2502
www.bectu.org.uk

The Costume Society
www.costumesociety.org.uk

MAKE UP ARTIST

The nature of the work
Make-up artists apply make-up and style hair for anyone appearing in front of a camera or a live audience. They can work in film, television, theatre, concerts, photographic sessions or fashion shows.

Most make-up artists start by taking a specialist course in make-up or beauty therapy and building up their practical experience.

As a make-up artist, you might create anything from a straightforward natural look to one using historical wigs and make-up. You could also create special effects such as scars and artificial pieces (prosthetics).

You could work alone, as an assistant to a senior colleague, or as part of a larger hair and make-up design team. Depending on the job, your tasks might include:

- researching and designing make-up and hairstyles to suit the job
- working to detailed notes or to general design instructions
- hair tidying and styling
- fitting wigs, hairpieces and bald caps
- applying prosthetic make-up to completely change someone's look
- making notes and taking photographs as reference so that you can recreate the look easily (continuity)
- standing by on set to redo make-up and hair
- keeping work areas and equipment clean and tidy.

You would work closely with production designers, costume designers, camera and lighting crew, and performers. See the Creative Choices website to read a theatre make-up artist's story.

What can you earn?

Freelance make-up artists are usually paid a fee for each contract. Rates can vary a lot and will usually depend on the type of production and the work you have done in the past. The Broadcasting Entertainment Cinematograph and Theatre Union (BECTU) publishes recommended pay rates on its website. For example, it recommends a rate of around £200 for a 10-hour day in TV or film. It also recommends that trainees are paid at least the minimum wage (or the London living wage, if in London).

Entry requirements

Most make-up artists start by taking a specialist course in make-up or beauty therapy and building up their practical experience.

There is a wide range of specialist courses available. College courses include Awards, Certificates and Diplomas at level 3 (and sometimes level 2) in fashion and photography make-up, and media make-up. Some universities offer foundation degrees and degrees in media make-up. You may need a level 2 qualification in hair and beauty to do some of these courses. Check entry requirements with course providers.

Courses in media make-up training are also run privately.

As well as taking a relevant make-up course, you should also try to gain practical experience, build a portfolio of your work to show to employers and get to know people in the industry (networking).

You could get useful experience in various ways, such as:

- amateur theatre
- student film, theatre and photography projects
- charity or student fashion shows
- with established make-up artists and photographers.

Once you have built up some experience and made some contacts, your first paid work in film or TV may be as a trainee or assistant to the make-up team.

You might also find casual work doing make-up and hair for extras in crowd scenes.

More information

Creative Skillset
Focus Point
21 Caledonian Road
London
N1 9GB
www.creativeskillset.org

Skillset Craft and Technical Skills Academy
Ealing, Hammersmith and West London College
The Green
Ealing
London
W5 5EW
info@craftandtech.org
www.craftandtech.org

Creative Skillset Careers
Tel: 08080 300 900 (England and Northern Ireland)
Tel: 0845 850 2502(Scotland)
Tel: 08000 121 815 (Wales)
www.creativeskillset.org/careers

National Association of Screen Makeup and Hair Artists (NASMAH)
68 Sarsfield Road
Perivale
Middlesex
UB6 7AG
www.nasmah.co.uk

Vocational Training Charitable Trust (VTCT)
3rd Floor
Eastleigh House
Upper Market Street

Eastleigh
Hampshire
SO50 9FD
Tel: 023 8068 4500
www.vtct.org.uk

International Therapy Examination Council
4 Heathfield Terrace
Chiswick
London
W4 4JE
Tel: 020 8994 4141
www.itecworld.co.uk

Get Into Theatre
www.getintotheatre.org

Hairdressing and Beauty Industry Authority (HABIA)
www.habia.org

Broadcasting Entertainment Cinematograph and Theatre Union (BECTU)
Tel: 0845 850 2502
ww.bectu.org.uk

****

16. THE POLICE FORCE

Jobs in the police force can be very rewarding indeed. However, you will need to be a certain type of person to fulfill what are demanding roles. There are a number of opportunities within the police force. In this chapter we cover:

- Police officer
- Police community support officer
- Forensic computer analyst

For the many other roles within the police service you should contact:

Police Recruitment Service

www.policerecruitment.homeoffice.uk
www. npia.police.uk

POLICE OFFICER

The nature of the work

You could work as a uniformed officer on foot or in a patrol car (known as on the beat), or at a police station. You would carry out a range of tasks, which could include:

- responding to calls for help from the public
- investigating crimes and offences, and making arrests
- interviewing witnesses and suspects, preparing crime reports and taking statements
- searching for missing people
- giving evidence in court
- going out to accidents and fires
- duties relating to custody
- working at the station reception desk dealing with the public
- two-way contact with officers on the beat from the communications room

- policing large public events, concerts and demonstrations
- visiting schools to give talks.

You would need to complete a trial (probationary) period as an officer. After that you could specialise in a specific branch such as the Criminal Investigation Department (CID), the drug squad or the traffic police.

What can you earn?

Salaries can vary between police forces. The starting salary is generally between £20,000 and £23,000 a year. With several years' experience, earnings can reach around £36,500 a year. A sergeant can earn around £40,000 a year and inspectors can earn around £50,000. There may be extra pay for working overtime. Police officers working in the London area may receive an additional cost of living payment.

Entry requirements

Police officer recruitment is handled by individual police forces, and their requirements can vary. In general you will need to:

- be a British citizen, a citizen of the Commonwealth, European Union (EU) or other European Economic Area (EEA) country, or a foreign national allowed to stay in the UK for an unlimited time.
- be at least 18 years old.
- pass background and security checks, and give details of any previous convictions.
- have above average physical fitness, and good vision and colour vision (with or without glasses or contact lenses).

In most cases, you will also need to have been resident in the UK for the three years before applying.

As well as meeting the standards above, you will also need to pass a series of tests before being accepted as a trainee police officer. These are in areas like working with numbers, communication, reading and writing skills, handling information, making decisions and making judgements. You will also have a physical fitness test and a health check.

As a probationer (trainee) or serving officer, you may be able to join the High Potential Development Scheme (HPDS). The scheme develops those with the potential to become future police leaders, and leads to a Masters qualification. Check the Police Service Recruitment website , or the National Policing Improvement Agency (NPIA) website for details.

More information

Police Recruitment Service
www.policerecruitment.homeoffice.uk
www. npia.police.uk

Scottish Police Forces
www.scottish.police.uk

Skills for Justice
Centre Court
Atlas Way
Sheffield
S4 7QQ
www.skillsforjustice.com

Police Service of Northern Ireland (PSNI)
http://www.joinpsni.co.uk/

Police Service Recruitment
www.policecouldyou.co.uk

POLICE COMMUNITY SUPPORT OFFICER

The nature of the work

Your duties would vary (depending on the needs of the police force and your local community), but they are likely to include:

- dealing with incidents of nuisance and anti-social behaviour, such as truants, vandalism and litter
- directing traffic and having vehicles removed
- guarding crime scenes
- offering advice on crime prevention
- issuing fixed penalty notices for anti-social behaviour
- detaining someone until a police officer arrives
- providing support at large public gatherings, such as sports events and public demonstrations
- other work relating to Neighbourhood Policing Teams and work around Anti-Social Behaviour
- work in partnership with other agencies.

You could work alone, in pairs or small teams, under the direction of the police commander in your area.

What can you earn?

Starting salaries can be around £16,000 a year. With experience, this can rise to around £19,000, plus a shift allowance. In some geographical areas PCSO salaries can be up to £25,000 a year.

Entry requirements

You will be selected for the role of PCSO based on your application and interview. You can apply if you have a permanent right to remain without restriction in the UK. Full security and reference checks will also be made.

Local police forces set their own entry requirements so the following is intended as a general guideline.

You will not usually need formal qualifications, but you will need good spoken and written communication skills. You need to be fit enough to carry out foot patrols, so you may be asked to take a fitness test.

A qualification in public service may give you an advantage when looking for work as a PCSO. Relevant qualifications include:

- NVQ Level 2 in Public Services
- BTEC First Diploma or National Diploma in Public Services
- BTEC National Certificate or Diploma in Uniformed Public Services
- foundation degree in Public Service.

Some police forces will also want you to have experience of working within the community (paid or voluntary), and it may be helpful if you have a driving licence.

Vetting of applicants is undertaken in line with HMG Personnel Security Controls. You can find local force contact details on the Police.uk site.

FORENSIC COMPUTER ANALYST

The nature of the work
As a forensic computer analyst, you could be involved in a range of investigations, such as:

- hacking, online scams and fraud
- political, industrial and commercial espionage
- terrorist communications
- possession of illegal pornography

You could work for the police or security services, a bank, or for an IT firm that specialises in computer security. You might also work in a broader security role, for example, testing the security of a company's information systems.

What can you earn?
Trainee forensic computer analysts can earn around £20,000 a year. Salaries for analysts with 12 months' experience can be between £25,000 and £35,000

a year. With four to five years' experience, this can rise to between £40,000 and £60,000 a year.

Entry requirements

To work as a forensic computer analyst you will need a background in IT. Employers may also ask for a degree, a postgraduate qualification or industry certification. For more details, see the Training and Development section.

You could start in this career by working for a company, for example as a network engineer or developer. By taking professional development courses and applying for opportunities as they come up, you may eventually be able to move into a more specialised security or analyst role.

You can find further information about this career on the Forums section of the Computer Forensics World website.

To get an idea of some of the technical skills you would need to apply, analysts suggest looking at the way different operating systems work and how they can be taken advantage of. You could download and practice on a free open-source system like Linux.

More information

Skills Framework for the Information Age (SFIA)
www.sfia.org.uk

UK Resource Centre for Women in Science, Engineering and Technology (UKRC)
Listerhills Park of Science and Commerce
40-42 Campus Road
Bradford
BD7 1HR
Tel: 01274 436485
www.theukrc.org

Skills for Justice
Centre Court

Atlas Way
Sheffield
S4 7QQ
www.skillsforjustice.com

e-skills UK
1 Castle Lane
London
SW1E 6DR
Tel: 020 7963 8920
www.e-skills.com

MI5 Careers
www.mi5careers.gov.uk

National Skills Academy for IT
www.itskillsacademy.ac.uk

****

17. RETAIL

The retail sector encompasses many and varied jobs. The work is challenging and can be exciting and the right candidates can forge a lively career in this area. Jobs vary from shop assistant to store managers and many more besides. in this section we look at:

- Retail Manager
- Sales Assistant
- Shopkeeper
- Store Demonstrator
- Post Office Customer Service Assistant
- Check Out operator
- Customer Service Assistant
- Customer Service Manager

For details of the numerous other opportunities in the area of retail you should go to:

Skillsmart Retail
Fourth Floor
93 Newman Street
London W1T 3EZ
Tel: 0800 093 5001
www.skillsmartretail.com

RETAIL MANAGER

The nature of the work

A retail manager is responsible for the day-to-day management of a store/retail outlet in line with overall company policy. The main focus of any retail manager's job is to improve the commercial performance of the store by increasing its turnover and maximising profitability. The major parts of the job on a day-to-day basis include managing and motivating staff, finding new ways to improve sales, and meeting customer demand.

Depending on the type of store and its opening times, unsociable hours are usually expected from weekends to late nights and early mornings. Managers are often in early to prepare for the day, and stay after closing to make sure systems and premises are closed down and secured properly. Some of your duties would depend on what the store sells and whether it is part of a chain, but your typical tasks would include:

- managing and motivating a team to increase sales including recruiting, training, day-to-day managing, appraisals, disciplining, dismissing, promotions and team building
- responsibility for maintaining the premises and displays
- organising stock checking and re-ordering as necessary, through computerised or manual systems
- organising sales and promotions
- dealing with queries, complaints and comments from customers
- analysing and interpreting consumer trends
- taking responsibility for seeing all security, health and safety and legal procedures
- analysing sales figures and forecasting future sales volumes to maximise profits
- ensuring standards for quality, customer service and health and safety are met
- regularly 'walking the sales floor' talking to colleagues and customers, and identifying or resolving urgent issues
- maintaining awareness of market trends in the retail industry, understanding forthcoming customer initiatives, and monitoring what local competitors are doing
- monitoring budgets and controlling expenditure
- dealing with takings and banking/security banking couriers
- serving customers when required.

What can you earn?

- Starting salaries start at around £20,000 a year

- With experience, typical earnings can rise to around £31,000
- Some senior store managers earn £47,000 a year.

You may also earn extra bonuses and commission for meeting sales targets.

Entry requirements

Entry requirements vary from company to company. Entrants may possess A levels/Highers or a degree or equivalent qualification. Experience of working with customers, especially in a retail environment, is very important and much more important in many cases than formal qualifications.

Entry is also possible through promotion – this is the most common entry method for store managers, entering as a retail sales assistant and through training and development gaining sufficient experience through the career path of sales assistant, supervisor, department manager, deputy store manager, store manager.

Apprenticeships and retail management schemes are also popular entry points for individuals with some retail experience who want to fast track their retail management career – individuals undertaking this path normally enter a store manager position after developing experience as a department manager and deputy store manager during their training.

Some national retail businesses run graduate trainee management schemes for entrants with a suitable degree. These are usually a combination of skills training and work placement in one or more of a company's stores. Individuals undertaking this path normally enter a store manager position after developing experience as a department manager and deputy store manager during their training.

More information

Skillsmart Retail
Fourth Floor
93 Newman Street
London W1T 3EZ

Tel: 0800 093 5001
www.skillsmartretail.com

SALES ASSISTANT

The nature of the work

To be a good sales assistant it's important that you're able to work as part of a team, and that you're helpful, friendly and polite. You also need to reliable, honest and responsible.

The places you could work include supermarkets, fashion stores and department stores, and you could be:

- serving and advising customers
- taking payment
- helping customers to find the goods they want
- advising on stock amounts
- giving information on products and prices
- stacking shelves or displaying goods in an attractive way
- arranging window displays
- promoting special offers or store cards
- ordering goods
- handling complaints or passing them on to a manager.

Some stores, for example mobile phone shops, DIY or electrical goods stores, would usually expect you to have a lot of knowledge about their products before you apply.

What can you earn?

- Full-time salaries can be between £11,000 and £15,000 a year
- Supervisors can earn between £15,000 and £20,000 a year

Many larger retail companies also offer benefits like staff discounts, extra pay depending on how much you sell (known as commission) and bonus schemes.

Entry requirements

When applying for jobs, it will help you if you already have experience of working with the public and of handling cash. Many stores employ temporary staff at busy times such as Christmas, and this can be a good way of getting experience that can lead to a permanent job.

You may be able to start this career through an Apprenticeship scheme. You will need to check which schemes run in your local area.

For more information, visit the Apprenticeships website.

More information

Skillsmart Retail
Fourth Floor
93 Newman Street
London
W1T 3EZ
Tel: 0800 093 5001
www.skillsmartretail.com

SHOPKEEPER

The nature of the work

Unlike sales assistants or store managers (who usually work for a large retailer), shopkeepers will normally have overall responsibility for a store. Independent retailers that employ shopkeepers include; green grocers, newsagents, butchers, bakers, booksellers, florists, and antique dealers.

As a shopkeeper, you would serve customers (either at a counter or checkout) and carry out other duties such as:

- taking payments, giving change and wrapping purchases
- answering enquiries and giving advice about products to customers

- listening to customers' needs and requests, which can indicate new sales opportunities
- calculating takings and wages
- depositing cash at the bank, book-keeping and stocktaking
- ordering stock from wholesalers, manufacturers, agents and importers.

Running your own shop would also involve keeping up to date with issues such as:

- your competitors' prices and products and using this knowledge to set the rates in your own shop
- the regulations covering trading and running a business, for example VAT and national insurance payments.

What can you earn?

Earnings can range from £13,000 to £30,000 a year. Income depends on the nature and size of the business, the product or service, and the shopkeeper's ability to make the business work in its location.

Entry requirements

You will not need any specific academic qualifications to become a shopkeeper. However, you will need good maths skills, people management and business skills. Experience of shop work, sales, administration or management would be particularly useful.

You could prepare for working as a shopkeeper by taking a part-time or short course in a subject such as sales or starting a business. You would also need financial backing in order to buy the business.

The Business Link network offers a range of business support and development services, including information about finding and setting up premises, VAT and tax, and becoming an employer.

More information

Scottish Enterprise
Tel: 0845 607 8787
www.scottish-enterprise.com

Skillsmart Retail
Fourth Floor
93 Newman Street
London
W1T 3EZ
Tel: 0800 093 5001
www.skillsmartretail.com

Business Link
Tel: 0845 600 9006
www.businesslink.gov.uk

British Independent Retailers Association
225 Bristol Road
Edgbaston
Birmingham
West Midlands
B5 7UB
www.bira.co.uk

STORE DEMONSTRATOR

The nature of the work

Store demonstrators work in department stores, supermarkets and other retail businesses, introducing products (which may new to the market or on promotion) to customers to help increase sales. They may demonstrate a wide range of different products including food and drink, domestic appliances, kitchen gadgets, cleaning products, beauty products, DIY products and tools, home improvement products and toys. Some may sell these products directly, while others may pass sales leads onto other sales team members depending on the type of product, venue and size of the organisation. Your job might involve:

- Setting up a counter or other area where demonstrations take place
- Arranging stock, posters and other publicity material to attract customers
- Demonstrating how to use a product
- Explaining the benefits of a product and answering questions about it
- Handing out leaflets, brochures, coupons and free samples
- Selling products, or passing customers to other members of the sales team.
- Talking to individual passers-by, or using a microphone to catch the attention of groups of people
- Monitoring stock levels
- Keeping sales records

You could be employed full-time by a store or retail chain, or you may be freelance and find work through an agency.

What can you earn?

- Store demonstrators starting out may earn between £10,000 and £11,000
- More experienced staff may earn around £13,500
- The highest salary for a store demonstrator in a retail chain is around £18,000 to £19,000
- Some store demonstrators earn commission or productivity bonuses. There may be other benefits such as free products, discounts and petrol allowances
- Freelanceand part-time work usually pays around £6 an hour or £60 up to £240 a day for senior specialised product demonstrators

Entry requirements

It is possible to become a store demonstrator without formal qualifications, but a lot of employers look for evidence of literacy, numeracy and excellent communication skills. Mature candidates with retail or customer service experience and great people skills are warmly welcomed. Recruiters look for people with good communication skills and an enthusiastic attitude.

You will find it useful to have previous experience of dealing with the public, and previous experience of working in retail, customer service and talking to groups of people may be required by some employers.

Although you do not usually need formal qualifications to work as a store demonstrator, for demonstrating certain products you may need to have undertaken specific training such as a Level 2 Award in Food Safety for Retail/ Manufacturing to work with unwrapped food products.

More information

Skillsmart Retail
Fourth Floor
93 Newman Street
London
W1T 3EZ
Tel: 0800 093 5001
www.skillsmartretail.com

POST OFFICE CUSTOMER SERVICE ASSISTANT

The nature of the work

Customer service assistants provide a wide range of services offered at main post offices. They may sometimes be known as post office counter clerks, or counter sales assistants.

As a customer service assistant, your day-to-day duties would include:

- selling stamps and dealing with letters and parcels
- paying out pensions and benefits
- banking and savings services

- accepting bill payments
- dealing with vehicle registrations and issuing tax discs
- travel services, such as checking passport applications and selling travel insurance and foreign currency.

In a main post office (or postshop) you would be involved in selling and advising customers on a wider range of products.

What can you earn?

- Salaries can be between £13,000 and £17,500 a year
- Post Office managers may earn up to £24,000.

Pay may vary according to the location of the post office. An allowance is paid for working in London.

Entry requirements

You do not need any specific qualifications to work in a post office, however, to pass the selection tests you are likely to need a reasonable standard of secondary education. GCSEs (A-D) in maths and English would be an advantage.

The first stage of the selection process is an online questionnaire to test your accuracy and number skills, followed by a telephone interview. If you pass these tests you will then be invited to attend a face-to-face interview.

Previous customer service experience in banks, building societies or retail would be particularly helpful.

More information

Royal Mail Group PLC
100 Victoria Embankment
London
EC4Y 0HQ
www.royalmailgroup.com

Post Office Limited
Helpline: 0845 722 3344
www.postoffice.co.uk

CHECKOUT OPERATOR

The nature of the work

If you enjoy being in a busy environment and like talking to different people, this job could be just right for you. As a checkout operator you would work on a till serving customers. This could be in a supermarket, convenience store or large retail store. They help customers with items that they have chosen and take payment for goods.

As a checkout operator, your work would normally include:

- Operating a computerised till system that has a barcode scanner
- Entering prices into the till system by scanning items chosen by customers
- Weighing and pricing certain items, such as fruit and vegetables
- Using special tools to remove security tags
- Packing and wrapping purchases
- Processing store loyalty cards, coupons and vouchers
- Taking payment.

You may also spend time away from the till, filling shelves, checking stock or working on a customer service desk.

You would need to work quickly and efficiently so that other customers in the queue do not have to wait too long. You would also need to be aware of some aspects of retail law, such as the age restrictions on buying goods like alcohol and knives. Working accurately is important, as the till must balance at the end of the day.

What can you earn?

Salaries for checkout operators may start at around £10,500 a year. More experienced staff may earn between £11,500 and £12,500, and a supervisor may earn around £16,000 a year. Some checkout operators receive benefits such as staff discounts and subsidised canteen meals.

Entry requirements

You do not usually need any qualifications to become a checkout operator, however you will need to have numeracy and communication skills. Some companies may want you to have four or more GCSEs (A*-C)/Standard Grades including maths and English. Employers like to see enthusiasm and good people skills, and it would help you if you have experience of handling cash and serving customers.

Qualifications that could be useful include:

- Level 1 Award or Certificate / SVQ in Retail Skills
- Level 1 or 2 Award, Certificate or Diploma in Retail Knowledge / SCQF Level 5 Certificate in Retail Knowledge.

You may be able to do this job through an Apprenticeship scheme. You will need to check which schemes are available in your area. To find out more, see the Apprenticeships website.

More information

Skillsmart Retail
Fourth Floor
93 Newman Street
London
W1T 3EZ
Tel: 0800 093 5001
www.skillsmartretail

CUSTOMER SERVICE ASSISTANT

The nature of the work

As a customer service assistant or adviser, you would deal with customer enquiries and any complaints. You would often be a customer's first point of contact with the company you work for.

Your work may include:

- answering customer enquiries or passing them on to another department
- giving information and helping to solve problems
- selling products or taking orders
- arranging services for customers, such as booking tickets or setting up insurance policies
- handling complaints and passing them on to a manager if required
- entering customer information onto a computer database
- taking payment for goods or services
- giving refunds.

What can you earn?

Salaries are around £18,000 a year for full-time work. Bonuses or commission may also be available in some types of business, like retail, sales or banking.

Entry requirements

Many employers will be more interested in your 'people skills' than your formal qualifications, although you should have a good general standard of education. You will find it useful if you have some experience of dealing with people face-to-face or over the telephone.

Some employers, such as banks and insurance companies, may ask for some GCSEs (A-C) or higher qualifications such as A levels or BTEC National Certificates/Diplomas.

You may be able to start this work through an Apprenticeship scheme. You will need to check which schemes are available in your area. For more information, visit the Apprenticeships website.

More information

Skillsmart Retail
Fourth Floor
93 Newman Street
London
W1T 3EZ
Tel: 0800 093 5001
www.skillsmartretail.com

Institute of Customer Service (ICS)
2 Castle Court
St Peter's St
Colchester
Essex
CO1 1EW
Tel. 01206 571716
www.instituteofcustomerservice.com

CUSTOMER SERVICE MANAGER

The nature of the work

As a customer services manager, it would be your job to make sure that customers' needs and expectations are satisfied. You could be responsible for anything from managing a customer service team and dealing with enquiries in person, to developing customer service standards for a large company.

Your typical duties would include:

- Helping to develop or update customer service policies and procedures

- Managing or leading a team of customer services staff
- Handling enquiries from customers
- Handling complaints from customers
- Advising customers on the organisation's products
- Investigating and solving customer problems escalated from other customer service staff
- Liaising with customers regarding an unexpected event, such as a security issue, a recall, or a customer being taken ill
- Authorising refunds or other compensation to customers
- Ensuring accurate records are kept of communications with customers
- Analysing key metrics to determine how well customers are being served
- Meeting with management to report on customer service and discuss improvements
- Preparing or writing information for customers
- Developing or improving feedback or complaints procedures
- Helping to recruit, train and appraise new staff
- Keeping up to date with the company's products
- Keeping up to date with developments in customer service best practice e.g. by reading journals, attending meetings and courses and any changes in relevant legislation.

What can you earn?

- Entry-level customer service managers may earn £15,000 to £25,000
- An experienced customer service manager may earn £25,000 to £40,000.

Bonuses or commission may also be available in some sectors like retail, sales or banking.

Figures are intended as a guideline only.

Entry requirements

There are no formal academic requirements to work in customer services, as most employers are more interested in 'people skills' and a positive attitude.

However, employers may require some GCSEs (or Standard Grades in Scotland), in particular English and maths, to demonstrate literacy and numeracy. Previous experience of working in a customer-facing role is valuable. Most people start as customer service assistants, and becoming a manager means demonstrating that you are willing and able to take on additional responsibility.

Apprenticeship schemes may be available, and are a great way to get into retail. Some firms offer customer services management training schemes, available to candidates with more GCSEs/Standard Grades or higher qualifications.

More information

Institute of Customer Service (ICS)
2 Castle Court
St Peter's St
Colchester
Essex
CO1 1EW
Tel. 01206 571716
www.instituteofcustomerservice.com

Institute of Leadership and Management (ILM)
Stowe House
Netherstowe
Lichfield
Staffordshire
WS13 6TJ
Tel: 01543 266867
www.i-l-m.com

Chartered Management Institute (CMI)
Management House
Cottingham Road
Corby
Northants
NN17 1TT

Tel: 01536 204222
www.managers.org.uk

Skillsmart Retail
Fourth Floor
93 Newman Street
London
W1T 3EZ
Tel: 0800 093 5001
www.skillsmartretail.com

18. SOCIAL WORK

This chapter covers five main social work jobs:

- Social worker
- Assistant social worker
- Residential social worker
- Drug and alcohol worker
- Youth and Community worker

The area of social work is very wide and there are other opportunities available. For information on the numerous other roles available contact:

General Social Care Council
2 Hay's Lane
London SE1 2HB
Registration helpline: 0845 070 0630

Skills for Care (England)
Albion Court 5
Albion Place Leeds
LS1 6JL
Tel: 0113 245 1716
www.skillsforcare.org.uk

SOCIAL WORKER

The nature of the work
As a social worker, you would provide people with advice and emotional support, and arrange care services to help people.

You could support a wide range of social service users, including:

- children and parents under pressure
- older people

- people with physical or learning disabilities
- people with mental health problems
- young adults
- homeless people
- people leaving hospital who need help to live independently
- people with drug or alcohol dependency.

You would normally specialise in working with children and families, or with adult service users.

What can you earn?

Starting salaries are often around £19,500 to £25,000 a year.

With more experience and responsibility, this can rise to between £26,000 and £40,000.

Entry requirements

To become a social worker in England, you will need to take a three-year undergraduate degree or a two-year postgraduate degree in social work that is approved by the General Social Care Council (GSCC). Many university courses are full time, although some work-based routes with part-time study may also be available. You will typically need the following qualifications in order to study for an undergraduate degree in social work:

- five GCSEs (A-C) including English and maths

- at least two A levels, or an equivalent such as a BTEC National Diploma or NVQ Level 3 in Health and Social Care.

However, you should check entry requirements as colleges and universities may accept alternatives like an Access to Higher Education qualification or substantial relevant work experience (paid or voluntary).

If you already have a degree, you could do a two-year postgraduate Masters degree in social work. All postgraduate Masters degrees in social work need to be applied for via the Universities and Colleges Admissions Service (UCAS).

For information on how to qualify as a social worker in Northern Ireland, see the Northern Ireland Social Care Council website.

Employment-based routes

Some local authorities may sponsor employees already working for them in a social care support role to take the social work degree part-time or through distance learning. Some local authorities also recruit people directly into work-based training schemes for new social workers. Check in your local area to see if schemes like these are available.

More information

General Social Care Council
2 Hay's Lane
London SE1 2HB
Registration helpline: 0845 070 0630

Skills for Care (England)
Albion Court 5
Albion Place Leeds
LS1 6JL
Tel: 0113 245 1716
www.skillsforcare.org.uk

Northern Ireland Social Care Council (NISCC)
www.niscc.info

Care Council for Wales (CCW)
www.ccwales.org.uk

Scottish Social Services Council (SSSC)
www.sssc.uk.com

NHS Business Services Authority

(NHSBSA) Social Work Bursary
Tel: 0845 610 1122
www.nhsbsa.nhs.uk/Students

SOCIAL WORK ASSISTANT

The nature of the work

As a social work assistant, you could work with a variety of people (known as clients), including:

- families under stress
- older people
- people with physical or learning disabilities
- people with mental health problems
- children at risk.

You may be known by other job titles, such as community support worker, home care officer or social services assistant.

What can you earn?

Starting salaries can be around £16,000 a year. With experience and relevant qualifications, salaries can rise to between £19,000 and £25,000.

Those taking on additional management responsibilities may earn up to £28,000 a year.

You may work for a specialist recruitment agency. Hourly rates for agency work can be between £8 and £14.

Entry requirements

You will increase your chances of finding work if you have some experience (paid or voluntary) of working with people in a caring role. You can get more information and search for volunteering opportunities on the Do-it website.

Employers will usually consider experience to be more important than your qualifications, although they may ask for a good standard of secondary education.

Before looking for work, you may find it helpful to take a full-time or part-time college course such as a BTEC National Certificate or Diploma in Health and Social Care. This is not essential, but most social care courses include work placements so this can be a good way of getting useful experience.

For any job where you would be working (paid or unpaid) with children or vulnerable adults, you will need to pass background checks by the Criminal Records Bureau (CRB). Previous convictions or cautions may not automatically prevent you from working in social care. A driving licence would be useful for jobs based in the community.

More information

Skills for Care (England)
West Gate
6 Grace Street
Leeds
LS1 2RP
Tel: 0113 245 1716
www.skillsforcare.org.uk

General Social Care Council
2 Hay's Lane
London SE1 2HB
Tel: 020 7397 5800
Registration helpline: 0845 070 0630
www.gscc.org.uk

Northern Ireland Social Care Council (NISCC)
www.niscc.info

Care Council for Wales (CCW)
www.ccwales.org.uk

Scottish Social Services Council (SSSC)
www.sssc.uk.com

Department for Education - Children and Young People
Castle View House
East Lane
Runcorn
Cheshire

RESIDENTIAL SUPPORT WORKER

The nature of the work

As a residential support worker, your clients could include children in care or adults with physical or learning disabilities, mental health problems, addiction issues or other emotional or social needs.

With experience, you could have extra responsibilities including supervising and leading a team, and managing a budget.

What can you earn?

Full-time salaries can be around £13,000 to £18,000 a year. Senior support workers can earn between £19,000 and £24,000 a year. Hourly rates for part-time and contract work can be between £7 and £14.

Salaries may be lower in the private sector.

Entry requirements

To work in residential support, you will need paid or voluntary experience in the social work and care sector. You could get relevant experience in a number of ways, such as:

- working or volunteering at a youth club
- personal experience of caring for a family member
- working as a social work assistant
- paid or voluntary work in a care home, nursery or relevant charity.

You can get more information and search for volunteering opportunities on the Do-it website.

Most social care employers will be more interested in your work and life experience than formal qualifications. However, before you look for paid work, you may find it helpful to take a college course in health and social care, youth work or childcare. This could be, for example, a BTEC National Certificate or Diploma in Health and Social Care or the 14-19 Diploma in Society, Health and Development.

Taking a social care qualification is not essential for finding work, but most courses include work placements so this could be a good way of getting experience.

Relevant qualifications are widely available at local colleges. You could do these full-time or part-time.

For any job where you would be working (paid or unpaid) with children or vulnerable adults, you will need to pass background checks by the Criminal Records Bureau (CRB). Previous convictions or cautions may not automatically prevent you from working in social care. See the CRB website for details.

More information

General Social Care Council
2 Hay's Lane
London
SE1 2HB
Tel: 020 7397 5800
Registration helpline: 0845 070 0630
www.gscc.org.uk

Skills for Care (England)

West Gate
6 Grace Street
Leeds
LS1 2RP

Tel: 0113 245 1716

www.skillsforcare.org.uk

Northern Ireland Social Care Council (NISCC)

www.niscc.info

Care Council for Wales (CCW)

www.ccwales.org.uk

Scottish Social Services Council (SSSC)

www.sssc.uk.com

Department for Education - Children and Young People

Castle View House

East Lane

Runcorn

Cheshire

WA7 2GJ

Tel: 0370 000 2288

www.education.gov.uk/childrenandyoungpeople

DRUG AND ALCOHOL WORKER

If you want to help people, and you are a calm and caring person, this job could be ideal for you. As a drug and alcohol worker, you would help people tackle their drug, alcohol or solvent misuse problems.

The nature of the work

As a drug and alcohol worker (also known as a substance misuse worker), you would help people tackle and recover from their dependence on drugs (illegal, prescription and over-the-counter), alcohol or solvents.

You would help clients to access services such as counselling, healthcare and education. Your job could also cover: out reach work – encouraging people (clients) with substance misuse problems to make contact with support services, assessing clients to understand their drug or alcohol misuse and identifying suitable ways of moving them towards recovery; counselling and rehabilitation – giving support and dealing with the causes of substance misuse; arrest referral work – supporting clients arrested for drug-related offences;; education and training – helping client access services to help them with reading, writing, maths, IT and job search skills; healthcare – working as a specialist nurse in an addiction clinic, where you might prescribe medication and supervise detox programmes; advocacy – helping clients to use housing, employment and healthcare services, and speaking up for clients in the justice system

In some jobs you may cover several of these areas or you might specialise.

What can you earn?

Employment officers, and outreach and drop-in centre workers earn between £20,000 and £25,000 a year. Counsellors and specialist nursing staff can earn between £23,000 and £28,000 a year, and team leaders and local service managers can earn up to £35,000 a year.

Entry requirements

You could have a variety of backgrounds for starting in this role, such as nursing, criminal justice, social care, youth work or counselling. For example, you may have dealt with drug or alcohol-dependent patients as a nurse, or worked in the probation service dealing with offenders after their release.

If you have personal experience of addiction or dependency you could also apply for this type of work, as applications are usually welcome from people who have been through treatment successfully.

Volunteering is an excellent way to gain relevant experience, make contacts and eventually find paid work. It gives the employer a chance to see your skills and motivation, and lets you decide whether this is the career for you. Most drug and alcohol support organisations offer volunteering opportunities and training.

You can find volunteering opportunities by contacting local substance misuse organisations. You can also visit the Do-it or Talktofrank websites to search for organisations by postcode or town.

For more information about working in this field, see the Federation of Drug & Alcohol Professionals (FDAP), DrugScope and Alcohol Concern websites.

More information

Federation of Drug & Alcohol Professionals
www.fdap.org.uk

DrugScope
www.drugscope.org.uk

Alcohol Concern
www.alcoholconcern.org.uk

YOUTH AND COMMUNITY WORKER

The nature of the work

You would generally work with young people aged 13 to 19, although in some jobs they might be as young as 11, or up to age 25. Your tasks would depend on the needs of the young people, but might include:

- organising sports, arts, drama and other activities
- advising and supporting young people
- offering counselling
- working with specific groups, such as young carers or those at risk of offending
- developing and running projects that deal with issues like health, bullying, crime or drugs
- managing volunteers and part-time workers
- keeping records and controlling budgets
- trying to get grants and funding

You might also be making contact with young people in meeting places like parks, shopping centres and on the streets. This is known as detached youth work.

What can you earn?

Youth support workers (those who are not fully qualified youth workers) can earn between £15,000 and £18,000 a year for full-time work. Salaries for qualified youth workers are usually between £22,000 and £34,000 a year. Senior and management salaries can be from £35,000.

Entry requirements

To become a professional youth worker in England you will need to gain at least a BA Honours degree in youth work that is recognised by the National Youth Agency (NYA). Depending on your previous qualifications, you could take either a BA Honours degree (three years full-time, or longer part-time) or a postgraduate certificate, diploma or MA if you already have a degree in any subject (one year full-time, or longer part-time)

Degree course entry requirements can vary, so check with each university or college. You may be accepted without formal qualifications if you have relevant work experience and the potential to succeed on the course.

If you have previous youth and community work qualifications at Diploma of Higher Education (Dip HE) or Foundation Degree level, you will not need to gain a degree in order to stay qualified.

It is important for you to get experience (paid or unpaid) of working with young people. You will often need at least one year's experience in order to apply for professional youth work courses and jobs. Find out about local opportunities for voluntary or part-time youth work by contacting your local youth service or by visiting the Do-it website.

Another option is to start as a part-time or volunteer youth support worker without any qualifications. You could then take work-based qualifications in youth support work, and if you wanted to, you could complete professional youth work training later on.

More information

National Youth Agency
Eastgate House 19-23
Humberstone Road Leicester
LE5 3GJ
www.nya.org.uk

Youth Council for Northern Ireland
Forestview Purdy's Lane Belfast
BT8 7AR
Tel: 028 9064 3882
www.ycni.org/

****

19· SPORT AND LEISURE

Sport related jobs are becoming more popular with young people and provide an entry into what is a fascinating area of employment. In this section we cover:

- Fitness Instructor
- Health Trainer
- Outdoor Activities Instructor
- Personal Trainer
- Sports Physiotherapist
- Swimming Coach/Teacher

For more details of opportunities in the sport and outdoors fields go to:

SkillsActive
Castlewood House
77-91 New Oxford Street
London
WC1A 1PX
Advice line: 08000 933300
www.skillsactive.com

FITNESS INSTRUCTOR

The nature of the work

As a fitness instructor, you would lead and organise group and individual exercise programmes to help people (clients) to improve their health and fitness. Your work could involve a range of activities or you could specialise in a particular one, like:

- keep fit
- aquacise (exercise in water)
- weight training

- yoga
- Pilates

You could also work with specialist groups of people, such as older adults, children, people with disabilities or people referred by doctors.

Your job could include:

- fitness assessments, consultations and introduction sessions for new clients
- demonstrating activities for clients to follow
- showing clients how to use exercise machines and free weights properly
- supervising clients to make sure that they are exercising safely and effectively
- leading group exercise classes, such as circuit training, aerobics or spinning
- creating personal exercise programmes
- giving advice on healthy eating and lifestyle

In smaller health or fitness clubs you may also carry out routine duties, such as at reception and the swimming pool, and health and safety checks.

What can you earn?

Starting salaries can be around £13,000 a year. This can rise to between £14,000 and over £20,000 a year. Freelance instructors can earn £10 to £20 an hour.

Entry requirements

To qualify as a fitness instructor, you could:

- either complete a nationally recognised qualification before starting work
- or start as an assistant instructor and complete work-based qualifications

Nationally recognised qualification

The Level 2 Certificate in Fitness Instructing is the preferred industry standard, and is approved by the Register of Exercise Professionals (also known as the Exercise Register). There are four categories for this certificate - gym, exercise to music, aqua, and physical activity for children.

The qualification will allow you to join the Register of Exercise Professionals (REPs) at level 2, which will show employers that you are competent and qualified to do your job. See the REPs website for more information.

Before you can work as an instructor, you will also need public liability insurance and a first aid certificate, which includes a cardiopulmonary resuscitation (CPR) certificate.

If you plan to work with children or other vulnerable groups, you will need Criminal Records Bureau (CRB) clearance. See the CRB website for details.

Work-based qualifications

You may be able to start as an assistant instructor and complete qualifications whilst working under the supervision of a qualified instructor. When you have completed your qualification you can apply to join the REPs at level 2.

You may be able to start in this job through an Apprenticeship scheme. You will need to check which schemes are available in your area. For more information about Apprenticeships, visit the Apprenticeships website.

More information

Register of Exercise Professionals (REPs)
3rd Floor
8-10 Crown Hill
Croydon
Surrey
CR0 1RZ
Tel: 020 8686 6464
www.exerciseregister.org

OCR Information Bureau
Tel: 024 7685 1509
www.ocr.org.uk

SkillsActive
Castlewood House
77-91 New Oxford Street
London
WC1A 1PX
Advice line: 08000 933300
www.skillsactive.com

YMCA Fitness Industry Training
www.ymcafit.org.uk

Vocational Training Charitable Trust (VTCT) 🖵
3rd Floor
Eastleigh House
Upper Market Street
Eastleigh
Hampshire
SO50 9FD
Tel: 023 8068 4500
www.vtct.org.uk

Central YMCA Qualifications (CYQ)
www.cyq.org.uk

Active IQ
www.activeiq.co.uk

City & Guilds
1 Giltspur Street
London
EC1A 9DD
Tel: 0844 543 0000
www.cityandguilds.com

NCFE
www.ncfe.org.uk

Edexcel
www.edexcel.com

HEALTH TRAINER

The nature of the work

As a health trainer, you would advise people about healthier lifestyle choices in order to improve their general health and wellbeing.

Your work within the community could focus on issues such as:

- improving the amount of exercise people take
- the importance of practising safe sex
- helping people stop smoking
- the positive effects of lowering alcohol intake
- the benefits of breastfeeding
- improving access to healthy lifestyles in communities with the greatest needs.

You would encourage people to understand and adapt their behaviour by providing information and practical support on a one-to-one basis, as well as in groups. Your work to improve the health of the community could also include:

- connecting people to relevant local services
- helping people understand how their behaviour effects their health
- supporting and motivating individuals to change harmful habits
- explaining the benefits of healthier food and lifestyle choices
- encouraging greater community integration and sense of togetherness
- recording activity levels and results, and using these to motivate clients.

What can you earn?

- Health trainers can earn between £15,600 and £18,600 a year
- Supervisors can earn between £21,000 and £27,500.

Many health trainer jobs are offered on a part-time basis, so earnings would be a portion of full-time rates (known as 'pro rata' payment). This means that actual annual income may be less than above.

Entry requirements

To become a health trainer, you will need:

- knowledge of the health issues facing the community
- good communication skills in English (and for some jobs, a second community language)
- experience (paid or voluntary) of working with local community groups.

For advice on voluntary opportunities, you can contact the voluntary services coordinator or manager at your local NHS Trust.

Some employers will prefer you to have GCSE grade C in English, and you may also be asked for an NVQ Level 3 or equivalent qualification.

You could have an advantage when looking for work if you have qualifications or work experience in an area such as:

- personal training
- fitness instructing
- nutritional therapy or dietetics.

See the related job profiles for details about qualifications and training in these careers.

More information

Skills for Health
Goldsmiths House
Broad Plain
Bristol
BS2 0JP
Tel: 0117 922 1155
www.skillsforhealth.org.uk

NHS Careers
PO Box 2311
Bristol
BS2 2ZX
Tel: 0345 60 60 655
www.nhscareers.nhs.uk

Health Learning and Skills Advice Line
Tel: 08000 150850

OUTDOOR ACTIVITIES INSTRUCTOR

The nature of the work

As an outdoor activities instructor, you could provide:

- activities to help people enjoy their leisure time
- self-development activities
- courses for youth, social and probation services

Your work would include:

- planning and preparing activities to suit needs, and abilities
- explaining, advising on and demonstrating activities
- instructing in one or more specialist areas, such as sailing or climbing
- making sure that all equipment and facilities are safe

- explaining safety procedures
- checking weather conditions, assessing hazards and managing risks.

You may also have to deal with accidents, and support people who may be nervous about taking part in activities.

What can you earn?

Starting salaries can be around £12,000 a year.

Experienced instructors can earn around £18,000 a year, and senior instructors can earn £25,000 a year or more.

Accommodation and food may be provided.

Figures are intended as a guideline only.

Entry requirements

You should be at least 18 (21 if you need to drive a minibus) and would usually need:

- skill in at least one outdoor activity - although the more activities you can offer the better
- coaching or instructor qualifications approved by the relevant national governing body
- a first aid certificate
- a life-saving certificate if you instruct water-based activities.

If you will be working with children, young people or other vulnerable groups, you will need Criminal Records Bureau (CRB) clearance.

It would be useful if you can drive a minibus and tow a trailer, as you may need to transport equipment.

It may also help you if you have been involved in activities such as Duke of Edinburgh's awards, membership of activity clubs, or volunteering at outdoor activities centres. Some instructors have previous experience in youth work, teaching, sports coaching or training, or as physical training instructors in the armed forces.

Examples of instructor qualifications include:

- Mountain Leaders Training Board Mountain Leader Award
- British Canoe Union Level 2 Coach Award (kayak, canoe or both)
- Ski Instructor and Snowboard Instructor qualifications.

You could complete the qualifications through sports or activity clubs, or at an accredited outdoor education centre. You would usually need at least 12 months' experience in the activity before you take the award. Check with the NGB for your sport for details of courses and qualifications. NGB contact details are on the Sport England website.

You may be able to complete NGB qualifications as part of a college or university course in sport, leisure and recreation. Courses include BTEC National and Higher National Certificates and Diplomas, foundation degrees and degrees and postgraduate qualifications.

See the Outdoor Sourcebook produced by the Institute for Outdoor Learning's (IOL) for details of colleges, universities and other organisations offering training for outdoor activities. The IOL website also has careers information and a job section.

More information

sports coach UK
www.sportscoachuk.org

SkillsActive
Castlewood House
77-91 New Oxford Street
London
WC1A 1PX
Advice line: 08000 933300
www.skillsactive.com

Institute for Outdoor Learning (IOL)
Warwick Mill Business Centre
Warwick Bridge
Carlisle
Cumbria
CA4 8RR
Tel: 01228 564580
www.outdoor-learning.org

PERSONAL TRAINER

The nature of the work

To become a personal trainer you would first need to be a fitness instructor with a high level of experience and advanced qualifications.

As a personal trainer, you would first talk to clients to find out about their fitness level and health history. You would then:

- set realistic short-term and long-term goals and plan programmes
- give clients advice on health, nutrition and lifestyle changes
- help clients with their workouts
- check and record clients' progress. In some cases you might work full-time as a gym instructor and do personal training outside your normal hours of work.

What can you earn?

Personal trainers are usually paid by the hour for each session with a client. There are no set salary scales and earnings depend on location, number of clients and whether the trainer is self-employed or works for a gym. Self-employed (also known as freelance) instructors can earn between £20 and £40 an hour. Some instructors with high profile clients can earn between £50 and £100 an hour.

Personal trainers in full time employment can earn between £18,000 and £40,000 a year.

Entry requirements

To become a personal trainer you would first need to be a fitness instructor with a high level of experience and advanced qualifications (at least a level 3 certificate).

Doing a course that allows you to be a member of the Register of Exercise Professionals (REPs) will improve your chances of employment. Membership of REPs shows employers and clients that you are a competent instructor who has recognised qualifications and meets good standards of practice. REPs is also known as the Exercise Register.

You can join the REPs at different levels, depending on your qualifications. With a Level 3 Certificate in Personal Training you can join at level 3. You can complete industry-recognised awards offered by some employers and universities, and you can complete courses through a number of colleges and private training providers. See the REPs website for information about membership and for details of qualifications and approved training providers.

You can also find advice on choosing courses on the National Register of Personal Trainers website.

Another option is to do relevant BTEC HNCs or HNDs, foundation degrees, degrees and postgraduate qualifications in exercise and sports science, sports therapy or sports studies. If you have a relevant degree and at least six months' up-to-date work experience you may be given provisional REPs membership at level 3. To gain full membership, you will need to show competence by completing a work-based qualification.

To work as a personal trainer you must have public liability insurance and a first aid certificate. This must include a cardio-pulmonary resuscitation certificate (CPR).

You may be able to do this job through an Apprenticeship scheme. You will need to check which schemes are available in your area. For more information, visit the Apprenticeships website.

More information

Register of Exercise Professionals (REPs)
3rd Floor 8-10 Crown Hill
Croydon
Surrey
CR0 1RZ
Tel: 020 8686 6464
www.exerciseregister.org

OCR
Tel: 024 7685 1509
www.ocr.org.uk

SkillsActive
Castlewood House
77-91 New Oxford Street
London
WC1A 1PX
Advice line: 08000 933300
www.skillsactive.com

YMCAfit
www.ymcafit.org.uk

Vocational Training Charitable Trust (VTCT)
3rd Floor
Eastleigh House
Upper Market Street
Eastleigh
Hampshire
SO50 9FD

Tel: 023 8068 4500

www.vtct.org.uk

Central YMCA Qualifications (CYQ)

www.cyq.org.uk

Active IQ

www.activeiq.co.uk

City & Guilds

www.cityandguilds.com

NCFE

www.ncfe.org.uk

National Register of Personal Trainers

www.nrpt.co.uk

SPORTS PHYSIOTHERAPIST

The nature of the work

To become a sports physiotherapist, you will need to have an interest in health science. You will need good communication and 'people' skills. You will also have the ability to look after the health and well being of patients.

As a sports physiotherapist, you could work with top professional sports people, amateurs or people who do sports as a leisure activity.

Your work would include:

- examining and diagnosing injuries
- planning treatment programmes
- using treatments such as manipulation, massage and heat treatment
- advising how long it could take to return to sport after injury
- keeping full records of patients' treatment and progress.

If you deal with sports professionals, you would work in a team with coaches, other health care professionals and sports scientists. You could specialise in a particular sport, or in a particular aspect of physiotherapy, such as rehabilitation.

What can you earn?

Physiotherapists working in the NHS earn between £20,710 and £26,839 a year. Specialist physiotherapists earn between £24,331 and £33,436 a year. Visit the NHS Careers website for full salary scales for physiotherapists in the NHS. Salaries in the private sector can be similar but may be higher.

Entry requirements

To become a sports physiotherapist, you first need to qualify as a chartered physiotherapist by completing a physiotherapy degree approved by the Health Professions Council (HPC). When you have completed the degree, you will be eligible for state registration and membership of the Chartered Society of Physiotherapy (CSP).

See the HPC and CSP websites for details of approved degree courses. Entry requirements may vary, so check with individual colleges or universities.

Competition for places on physiotherapy degree courses is strong, so it would help you if you have relevant health care experience before applying, for example as a physiotherapy assistant. As a physiotherapy assistant, you may be able to take a part-time degree alongside your job. Ask your local NHS Trust for details.

For all courses you will need Criminal Records Bureau (CRB) clearance at the beginning of the course, and again before registering with the HPC.

The NHS would usually pay your course fees, and there is also a means-tested bursary to help with the cost of living while you train. Visit the NHS Business Services Authority website for detailed information about eligibility for the NHS bursary scheme.

If you have a first or upper second class honours degree in a relevant subject (such as a biological science, psychology or sports science) you may be eligible for an accelerated postgraduate programme. Contact the CSP for more details.

More information

NHS Careers
PO Box 2311
Bristol
BS2 2ZX
Tel: 0345 60 60 655
www.nhscareers.nhs.uk

SkillsActive
Castlewood House
77-91 New Oxford Street
London
WC1A 1PX
Advice line: 08000 933300
www.skillsactive.com

Health Learning and Skills Advice Line
Tel: 08000 150850

Association of Chartered Physiotherapists in Sports Medicine
www.acpsm.org

Chartered Society of Physiotherapy
14 Bedford Row
London
WC1R 4ED
Tel: 020 7306 6666
www.csp.org.uk

SWIMMING TEACHER OR COACH

The nature of the work

As a swimming teacher or coach you would:

- teach or coach one-to-one or in groups
- identify participants' abilities
- plan and deliver sessions appropriate to the level of swimmer
- make sure safety standards are followed in all sessions
- check that life-saving equipment is in working order
- provide explanations and demonstrate swimming techniques
- set ground rules for each session
- correct faults in swimming techniques and improve performance
- evaluate sessions and give feedback
- organise and supervise assistants and helpers.

You may also need to deal with minor injuries and accidents.

What can you earn?

Most swimming teachers and coaches work part-time and are paid an hourly rate. Rates can be between £10 and over £30 an hour.

Entry requirements

You can qualify as a swimming teacher by completing qualifications awarded by:

- the Amateur Swimming Association (ASA)
- the Swimming Teachers Association (STA).

The ASA also awards swimming coaching qualifications.

You would start with either of the following:

- ASA/UKCC Level 1 Certificate for Teaching Aquatics
- ASA/UKCC Level 1 Certificate for Coaching Swimming.

Completing a qualification at level 1 will qualify you to support fully-qualified teachers or coaches.

Visit the ASA website for details of qualifications and centres offering training.

Alternatively, you can qualify as a swimming teacher by doing STA teaching qualifications. See the STA website for full details.

To work with children or other vulnerable people you will need clearance from the Criminal Records Bureau (CRB).

More information

Swimming Teachers' Association (STA)
Anchor House
Birch Street
Walsall
West Midlands
WS2 8HZ
Tel: 01922 645097
www.sta.co.uk

SkillsActive
Castlewood House
77-91 New Oxford Street
London
WC1A 1PX
Advice line: 08000 933300
www.skillsactive.com

****

20. TEACHING

This chapter covers three main teaching jobs:

- Primary School Teacher
- Secondary School Teacher
- Teaching Assistant

The area of teaching is very wide and there are other opportunities available, such as college lecturing. For information on the numerous other roles available contact:

Teaching Agency - Get into Teaching
Teaching Information Line (freephone): 0800 389 2500
www.education.gov.uk/get-into-teaching

PRIMARY SCHOOL TEACHER

The nature of the work
You would work with children aged between five and eleven in state and independent schools, and be responsible for their educational, social and emotional development while in your care.

You would teach subjects covered by the primary national curriculum at Key Stage 1 (ages 5 to 7) and Key Stage 2 (7 to 11) — subjects such as English, science, music and art. In some classes, you may have a teaching assistant to help you.

Depending on your qualifications and experience, you may work as a subject specialist teacher.

As well as teaching you would:

- plan lessons and teaching materials
- mark and assess children's work
- manage class behaviour
- work with other professionals, such as education psychologists and social workers
- discuss children's progress and other relevant matters with parents and carers
- attend meetings and training
- organise outings, social activities and sports events.

As a primary teacher, you could also work with children under the age of five (Early Years Foundation Stage) in settings like a children's centre or a reception class in a school.

What can you earn?

The main salary scale is from £21,588 to £31,552 a year (£27,000 to £36,387 in inner London and £25,117 to £35,116 in outer London). Teachers who reach the top of the main salary scale may be able to move on to a higher scale, ranging from £34,181 to £36,756 (£40,288 to £43,692 in inner London). There are also separate scales for teachers who have advanced skills or progress into leadership roles, and additional payments for those who take on extra responsibilities.

Entry requirements

The most common way to become a primary school teacher is to do Initial Teacher Training (ITT) and gain Qualified Teacher Status (QTS). The following ITT routes lead to QTS:

- undergraduate degree
- postgraduate award
- work-based programme.

For all routes you will need:

- GCSEs (A-C) in English, maths and a science subject or equivalent qualifications. Check with course providers which qualifications they will accept
- passes in numeracy and literacy skills tests
- Enhanced Disclosure checks through the Criminal Records Bureau (CRB).

You will also need experience of working with young children through paid work or volunteering for example, at a local school or on a holiday play scheme. The Teaching Agency has useful advice about contacting schools for work experience.

Work-based routes

There are several options you can look at if you prefer to train and work in a school at the same time. These options are very popular and there is a lot of competition for places.

School-Centred Initial Teacher Training (SCITT)

SCITT is a classroom-based training programme that takes one year, and is aimed at those who already have a degree related to a national curriculum subject.

The programmes are run by groups of schools and colleges within a local area and you would spend time in one or more of the schools while doing your training.

School Direct

This option replaces the Graduate Teaching Programme and has two alternatives:

- School Direct Training Programme
- School Direct Training Programme (with salary – starting in September 2013).

You will need a degree for either option, and for the paid training route you will also need a minimum of three years' working experience. The aim is to attract people into teaching, who can bring in skills and knowledge from commerce and industry.

You can apply directly to schools offering the programmes and work while you are training. Both options take around 12 months to complete and lead to QTS.

Contact the Teaching Agency for a list of schools taking part in School Direct.

Teach First

Teach First is a charity that runs a two-year teacher training and leadership programme for graduates with a good degree (2:1 or higher). Training is based within schools located in areas facing social and economic challenges. See the Teach First website for more details.

Teachers who have teaching qualifications from another country should check the career pportunities pages of the Department of Education website for details about extra training that may be needed to work in schools in England and Wales.

Moving from further education into school teaching

Since April 2012, lecturers in further education who hold Qualified Teacher Learning and Skills (QTLS) status, and are members of the Institute for Learning, can be employed in primary or secondary schools as fully qualified teachers. See the Department of Education pages on QTLS recognition for more information.

Visit the Teaching Agency website for full details of all entry routes into teaching and funding for training.

Northern Ireland

For details of routes into teaching in Northern Ireland see the Department of Education Northern Ireland website.

Transferring to another age group

You do not need to do further training to transfer to teaching another age group. However, schools recommend that you get some experience of the age group you are intending to teach. This could be on a voluntary basis.

Some local education authorities and teacher training institutions may offer short conversion or refresher courses.

Returning to teaching

If you are a qualified teacher wanting to return to teaching after a career break you can find information on the Teaching Agency website. This includes details of returners' courses and other available support.

More information

Teaching Agency - Get into Teaching 🖰
Teaching Information Line (freephone): 0800 389 2500
www.education.gov.uk/get-into-teaching

Department of Education Northern Ireland (DENI) 🖰
Rathael House
Balloo Road
Bangor
BT19 7PR
Tel: 028 9127 9279
www.deni.gov.uk

Graduate Teacher Training Registry (GTTR)
Rosehill New
Barn Lane

Cheltenham
Gloucestershire
GL52 3LZ
Tel: 0871 4680 469
www.gttr.ac.uk

SECONDARY SCHOOL TEACHER

The nature of the work

Your work would be in state or independent schools, teaching children aged from 11 to 16, or up to 19 in schools with sixth forms. You would:

- specialise in teaching one or two subjects
- teach classes of different ages and abilities throughout the school
- prepare pupils for exams like GCSEs and A levels.

Some areas of England and Wales have middle schools. These take children from ages eight or nine up to ages 12 or 13. As a teacher in a middle school you would teach the primary or secondary curriculum, depending on the age of children in your class.

What can you earn?

The main salary scale is from £21,588 to £31,552 a year (£27,000 to £36,387 in inner London and £25,117 to £35,116 in outer London).

Teachers who reach the top of the main salary scale may be able to move on to a higher scale, ranging from £34,181 to £36,756 (£40,288 to £43,692 in inner London).

There are also separate scales for teachers who have advanced skills or progress into leadership roles, and additional payments for those who take on extra responsibilities.

See details of all the salary scales on the Teaching Agency website.

Entry requirements

The most common way to become a secondary school teacher is to do Initial Teacher Training (ITT) and gain Qualified Teacher Status (QTS). The following ITT routes lead to QTS:

- undergraduate degree
- postgraduate award
- work-based programme.

For all of these routes, you will need:

- GCSEs (A-C) in English and maths (and science, depending on your teaching subject) or equivalent qualifications

- passes in numeracy and literacy skills tests
- Enhanced Disclosure checks through the Criminal Records Bureau (CRB).

You will also need experience of working with young people through paid work or volunteering for example, at a local school, through youth work or on a holiday scheme. The Teaching Agency has lots of advice about contacting schools for work experience. It also offers up to 10 days' classroom experience in certain secondary subjects through the School Experience Programme.

Undergraduate degree route

You can study for a university degree and gain QTS at the same time by doing one of the following courses:

- BA (Hons) degree or BSc (Hons) degree with QTS
- Bachelor of Education (BEd) degree course.

These are usually full-time courses and take three to four years.

To get onto a degree course, you will usually need at least two A levels and at least five GCSEs (A-C). Universities may accept other qualifications such as an Access to Higher Education course. Check with course providers for their exact requirements.

Postgraduate routes

If you already have a degree related to the national curriculum, you can gain QTS by doing a Postgraduate Certificate of Education (PGCE) course. Courses take one year, full-time or two years, part-time. A small number of flexible courses are available mainly aimed at those already working as unqualified teachers.

You can search for all PGCE courses and apply online on the Graduate Teacher Training Registry (GTTR) website.

Find out more about national curriculum subjects on the following website:

Work-based routes

There are several options you can look at if you prefer to train and work in a school at the same time. These options are very popular and there is a lot of competition for places.

School-Centred Initial Teacher Training (SCITT)

SCITT is a classroom-based training programme that takes one year, and is aimed at those who already have a degree related to a national curriculum subject.

The programmes are run by groups of schools and colleges within a local area and you would spend time in one or more of the schools while doing your training.

School Direct

This option replaces the Graduate Teaching Programme and has two alternatives:

- School Direct Training Programme
- School Direct Training Programme (with salary – starting in September 2013).

You will need a degree for either option, and for the paid training route you will also need a minimum of three years' working experience. The aim is to attract people into teaching, who can bring in skills and knowledge from commerce and industry.

You can apply directly to schools offering the programmes and work while you are training. Both options take around 12 months to complete and lead to QTS.

Contact the Teaching Agency for a list of schools taking part in School Direct.

Teach First

Teach First is a charity that runs a two-year teacher training and leadership programme for graduates with a good degree (2:1 or higher). Training is based within schools located in areas facing social and economic challenges. See the Teach First website for more details.

Overseas Trained Teacher Programme (OTTP)

Teachers who have teaching qualifications from another country should check the career opportunities pages of the Department of Education website for details about extra training that may be needed to work in schools in England and Wales.

Moving from further education into school teaching

Since April 2012, lecturers in further education who hold Qualified Teacher Learning and Skills (QTLS) status, and are members of the Institute for Learning, can be employed in primary or secondary schools as fully qualified teachers. See the Department of Education pages on QTLS recognition for more information.

Visit the Teaching Agency's Get into Teaching website for full details of all entry routes into teaching and funding for training.

Northern Ireland

For details of routes into teaching in Northern Ireland see the Department of Education Northern Ireland website.

More information

Teaching Agency - Get into Teaching
Teaching Information Line (freephone): 0800 389 2500
www.education.gov.uk/get-into-teaching

Department of Education Northern Ireland (DENI)
Rathael House
Balloo Road
Bangor
BT19 7PR
Tel: 028 9127 9279
www.deni.gov.uk

Graduate Teacher Training Registry (GTTR)
Rosehill
New Barn Lane
Cheltenham
Gloucestershire
GL52 3LZ
Tel: 0871 4680 469
www.gttr.ac.uk

TEACHING ASSISTANT

The nature of the work

As a teaching assistant you would support teachers and help children with their educational and social development, both in and out of the classroom. Your exact job will depend on the school and the age of the children.

Your job may include:

- getting the classroom ready for lessons
- listening to children read, reading to them or telling them stories
- helping children who need extra support to complete tasks
- helping teachers to plan learning activities and complete records
- supporting teachers in managing class behaviour
- supervising group activities
- looking after children who are upset or have had accidents
- clearing away materials and equipment after lessons
- helping with outings and sports events
- taking part in training
- carrying out administrative tasks.

You would also support children with particular needs, working with them individually or in small groups.

In some schools you could have a specialism, such as literacy, numeracy or special educational needs (SEN). If you are bilingual, you might do more work with children whose first language is not English. At secondary level, you're likely to concentrate on working with individuals and small groups and, depending on the subject, you may assist with practicals, for example in science. A teaching assistant might also be called classroom assistant or learning support assistant.

Higher Level Teaching Assistant

As a Higher Level Teaching Assistant (HLTA) you would have more responsibility. This could include:

- working along side teachers to support learning activities

- helping to plan lessons and prepare teaching materials
- acting as a specialist assistant for particular subjects
- leading classes under the direction of the teacher
- supervising other support staff.

You would also assess, record and report on the progress of children you work with.

What can you earn?

Salaries for full-time teaching assistants range from £12,000 to over £17,000 a year. Salaries for full-time HLTAs can be between £16,000 and £21,000 a year. This will vary depending on the Local Education Authority (LEA) and the responsibilities of individual jobs. There is no national pay scale and wage rates are set by each LEA. Teaching assistants who work part-time, or are paid only for term-time, earn a proportion of full-time rates. This is known as pro rata payment.

Entry requirements

LEAs and individual schools decide which qualifications and experience they want applicants to have. You can get an idea of what you are likely to need by looking at jobs advertised locally or by checking your LEA's vacancies online.

Previous qualifications in nursery nursing, childcare, play work or youth work can be useful for finding work. If you have enough experience of working with children or can show employers that you have the right personality and potential, you may be able to start work without qualifications. Volunteering to help in a local school for a few hours a week is a good way to start.

The following qualifications are also available for those not yet employed in the role and for those just new to the job, whether paid or volunteering:

- Level 2 Award in Support Work in Schools
- Level 3 Award in Supporting Teaching and Learning in Schools.

Most paid jobs will require you to have qualifications in literacy and numeracy at GCSE or equivalent.

You may be able to become a teaching assistant through an Apprenticeship scheme. The range of Apprenticeships available in your area will depend on the local jobs market and the types of skills employers need from their workers.

You can find more information on careers and qualifications for school support staff on the Department for Education and Skills4Schools websites.

More information

Department for Education - support staff
Support Staff Enquiry Line (freephone): 0800 389 5335
www.education.gov.uk/get-into-teaching

Local Government Careers Information
www.lgcareers.com

****

21. TRAVEL AND TOURISM

The areas of travel and tourism generally attract dynamic people with a sense of adventure. the field is wide, from travel agent to tourist guide. For the right people the rewards are great. In this section, we cover the following jobs:

- Travel Agent
- Tour manager
- Tourist Guide
- Resort Representative
- Air cabin crew
- Airline Customer Service Agent
- Cruise Ship Steward
- Hotel Manager
- Hotel Porter

For more details of jobs in the tourism industry go to:

International Association of Tour Managers (IATM)
397 Walworth Road
London
SE17 2AW
Tel: 020 7703 9154
www.iatm.co.uk

TRAVEL AGENT

The nature of the work

As a travel agent, you could be based at places like high street travel agents or call centres. Your work would include:

- helping customers to find a suitable package holiday or to plan independent travel

- checking the availability of the chosen holiday by telephone or computer
- making bookings using a computer system
- collecting deposits (a portion of payment) and filling in booking forms
- contacting customers when their tickets arrive, and collecting final payments
- informing customers of any changes such as cancelled flights, and arranging alternatives.

You would also advise customers about passports, travel insurance, visas, vaccinations and tours. You may also arrange refunds and handle complaints.

What can you earn?

Starting salaries can be around £13,000 a year. Experienced travel agents can earn between £15,000 and £25,000 a year, and salaries for those in senior jobs can be £30,000 a year or more. Travel agents often get commission based on meeting performance targets. They may also get discounts on holidays.

Entry requirements
You would not usually need any particular qualifications, although it may be useful if you have GCSEs. Employers will want to see that you are enthusiastic, and have the right personal qualities and skills for the job.
It could help you if you have experience in customer services or sales, and if you are able to speak other languages.

The most common way to start as a travel agent is to find work with a travel agency and train on the job. However, you could take a full-time college course before you look for work. This is not essential, but it may help you get a job. Relevant courses include:

- Level 2 Diploma in Travel and Tourism
- Level 3 Diploma in Travel and Tourism
- Level 2 Certificate in Travel Services.

You may be able to start this job through an Apprenticeship scheme, such as the Level 2 Apprenticeship in Travel Services. For more information, see the Apprenticeships and UKSP websites.

More information
People first
2nd Floor
Armstrong House
38 Market Square
Uxbridge
Middlesex
UB8 1LH
Tel: 01895 817 000
www.people1st.co.uk

UKSP
www.uksp.co.uk (careers information)

Springboard UK
http://springboarduk.net

City & Guilds
1 Giltspur Street
London
EC1A 9DD
Tel: 0844 543 0000
www.cityandguilds.com

TOUR MANAGER

The nature of the work

As a tour manager, you would be responsible for making sure that travel arrangements for groups of holiday-makers run as smoothly and enjoyably as possible. You would accompany passengers throughout their tour, keeping them informed about details like arrival and departure times and places of interest.

You would usually work on coach tours that can last from between two or three days to over a month, but could also work on tours by rail or cruise ship.

Your job would involve:

- joining the group at the start of their journey, welcoming them, and announcing details of travel arrangements and stopover points
- making sure all travel arrangements run according to plan, and that the accommodation, meals and service are satisfactory
- helping with passport and immigration issues
- helping with check-in to accommodation
- giving a spoken commentary on places travelled through or visited (although local guides may also be used)
- promoting and selling excursions to tour members
- advising about facilities such as sights, restaurants and shops at each destination
- organising entry to attractions and additional transport, such as car hire
- keeping records.

You would need to be available at almost any time to give advice, solve problems and deal with emergencies like loss of passports or money, illness or difficulties with accommodation.

In some companies you may be known as tour director rather than tour manager.

What can you earn?

Tour managers salaries can start at around £15,000 a year, rising to around £20,000 with experience.

Income varies considerably from company to company, and also depends on the areas and types of tour the manager covers. Earnings are often based on a daily allowance, plus free board and lodgings for the duration of the tour and other relevant expenses.

Entry requirements

You would not usually need any particular qualifications to become a tour manager, but you would need a good standard of general education.

You would also usually need:

- experience of working with people
- an interest in geography, history and history of art, and the ability to research these for the region covered by the tour
- a good working knowledge of foreign languages if working overseas
- experience of working abroad (if the job you are applying for is based overseas).

Qualifications related to leisure, travel and tourism are available at all levels, including GCSEs, A levels, NVQs, BTECs, degrees and postgraduate qualifications. You could find it useful to complete one of these, but this is not essential.

You may be able to get into this job through an Apprenticeship scheme. The range of Apprenticeships available in your area will depend on the local jobs market and the types of skills employers need from their workers. To find out more about Apprenticeships, visit the Apprenticeships website.

More information

International Association of Tour Managers (IATM)
397 Walworth Road
London
SE17 2AW
Tel: 020 7703 9154
www.iatm.co.uk

People 1st
2nd Floor
Armstrong House
38 Market Square
Uxbridge

Middlesex
UB8 1LH
Tel: 01895 817 000
www.uksp.co.uk/ (careers information)
www.people1st.co.uk

Institute of Travel and Tourism
PO Box 217
Ware
Hertfordshire
SG12 8WY
Tel: 0844 4995 653
www.itt.co.uk

TOURIST GUIDE

The nature of the work

Tourist guides show visitors around places of interest, such as towns and cities, historic buildings, gardens, religious sites or museums and art galleries.

As a tourist guide you could:

- work in one place such as a castle or historic house, or
- accompany groups on day tours to interesting places or sites.
- You would escort groups around the site or area, and give information about history, purpose, architecture or other points of interest.
- Guided tours could be:
- sightseeing tours
- tours for special interest groups
- themed walks.

You could also work as a 'driver guide', taking small groups of tourists on guided tours around places of interest in a car or minibus.

What can you earn?

Rates of pay vary depending on the employer and the location. Most tourist guides are self-employed and charge fees. See the Association of Professional Tourist Guides website for details of recommended fees for qualified guides.

Entry requirements

You would not need any set qualifications to start training as a tourist guide, but you would need a good standard of general education.

It would be an advantage if you have experience in jobs that involve dealing with the public and giving presentations. It could be useful if you speak a foreign language fluently, but this is not usually essential.

You can do courses and take exams which are accredited by the Institute of Tourist Guiding. Depending on the type of guiding you want to do, you could work towards qualifications such as:

- Level 2: Fixed Route Commentary, Interpretation and Presentation – for paid or voluntary work, guiding visitors round attractions such as galleries, cathedrals or stately homes, or on fixed route tours such as river trips and open top bus trips
- Level 3 Flexible Route Commentary, Heritage Interpretation and Presentation – for work as a guide in areas such as city and town centres, or in visitor attractions, historic buildings or heritage sites
- Level 4: Blue Badge in Tourist Guiding – for all aspects of guiding.

In some places, such as Westminster Abbey and York Minster, Blue Badge guides are the only guides allowed (apart from in-house staff).

Courses are run by local and regional tourist bodies, colleges and other institutions. Visit the Institute of Tourist Guiding website for details of accredited courses. See the Guild of Registered Tourist Guides website for details of regional tourist boards.

Most courses are around 20 weeks long, although some can take up to two years. They are part-time, with evening lectures and practical training at weekends. Blue Badge courses in London run once a year, but in other areas they only run when there is a demand for guides.

If you work on a site where in-house guides are employed, you may receive training from the owner of the site.

More information

Institute of Tourist Guiding
Coppergate House
16 Brune St
London
E1 7NJ
Tel: 020 7953 8397
www.itg.org.uk

People 1st
2nd Floor
Armstrong House
38 Market Square
Uxbridge
Middlesex
UB8 1LH
Tel: 01895 817 000
www.uksp.co.uk/ (careers information)
www.people1st.co.uk

Association of Professional Tourist Guides
33-37 Moreland Street
London
EC1V 8HA

RESORT REPRESENTATIVE

The nature of the work

As a resort representative, you would look after holiday-makers at their holiday destination (usually abroad).

Your work would include:

- meeting groups of holiday-makers when they arrive at the airport
- accompanying holiday-makers by coach to their accommodation
- holding a welcome meeting to give information about resort facilities and local attractions
- meeting holiday-makers at pre-arranged times to make announcements and deal with enquiries and problems
- keeping an information board and a folder of useful information up-to-date at each hotel
- arranging, and sometimes accompanying, excursions and sightseeing trips
- arranging car or ski hire if necessary
- being on-call to give advice and deal with emergencies like lost passports or money, illness or difficulties with accommodation.

You would also keep records, and write reports of complaints and incidents such as illness.

What can you earn?

- Resort representatives can start at around £12,000 a year
- Experienced representatives can earn £16,000 or more.

Resort representatives are also provided with free accommodation and insurance, and sometimes earn commission, for example by selling tours and arranging car hire.

Entry requirements

You would not need any set qualifications to become a resort representative, although employers may expect you to have GCSEs (A-C) or similar qualifications, particularly in English and maths. You would usually need a good working knowledge of one or more foreign languages.

For most jobs you should be at least 20 years of age. To work as a children's representative you may be accepted from the age of 18 or 19, and would usually be expected to have a qualification in childcare.

You could have an advantage if you have relevant experience, such as in another area of travel and tourism, or in customer service or administration. You may need specialist knowledge or skills for some holidays – for example, as a winter sports representative you may need to be able to ski at an advanced level.

Colleges offer a range of courses related to travel and tourism, including BTEC certificates and diplomas, BTEC HNCs/HNDs, foundation degrees and degrees. Although you may find these useful when looking for work, they are not essential.

More information

People 1st
2nd Floor
Armstrong House
38 Market Square
Uxbridge
Middlesex
UB8 1LH
Tel: 01895 817 000
www.people1st.co.uk
www.uksp.co.uk/ (careers information)

Springboard UK
http://springboarduk.net

Association of Independent Tour Operators
www.aito.co.uk

Federation of Tour Operators
www.fto.co.uk

Guild of Registered Tourist Guides
The Guild House
52d Borough High Street
London
SE1 1XN

Tel: 020 7403 1115
www.britainsbestguides.org

AIR CABIN CREW

The nature of the work

As an air cabin crew member you would help make sure that airline passengers have a comfortable, safe and pleasant flight. Before a flight you would:

- go a meeting about the flight and schedule
- check that there are enough supplies on the plane and that emergency equipment is working properly
- greet passengers and direct them to their seats
- demonstrate emergency equipment and procedures to passengers.
- During a flight you would:
- make sure that passengers are comfortable and deal with any requests
- serve food and drinks, and sell duty-free items
- make announcements on behalf of the pilot
- reassure passengers in the event of an emergency, and make sure that they follow safety procedures.

At the end of a flight you would:

- make sure that passengers leave the plane safely and with all their hand luggage
- write a flight report, including about any unusual incidents
- add up and record food and drink orders, and duty-free sales.

Between flights, you may have some spare time to relax and explore the destination you have flown to.

What can you earn?

Starting salaries can be between £12,000 and £14,000 a year. With experience, this rises to between £15,000 and £21,000 a year. Senior crew can earn up to £25,000 a year. Overtime and flight allowances can increase salaries.

Entry requirements

Entry requirements can vary between airlines so you should check with them directly. You will usually need to have a good standard of basic maths and English. Some airlines may ask for GCSEs (grades A-C) in maths and English, or equivalent qualifications.

You will also need:

- a good level of fitness, normal colour vision and good eyesight
- the ability to swim at least 25 metres
- a smart appearance
- a valid passport that allows you to travel anywhere in the world.

You should not have any visible tattoos or body piercings.

You must be over 18 to work as an air cabin crew member, and some airlines set the minimum entry age at 21. Height and weight requirements also vary between airlines, so you should check with them.
Some airlines look for air cabin crew who can speak a second language. Previous experience in customer service is also helpful, and nursing, or hotel and catering experience may be particularly useful.

Although not essential, there are several college courses that could help you gain useful skills for this career. These include:

- BTEC Level 2 Certificate in Preparation for Air Cabin Crew Service
- City & Guilds Level 2 Certificate/Diploma in Air Cabin Crew (New Entrants)
- NCFE Level 2 Certificate for Airline Cabin Crew.

Check with local colleges for more information.

More information
People first
2nd Floor

Armstrong House
38 Market Square
Uxbridge
Middlesex
UB8 1LH
Tel: 01895 817 000
www.people1st.co.uk

NCFE
www.ncfe.org.uk

Royal Aeronautical Society
4 Hamilton Place

AIRLINE CUSTOMER SERVICE AGENT

The nature of the work
As an airline customer service agent, you would usually work for an airline, or for a ground services agent on behalf of an airline. Your job would include:

- dealing with passenger enquiries about flight departures and arrivals
- checking passengers in
- giving seat numbers
- providing boarding passes and luggage labels
- telling passengers about luggage restrictions
- weighing baggage and collecting any excess weight charges
- taking care of people with special needs, and unaccompanied children
- calming and reassuring nervous passengers.

You may sometimes help passengers through immigration and customs, or escort passengers who have night flight connections. You could also specialise in different areas of airport work, such as computer control.

What can you earn?
Airline customer services agents can earn between £12,000-£18,000

Entry requirements

There are no fixed entry requirements for becoming an airline customer service agent. However, employers may ask for GCSEs (A-C) in subjects like English and maths, or equivalent qualifications. Some may ask you to take a medical test.

Employers may want you to have previous experience of working in a customer service role and the ability to speak a foreign language. They may also look for applicants who live near the airport or have their own transport. This can often be important as shifts may be outside normal public transport hours.

You may be able to get into this job through an Aviation Operations Apprenticeship. You will need to check if this is available in your area. For more information, visit the Apprenticeships website.

For more details about airline careers, see the GoSkills website.

More information
People 1st
2nd Floor
Armstrong House
38 Market Square
Uxbridge
Middlesex
UB8 1LH
Tel: 01895 817 000
www.people1st.co.uk

CRUISE SHIP STEWARDS

The nature of the work

Cruise ship stewards work either in cabin service or in the bar area of cruise liners.

As a cabin steward your work would include:

- keeping guests' cabins clean and tidy
- making beds
- supplying fresh linen
- vacuuming floors
- replacing stocks of supplies such as shampoo and soap.

Working in the bar area, you would:

- serve passengers with drinks
- clear and wash glasses
- help keep the bar well stocked and tidy
- deal with payments and operate the till.

You would work as part of a team, under the supervision of a head housekeeper or bar manager.

With some cruise companies the job title 'steward' refers to customer service or reception staff. In these roles, your duties could include informing passengers about the services offered on board, arranging excursions and dealing with guests' queries and complaints.

What can you earn?

Rates of pay vary between shipping companies, and according to duties. Bar staff may earn around £800 a month, plus free accommodation and meals. Cabin stewards may earn between £600 and £1,100 a month, depending on experience.

Earnings may be supplemented by tips.

Entry requirements

You will not need any particular qualifications to become a passenger liner steward. However, there is a lot of competition for jobs, so it would be useful to have previous relevant experience, for example in catering, hotel or bar work.

Some employers might prefer you to have qualifications, such as:

- Level 2 Certificate in General Food and Beverage Service Skills
- Level 1 NVQ Certificate in Accommodation Services.

Your ability to work towards certain qualifications may be considered, such as:

- Level 2 NVQ Diploma in Food and Beverage Service Skills
- Level 2 NVQ Diploma in Housekeeping.

You can apply to companies directly, or through agencies that recruit for cruise liners.

More information

Springboard UK
http://springboarduk.net

People 1st
2nd Floor
Armstrong House
38 Market Square
Uxbridge
Middlesex
UB8 1LH
Tel: 01895 817 000
www.people1st.co.uk

HOTEL MANAGER

The nature of the work
Hotel managers oversee all aspects of running a hotel, from housekeeping and general maintenance to budget management and marketing.

Large hotels may have a manager for each department, reporting to the general manager. In smaller hotels, the manager is more involved in the day-to-day running of the hotel, often dealing directly with guests.

As a hotel manager, your tasks would typically include:

- setting annual budgets
- analysing financial information and statistics
- setting business targets and marketing strategies
- managing staff
- organising building maintenance
- making sure security is effective
- dealing with customer complaints and comments
- making sure the hotel follows regulations such as licensing laws
- securing corporate bookings for entertainment and conference facilities.

In larger hotels you will spend a lot of time in meetings with the heads of departments.

What can you earn?

Trainee and assistant hotel managers can earn around £19,000 a year. Managers of small hotels or deputy managers of larger ones can earn from £20,000 to around £35,000. Senior or general managers can earn £60,000 or more.

Entry requirements

You could become a hotel manager in either of the following ways:
- working your way up to management level from a more junior position
- entering management after completing a HNC/HND, degree or postgraduate qualification.
- Relevant degree and HNC/HND subjects include:
- Hospitality Management
- International Hospitality Management

- Hotel and Hospitality Management
- Hospitality and Licensed Retail Management.

You can also complete foundation degrees in subjects such as Hospitality Business Management. These are vocational courses that are usually studied over two years. You can study part-time whilst in relevant employment or full-time with work placements. To search for foundation degrees, HNDs and degrees see the UCAS website.

An Apprenticeship might help you build the skills you need towards this role. You may be able to get into this job through an Apprenticeship scheme such as the Level 3 Apprenticeship in Hospitality & Catering (Supervision & Leadership). The range of Apprenticeships available in your area will depend on the local jobs market and the types of skills employers need from their workers.

More information

Springboard UK
http://springboarduk.net

People 1st
2nd Floor
Armstrong House
38 Market Square
Uxbridge
Middlesex
UB8 1LH
Tel: 01895 817 000
www.people1st.co.uk

Institute of Hospitality
www.instituteofhospitality.org

HOTEL PORTER

The nature of the work

As a hotel porter, based in reception or at the porters' desk, you will often be the first person to greet guests at a hotel.

Your work will include:

- helping guests by carrying luggage
- advising on hotel facilities
- arranging taxis
- running errands, such as taking and picking up dry cleaning
- taking messages
- giving directions
- answering queries and making reservations.

If the hotel has a conference suite, you may be responsible for moving and setting up equipment. In a large hotel, your duties may be more specialised.

What can you earn?

- Starting salaries can be around £12,000 a year.
- With experience, this can rise to around £16,000.
- Head porters at large hotels can earn around £22,000.

Shift allowance, overtime and tips can increase earnings.

Entry requirements

You do not need qualifications to be a hotel porter, although employers will usually expect you to have a good general education and the following may be an advantage:

- Level 2 Award in Introduction to Employment in the Hospitality Industry
- Level 2 Award in the Principles of Customer Service in Hospitality, Leisure, Travel and Tourism

You may have an advantage when looking for work if you have experience of working with the public and a knowledge of the local area will be useful so that you can answer guests' questions and give them directions.

- You may be able to get into this job through an Apprenticeship scheme such as a Level 2 Apprenticeship in Hospitality & Catering (Front of House Reception). The range of Apprenticeships available in your area will depend on the local jobs market and the types of skills employers need from their workers.

More information

Springboard UK
http://springboarduk.net

People 1st
2nd Floor
Armstrong House
38 Market Square
Uxbridge
Middlesex
UB8 1LH
Tel: 01895 817 000
www.uksp.co.uk/ (careers information)
www.people1st.co.uk

****

22. VETINARY

To work in this area, a main prerequisite is a love of animals. The rewards are great for the right person. In this section we cover the following jobs:

- Vetinary Nurse
- Vetinary Surgeon
- Vetinary Physiotherapist

For more details about careers in the vetinary profession go to:

British Veterinary Nursing Association (BVNA)
82 Greenway Business Centre
Harlow Business Park
Harlow
Essex
CM19 5QE
Tel: 01279 408644
www.bvna.org.uk

VETINARY NURSE

The nature of the work

Veterinary nurses help veterinary surgeons (vets) by providing nursing care for sick, injured and hospitalised animals. They also play an important role in educating owners on good standards of animal care and welfare. If you love animals and want to look after their health, this could be ideal for you.

As a veterinary nurse, your duties would include:

- preparing and carrying out nursing care plans
- holding animals and keeping them calm during treatment
- giving injections and drugs (as instructed by the vet)

- getting blood, urine and other samples from animals, and carrying out laboratory work at the practice
- sterilising instruments
- taking x-rays
- preparing animals for operations
- helping vets during operations
- carrying out minor procedures such as removing stitches.
- talking to clients about the care and progress of their animals

You would often have other responsibilities, including:

- taking care of animals staying in house (feeding, cleaning their accommodation, grooming and exercising)
- holding clinics for suture removal, post operation checks and weight management
- giving owners advice about caring for their animals

You could also have administration and reception duties.

What can you earn?

Veterinary nurses can earn between £14,000 and £22,000 a year, depending on experience. Senior veterinary nurses can earn around £25,000 a year. Accommodation may be provided.

Entry requirements

You can qualify as a veterinary nurse either through work-based training or through higher education. Both of these lead to Royal College of Veterinary Surgeons (RCVS) registration as a veterinary nurse.

Work-based training
You could work towards the RCVS Level 3 Diploma in Veterinary Nursing whilst you are working. This is an apprentice style option, and you will need to find employment at a training practice first. To find training practices in your area, contact RCVS Awards or check their website.

To undertake the diploma, you would need to have five GCSEs at grade C or above, including English, maths and two science subjects, or equivalent qualifications, which include:

- ABC Level 2 Certificate for Animal Nursing Assistants
- City & Guilds Level 2 Diploma For Veterinary Care Assistants.

When you are looking for work as a trainee or assistant, it could help you if you have relevant experience. This could be as a volunteer with a local vet, or in other kinds of work with animals, such as at local kennels or RSPCA centres.

Higher education

Instead of work-based training, you can complete an RCVS-approved veterinary nursing degree or foundation degree, which includes work experience placements. This combines RCVS-approved training with the academic qualification. It will take you longer to qualify than through work-based training, but it could give you more career opportunities, such as research or teaching. To do a higher education course you would usually need:

- at least two A levels or equivalent qualifications, preferably in chemistry and biology
- and five GCSEs (A-C) including English language, maths and two sciences

Check the exact requirements with individual colleges and universities.
See the RCVS website for a list of approved courses. You can search for course providers on the UCAS website.

More information

Lantra
Lantra House
Stoneleigh Park
Nr Coventry
Warwickshire

CV8 2LG
Tel: 0845 707 8007
www.lantra.co.uk

Royal College of Veterinary Surgeons (RCVS)
Belgravia House
62-64 Horseferry Road
London
SW1P 2AF
Tel: 020 7222 2001
www.rcvs.org.uk

British Veterinary Nursing Association (BVNA)
82 Greenway Business Centre
Harlow Business Park
Harlow
Essex
CM19 5QE
Tel: 01279 408644
www.bvna.org.uk

British Equine Veterinary Association (BEVA)
Mulberry House
31 Market St
Fordham
Ely
Cambridgeshire
CB7 5LQ
Tel: 01638 723555
www.beva.org.uk

VETINARY SURGEON

The nature of the work
If you would love working with animals and want a challenging medical job, this could be perfect for you. Veterinary surgeons, also known as vets, look

after the health and welfare of animals. Most work in general practice, with domestic pets, farm and zoo animals.

As a vet in general practice you would:

- diagnose and treat sick and injured animals
- operate on ill or injured animals
- carry out a range of tests such as X-rays and scans
- provide care for in-patients
- carry out regular health checks, give vaccinations and give owners advice on care and diet for their animals
- check farm animals and advise how to stop diseases spreading
- neuter animals to stop them breeding
- carry out euthanasia (painless killing) for terminally ill and severely injured animals
- supervise veterinary nurses and support staff
- keep records of the treatments that you carry out.

You could also be involved in inspecting hygiene and care standards in zoos, kennels, catteries, riding stables, pet shops and cattle markets.

Some vets work full-time for the Department for Environment, Food and Rural Affairs (DEFRA), helping to control animal diseases and protect public health interests. In this role they would work in either the Veterinary Field Service (VFS) or at Veterinary Investigation Centres (VICs).

Vets who work in public health aim to prevent and control animal and human diseases. Their work could involve investigating animal and human disease outbreaks, such as foot and mouth disease, or assessing the safety of food processing plants and abattoirs.

Vets in industry develop, test and supervise production of drugs, chemicals and biological products.

What Can you earn?
Newly qualified vets can earn around £30,000 a year. Experienced vets can earn around £48,000 a year. Earnings for senior partners in a practice can be

over £50,000 a year, depending on the size of their practice. Employers may provide accommodation and transport.

Entry requirements

To work as a vet you must be registered with the Royal College of Veterinary Surgeons (RCVS).

To register, you must have a degree from a veterinary school at one of the UK universities approved by RCVS, or an equivalent overseas qualification that the RCVS recognises. See the RCVS website for details of approved degree courses.

Your degree would take five years to complete (six years at Cambridge), and include both clinical and practical training.

To do a degree course you would usually need:

- five GCSEs (A-C) including English, maths, chemistry, biology and physics (or a combined science, double award)
- and at least three A levels (AAB), including chemistry and one or two in biology, physics or maths.

Some universities will consider other relevant qualifications, such as a BTEC Diploma in Animal Science/Animal Management with distinction grades. You will need to check exact entry requirements with universities.

If you do not have the required grades or subjects, some universities offer a six-year course. The first year will prepare you for the five-year degree.

If you have a first or upper second-class honours degree in a science-related subject, you may be exempt from part of the veterinary degree course.

You would also need to gain a considerable amount of work experience in different veterinary practices, and in handling healthy animals on livestock farms or other animal establishments.

More information

Royal College of Veterinary Surgeons (RCVS)
Belgravia House
62-64 Horseferry Road
London
SW1P 2AF
Tel: 020 7222 2001
www.rcvs.org.uk

British Equine Veterinary Association (BEVA)
Mulberry House
31 Market St
Fordham
Ely
Cambridgeshire
CB7 5LQ
Tel: 01638 723555
www.beva.org.uk

British Veterinary Nursing Association (BVNA)
82 Greenway Business Centre
Harlow Business Park
Harlow
Essex
CM19 5QE
Tel: 01279 408644
www.bvna.org.uk

Society of Practicing Veterinary Surgeons
The Governor's House,
Cape Road,
Warwick,
Warwickshire,
CV34 5DJ
Tel: 01926 410454
Email: office@spvs.org.uk
www.spvs.org.uk

VETINARY PHYSIOTHERAPIST

The nature of the work

As an veterinary physiotherapist (also known as an animal physiotherapist), you would assess and treat animals with injuries or movement problems.

As a veterinary physiotherapist, you would mainly treat horses and dogs, including both pets and 'working animals', such as race horses and greyhounds. However, you could also work with other animals such as cats and farm or zoo animals.

Your tasks would typically include:

- planning exercise programmes
- using manual and electro-therapy methods to reduce pain, increase flexibility and restore normal movement
- giving advice on changes to animals' environments to help them perform tasks more easily.

You would only be legally allowed to carry out treatment for diagnosed conditions or injuries if animals are referred by (or with the permission of) a veterinary surgeon.

What can you earn?

Salaries vary enormously for this type of work, and for self-employed private practitioners they will depend on workload. As an example, a survey of ACPAT (Association of Chartered Physiotherapists in Animal Therapy) members showed a wide range of charges for physiotherapy sessions:
initial consultations (from 30 minutes to 2 hours) from £20 to £70.50
follow-up consultations (from 30 minutes to 1.5 hours) from £20 to £60.

Entry requirements

There are two ways to become a veterinary physiotherapist:

- Chartered physiotherapist working with animals

You must first qualify and gain experience as a chartered physiotherapist in human physiotherapy. See the physiotherapist profile, and the Chartered Society of Physiotherapy website, for details.

You would then need to learn to apply your professional and practical therapy skills as a chartered physiotherapist to working with animals, by completing postgraduate training in veterinary physiotherapy.

- Postgraduate Diploma and MSc courses in Veterinary Physiotherapy are offered by the Royal Veterinary College (RVC) and the University of the West of England (run at Hartpury College, Gloucestershire). Check with the universities for their entry requirements.

To complete the course you must:

- attend one weekend a month over 18 months at the Royal Veterinary College in Hatfield, Hertfordshire
- complete 25 hours' private study, including completion of assessed coursework
- pass an exam.

As a MSc student you would also complete a thesis or dissertation.

Successful completion of either the Diploma or MSc would entitle you to become a Category A member of the ACPAT and to use the title veterinary physiotherapist.

Alternatively, you may be able to train with a fully qualified (Category A) member of the Association of Chartered Physiotherapists in Animal Therapy (ACPAT) and complete the ACPAT education course over a period of two years. To do this, you must have trainee (Category B) membership of the ACPAT.

When you have completed the training, you would be able to apply to upgrade to Category A membership of the ACPAT, and become an independent practitioner.

Training without a qualification in human physiotherapy

If you have a good working knowledge of animal care and handling, and a higher or further education qualification, you could complete the Canine and Equine Physiotherapy Training (CEPT) Advanced Certificate in Veterinary Physiotherapy. Check the CEPT website for details.

More information

Royal Veterinary College
Hawkshead Lane
North Mymms
Hatfield
Herts
AL9 7TA
Tel: 01707 666333
www.rvc.ac.uk

Chartered Society of Physiotherapy
14 Bedford Row
London
WC1R 4ED
Tel: 020 7306 6666
www.csp.org.uk

Association of Chartered Physiotherapists in Animal Therapy (ACPAT)
www.acpat.org

****

Index